Class and Community in Malaysia

Hua Wu Yin

Class and Communalism in Malaysia

Politics in a Dependent Capitalist State

Hua Wu Yin

 Zed Books Ltd., 57 Caledonian Road, London N1 9BU.

in conjunction with

 Marram Books, 101 Kilburn Square, London NW6 6PS.

Class and Communalism in Malaysia was first published by Zed Books Ltd., 57 Caledonian Road, London N1 9BU in conjunction with Marram Books, 101 Kilburn Square, London NW6 6PS in 1983.

Copyright © Hua Wu Yin, 1983

Typeset by Grassroots Typeset
Cover design by Len Breen
Printed by The Pitman Press, Bath, U.K.

British Library Cataloguing in Publication Data

Hua, Wu Yin
  Class and communalism in Malaysia
  1. Dependency   2. Imperialism
  3. International economic relations
  4. Malaysia—Politics and government
  5. Malaysia—Economic development
  I. Title
  337'.09595   HF1413
ISBN 0-86232-181-6
ISBN 0-86232-182-4 Pbk

US Distributor:
Biblio Distribution Center, 81 Adams Drive, Totowa,
New Jersey 07512.

Contents

List of Tables

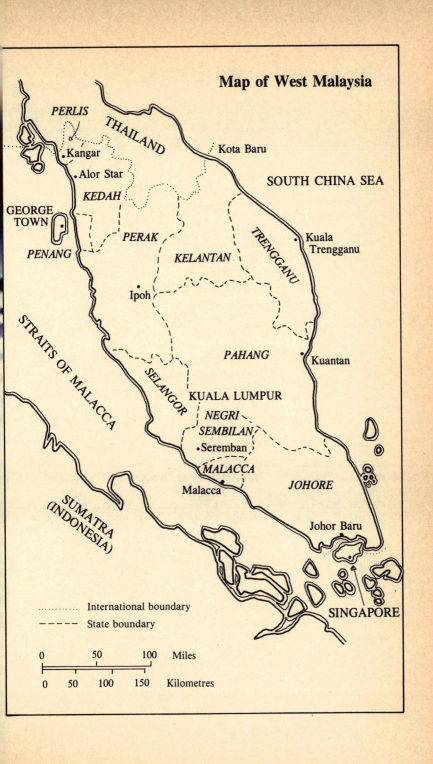

Map of West Malaysia

PERLIS

THAILAND

•Kangar

•Alor Star

KEDAH

Kota Baru

SOUTH CHINA SEA

GEORGE TOWN

PERAK

PENANG

KELANTAN

TRENGGANU

Kuala Trengganu

•Ipoh

PAHANG

Kuantan•

STRAITS OF MALACCA

SELANGOR

KUALA LUMPUR

NEGRI SEMBILAN

•Seremban

MALACCA

Malacca

JOHORE

SUMATRA (INDONESIA)

Johor Baru

SINGAPORE

.... International boundary

- - - - - State boundary

| 0 | | 50 | | 100 | Miles |

| 0 | 50 | 100 | 150 | Kilometres |

Glossary of Local Terms

anak	child
anak dagang	foreigner
anak negeri	citizen
anak raja	royal born
baba (Chinese)	Straits-born Chinese
bangsal	labour line, shed
barisan	front
bumiputra	'son of the soil' (literally 'prince of the soil')
bunga emas	traditional tribute of gold to the Siamese king from the northern Malay states.
chettiar	Indian moneylender
coolie	derogatory term for labourer (literally 'servant')
daerah	district
dakwah	'missionary'; refers to the Islamic fundamentalist movement.
dekat/jauh	near/far; refers to social relationship in the kampong.
duit kopi/teh	coffee/tea money (inducement for favour)
dulang	washing or panning method of tin mining used by the Malays.
gadai	usufructuary loan
gantang	1 gantang = 1 English gallon
gotong royong	co-operation
haji	status conferred on one who has made a pilgrimage to Mecca.
hartal	economic boycott
hokkien	Chinese dialect from the Fukien province of China.
hui guan	(Chinese) association
imam	prayer leader or priest of mosque
jual janji	usufructuary mortgage
kadi	judge in Muslim affairs
kafir	infidel
kampong	Malay village

kangany (system)	A foreman was sent by the estate employer back to his native village in India and paid free passage and a commission for each labourer recruited.
kangchu (system)	The contract system of employment of Chinese immigrant labour.
kapitan	captains or community overseers
kaum muda	modernist group
kaum tua	traditionalists
kenduri	feast
kerah	corvee system
ladang (cultivation)	shifting cultivation
masuk Islam	be a Muslim convert
masuk Melayu	become a Malay, synonymous with *masuk Islam*
masjid	mosque
mentri besar	chief minister (may be a non-aristocrat)
merdeka	'freedom' or Independence
mufti	the religious head after the Sultan.
mukim	smallest administrative unit, equivalent to English parish.
nanyang	'South Sea'; refers to the overseas Chinese in SE Asia.
nusantara	political union with Indonesia
orang asli	the aborigines
padi berat, padi merah	higher quality rice
pajak	lease
pawah	cropsharing
penghulu	village headman
pertarohan	cash deposit
pesaka	trust arrangement
picul	1 picul = 133 pounds
pondok (school)	'hut' school for religious education, usually after school hours.
rakyat	citizens or 'people'
rukun negara	national ideology
sakai	derogatory reference to the aborigines (literally 'slave').
semenajung	peninsula, usually refers to Peninsula Malaya.
sendiri	sole (ownership)
sewa	cash or padi rent
siasat	politics, equated with 'government business'
surat kuasa	Sultan's seal of office
surau	prayer-house, usually beside the mosque

tenaga	labour services
teochew	Chinese dialect spoken in the Kwangtung Province bordering Fukien.
towkay	Chinese boss or businessman
ulama	Islamic theologian
zakat	religious tithe incumbent upon Malay rice growers.

Abbreviations

API	Angkatan Pemuda Insaf—Organisation of Youth for Justice. ('Api' is Malay for fire)
ASEAN	Association of South East Asian Nations (Malaysia, Singapore, Indonesia, Philippines, Thailand)
Berjasa	Barisan Jumaah Islamiah Malaysia Bersatu
Berjaya	Sabah United Peoples' Party
BMA	British Military Administration
BN	Barisan Nasional
CIAM	Central Indian Association of Malaya
CLC	Communities Liaison Committtee
CO	Colonial Office
DAP	Democratic Action Party
DID	Drainage and Irrigation Department
ESCAR	Essential (Security Cases) Amendments Regulations
FAMA	Federal Agricultural Marketing Authority
FEER	*Far Eastern Economic Review*
FELDA	Federal Land Development Authority
FFYP	First Five-Year Plan
FIDA	Federal Industrial Development Authority, now MIDA
FIMA	Food Industries of Malaysia
FMP	First Malaysia Plan
FMS	Federated Malay States (Perak, Pahang, Negri Sembilan, Selangor)
FO	Foreign Office
FOA	Farmers Organisation Authority
F T Z	Free Trade Zone
GATT	General Agreement on Tariff and Trade
GLU	General Labour Union
IBRD	International Bank for Reconstruction and Development (World Bank)
ICA	Industrial Co-ordination Act (1975)
IIL	Indian Independence League (civilian wing of INA)

IMF	International Monetary Fund
IMP	Independence of Malaya Party
INA	Indian Nationalist Army
ISA	Internal Security Act
JMBRAS	Journal of the Malayan Branch of the Royal Asiatic Society
KMM	Kesatuan Melayu Muda (Union of Malay Youth)
KRIS	Kesatuan Rakyat Indonesia Semenanjung—Union of Indonesia and Malayan People. ('kris' is the symbolic Malay dagger.)
KSM	Malaysian Multi-Purpose Co-operative Society
LPN	Lembaga Padi Negara—National Padi Authority
MAJUIKAN	Fisheries Development Authority
MAJUTERNAK	Livestock Development Authority
MARA	Majlis Amanah Rakyat—Council of the People's Trust
MARDI	Malaysian Agricultural Research and Development Institute
MCA	Malayan Chinese Association
MCP or CPM	Malayan Communist Party
MDU	Malayan Democratic Union
MER	*Malayan Economic Review*
MIC	Malayan Indian Congress
MIDA	Malaysian Industrial Development Authority
MIDF	Malaysian Industrial Development Finance
MMEA	Malayan Mining Employers Association
MNC	Multinational corporation
MNLA	Malayan National Liberation Army
MNP	Malay Nationalist Party
MPAJA	Malayan Peoples Anti-Japanese Army
MPAJU	Malayan Peoples Anti-Japanese Union (civilian wing of MPAJA)
MPH	Multi-Purpose Holdings
MPIEA	Malayan Planting Industry Employers Association
MPU	Malayan Planning Unit
MTUC	Malayan Trade Union Congress
NEP	New Economic Policy
NST	*New Straits Times* (Kuala Lumpur)
NUPW	National Union of Plantation Workers
PAP	Peoples Action Party (Singapore)
PAS	Partai Islam (formerly PMIP)
PBB	Partai Pesaka Bumiputra Bersatu (Sarawak)
Pekemas	Persatuan Kebangsaan Melayu Singapura—Malay National Union of Singapore

PERNAS	Perbadanan Nasional—National Corporation
PESAKA	Partai Pesaka Anale Sarawak
PMCJA	Pan-Malayan Council of Joint Action
PMFTU	Pan-Malayan Federation of Trade Unions
PMIP	Pan-Malayan Islamic Party
PMU	Peninsula Malay Union—Persatuan Melayu Semenanjung
PN	Party Negara
PPP	Peoples' Progressive Party
PSRM	Partai Sosialis Rakyat Malaya
PUTERA	Pusat Tenaga Rakyat—Council of People's Action
RIDA	Rural and Industrial Development Authority
RISDA	Rubber Industry Smallholders Development Authority
RRI	Rubber Research Institute
SATU	Singapore Association of Trade Unions (Barisan-led)
SCA	Sabah Chinese Association
SEDC	State Economic Development Corporation
SFTU	Singapore Federation of Trade Unions
SFYP	Second Five-Year Plan
SNAP	Sarawak National Party
SS	Straits Settlements (Penang, Malacca, Singapore)
ST	*Straits Times* (Singapore)
STUC	Singapore Trade Union Congress (PAP-led)
SMP	Second Malaysia Plan
SUPP	Sarawak United Peoples Party
TMP	Third Malaysia Plan
UDA	Urban Development Authority
UMNO	United Malays National Organisation
UPAM	United Planters Association of Malaya
USNO	United Sabah National Organisation
WB	World Bank
WCC	World Council of Churches

Introduction

This book is about the politics of imperialist domination. It seeks to highlight the mechanisms of oppression that maintain the conditions responsible for Malaysia's economic subordination to metropolitan capital. It does not, therefore, address itself to the question that has come to dominate academic literature on the Third World: that is, whether or not industrial development is taking place. The principal issue for the anti-imperialist forces is not the pace and scale of industrialization, or the size of the GNP, but the relations of economic exploitation and political oppression which condemn the vast majority of the peoples of the Third World to poverty and an absence of basic political rights, irrespective of whether or not their countries are undergoing industrial development.

This book sets out to answer the question: 'What is preventing the masses in Malaysia from gaining control over the use of their labour and material resources?' If this raises a different set of issues from those discussed in most economic and sociological texts on 'development', it is, nevertheless, closer to the tasks faced by the liberation struggles in the Third World.

In Malaysia, as elsewhere in the neo-colonial world, the transformation of imperialist domination depends on the formation of the masses—first and foremost the working class and the peasantry—into a political force, and an agent of historical change. On this development hinges the achievement of the National Democratic Revolution—land to the tillers and democratic rights to the masses. In contrast, the continuation of capitalist development depends on political domination of the masses, and on preventing them from becoming a political force in their own right. This is common both to the metropolitan centres and the peripheral countries of the imperialist system. The mechanisms for securing this political condition are, however, strikingly different in the two cases.

Helped by super-profits and an intricate system of cooption and coercion, in Lenin's words 'buying off' sections of the subordinate classes, domination over the working class and the petty bourgeoisie in the heartland capitals has been put on a stable footing. This has permitted working-class opposition to be contained within the framework of bourgeois democracy. In Malaysia, within the conditions of peripheral capitalism, no such political concessions could be made. For metropolitan capital and its local agents to maintain their exploitation they have had to deny even the limited freedoms that bourgeois democracy permits. That is why the National Democratic Movement remains on the agenda and why the struggle for the democratic rights threatens the very basis of imperialist domination.

In Malaysia, the ruling class' political domination has been established through communalism: the division of the masses along national lines in order to prevent them from acting as a unified political force. The form of this domination has been organized, on the one hand around the denial of democratic rights to the minority nationalities—the Chinese and the Indians—and on the other, around the mobilization of the Malay masses behind the demand of correcting the 'racial imbalance' of the economy. The latter, obscures the relations of class exploitation by portraying economic inequalities as the product of unequal distribution among the national groups.

As we will have occasion to show, the practice of the Malay ruling class itself refutes this ideological manoeuvre, for it continues to collaborate with the Chinese big bourgeoisie and, of course, could not attack the economic basis of this class without challenging capitalism itself on which it also depends. Communalism in Malaysia seeks to deflect the economic grievances of the Malay masses from its objectively anti-imperialist and anti-capitalist content into an ideological support of the Malay ruling class.

Today, at the forefront of the struggle against communalism are the minority nationalities—rather sizeable minorities—who, in their demands for cultural rights, are furthering the democratic rights of the masses. Only through recognition of the rights of the national minorities can the masses be united on a democratic and equal basis, and the Malay workers and peasants be freed from the ideology that ties it to its own ruling class.

Pluralist Analyses of Communalism in Malaysia

There is a plethora of social science studies of Malaya/Malaysia based on pluralism and the problematic of 'race relations'.[1] But if the error of certain Marxist schools has been to consider the bourgeoisie and the state without reference to how their power organizes the subordinate classes, pluralists and other bourgeois social scientists look at the communal divisions within the society and completely ignore the role of the state and the dominant classes. Pluralists take the national divisions within the society as assumed rather than something that needs to be explained. The divisions on national lines are not based on a difference of culture but on class oppression.

Communalism and other manifestations of social conflict cannot be taken for granted as the inevitable consequence of a multiethnic society, but must be explained as an ideology produced under concrete historical circumstances and by social classes. As such, we have to discover the origins of that ideology and the social forces which sustain it. In the Malaysian case, we find that the character of communal relations changes profoundly from its relatively non-antagonistic aspect during pre-colonial days to a serious communal problem during the colonial and subsequent periods. This is related intrinsically to the very different class contradictions inherent in imperialist domination. With the subordination of the non-Malay merchants and traders to imperialist capital, the contradiction between them and the Malay peasantry was now ideologically reorganized to make it appear as the principal contradiction. The problem of communalism then arose concomitantly with the strategy of imperial rule. The segregation in occupation and domicile of the various communities can also be seen as the result of imperial policy, rather than the 'natural' orientation of different ethnic groups.

The pluralists' conceptualization of the state as a neutral element is evident not only in their analysis of colonialism but also of the neo-colonial period. It further leads them to be conceptually blind to the institutionalization of communalism in the country's Constitution, and more recently, in the New Economic Policy (NEP). Communalism has become enshrined in the state; it was a major consideration in post-war politics and in the imperialist strategy to effect the changeover to a neo-colonial situation. From the 1930s onwards, through the Malayan Union crisis of 1946 and up to the opposition to the merger (Malaysia) plans in 1963, the state had to confront a left-wing, anti-colonial movement strongly rooted in the working class. Communalism was the strategy it consistently relied upon to defuse that threat.

However, the pluralists' view of the state as a neutral element cannot simply be attributed to their empiricist practice. Their characterization of Malayan/Malaysian society occasionally bordering on 'despair', cloaks political objectives:[2]

> There is also a complete lack of cultural homogeneity, each community having its own religion, language, customs, and habits. This naturally constitutes a serious obstacle to unification; it is also the reason why certain 'cultural' matters (particularly language) have come to constitute some of the most difficult political issues of present-day Malaya.

Pluralists have, in fact, provided legitimacy for the existence of communalism itself by the way in which 'race relations' has become a 'problem' to be solved only by a government department or yet another academic department.[3] Pluralist accounts, at other times, seem naive, if not apologetic for the status quo:[4]

The Malaysian (Malayan) leaders, however, had also another notable predilection, a preference for democratic politics. They knew, of course, the tactical value of such a posture in negotiations with British authorities and even recognised the strategic advantages in relations with the indigenous traditional rulers, the sultans... they all considered the use of violence bad form and poor judgement, and coercion only the last resort of public policy....

To discuss obstacles to national unity on the basis of heterogeneity of cultures is to make assumptions about precisely that which needs to be explained; and to see cultural and political liberties for the various national groups in the society as in some way constituting a difficult choice for the government is completely fallacious. The assumption implicit in the first assertion is already contradicted by evidence of 'horizontal solidarity' amongst the ruling class presented by the pluralists themselves.[5] The second is easily contradicted by ample historical instances in this book when these issues were purposefully overridden by the state primarily to preserve the climate of communalism.

The neo-colonial state has consistently denied basic bourgeois democratic rights to the people, a characteristic of most Third World countries under the domination of imperialism. The institutionalization of the *bumiputra* (son/prince of the soil) policy dates back to the colonial state's refusal to grant equal democratic liberties to the non-Malay masses in the Federation of Malaya proposals of 1948. The entire neo-colonial period has witnessed all manner of repressive legislations, and the most recent communalist policies of the Malaysian state have involved further measures aimed at national oppression (see Chapter 8, pp. 190-3).

Brutal state coercion has been exercised often enough in the history of class struggles of the Malayan people, most notoriously, the national liberation war of 1948-60, although it had wielded its suppressive powers from the first days of colonialism itself to crush Malay resistance. The use of police and armed forces to break workers' actions and demonstrations have also been well-documented.[6]

The 'Radical' Response to the Pluralists

In recent years, Malaysian academics have attempted to redress the pluralists' domination of social scientific analyses of Malaysian society.[7] While many of them have correctly identified the roots of communalism in British colonial practice, this 'radical' response has, in varying degree, tended to counterpose the cultural determinism of the pluralists with an economistic understanding of the relationship between class and communalism.

B.N. Cham's article (1975) was one of the earliest to challenge pluralist accounts of Malayan/Malaysian society. His attempts to reveal the roots of communalism in British colonialism and the 'determination in the last instance' of class, however, remain within the problematic of 'elite manipulation' because he does not theoretically analyse the state. In this view, communalism is seen merely as a superstructural phenomenon resting on an abstracted economic base:[8]

> ...communal politics is still very much alive. This is, of course, very natural not only because of the fact that the economic base of communalism has not been changed, but also because the manipulation of communal sentiment serves the purpose of divide and rule, thus strengthening class domination.

M.H. Lim (1981) does attempt to discuss the state, but by making the same mistakes as the Western academic Marxist theorists of the 'post-colonial state', he has chosen to focus on the ruling class and 'its' state; to ascertain which faction(s) of the ruling class 'dominates' or 'controls' the state, since this is seen as a key to understanding how the Malaysian state deploys communalism. The state is seen as the 'prize' of the contending factions of the ruling class, and even:[9]

> It is argued that the primary contradiction in Malaysian society at this point is not between capital and labour but between fragments of the dominant class...

Similarly, he claims a 'relative autonomy' for the Malaysian state, which leads to a 'crisis of hegemony':[10]

> [The state is beset by] a 'crisis of hegemony' in which no fragment of the dominant class is able to attain the position of a hegemonic bloc in power so that it can develop and determine its own path of capital accu-mulation... not even the metropolitan or international bourgeoisie.[!]

This 'relative autonomy' of the Malaysian state is similarly mechanistically invoked by K.S.Jomo (mimeo).

While the Poulantzas/Miliband debate may be instructive in showing the non-empiricist linkage between the state and social classes and the manner in which class oppression permeates through the various state ideological apparatuses, the question of the state's 'relative autonomy' can be pertinent only to specific conjunctures. The relative autonomy (or otherwise) of the state has to be established as a product of the class struggle, of history, rather than taken *a priori*, as if it was some structural feature that is a constant factor of the class struggle.

For the neo-Marxists, the 'relative autonomy' of the state serves to detach the analysis of the state from its relation to the oppressed. The concomitants of this are: firstly, that the economy is detached from the relation of domination/subordination maintained by the ruling class, thus, communalism as the particular *political* form in which the economic exploitation of the oppressed is organized, is obscured; secondly, the anti-democratic character of the state, realized principally through communalism recedes into the background behind considerations of how the state relates to different factions of the bourgeoisie.

The incapacity of these Malaysian academics to locate communalism in relation to the state leads them to present the state as standing 'above' communal conflict. Their examination of the NEP gives the impression that communalism is more or less the 'unintended consequences' of the state bourgeoisie's economic policy, or, at most, the product of an intra-ruling class conflict:[11]

> ...fragments of the dominant class, each of which has its own distinct ethnic or national identity.... As a result, ethnic conflicts have become the most prevalent form of contradiction in Malaysian society.

This conception misses the central point about the nature of the state and its communalist strategy. It wavers between mechanistic Marxism and a Weberian 'solution'—class and communalism are eclectically combined[12] '...to emphasize the *interplay* between class and ethnicity'.

In this respect, the very aim of the NEP—couched in terms of 'correcting the racial imbalance of wealth'—is seen as the latest attempt by the state to institutionalize communalism. The failure of these Marxists to see the fundamental role of the state in dividing and disorganising the masses also leads them to speculate about whether or not the increasing proletarianization of the Malay peasantry will lead them 'naturally' to realize their common class identity and destiny with the non-Malay workers.[13] 'When the Malay proletariat come into maturity, ethnic populism could lose its saliency and a crisis of legitimacy would be likely...' This 'immiseration thesis', common in Trotskyist analysis and practice, betrays its economism and fails to take into full account the state's role in creating divisions among the masses, and the different levels of contradictions.

In the same vein, one can detect in these various writers a hint that there is a 'progressive' aspect in the way the state bourgeoisie's policies are helping to proletarianize the Malay peasantry, and 'sweeping away the obfuscation of communal divisions' in its competition with the Chinese commercial bourgeoisie.[14] Based on its record, however, there is no doubt that the state will simply update the same communalist strategy (as it has through its recent communalist policies) in order to divide the masses.

It is incorrect to counterpose communalism against class division. Neither the cultural determinism of the pluralists nor the economistic and mechanistic interpretations of these Marxists have properly integrated class and ideology. Marxist analysis must take into account the significance of social divisions other than class but determined by class oppression, in all capitalist societies. Communal division in Malaysian society is a material reality and is utilized by the state, especially during periods of acute class struggle. The peculiar ideological power of communalism in Malaysia resides in the particular conditions the bourgeoisie must secure in order to maintain its domination: from the Malay *kampong* (village) social and religious institutions to the popular, everyday rhetoric regarding the racial myths propagated through the years. These have been further consolidated in the various communal clashes, the most tragic of which was on 13 May 1969. The communal division of labour and segregation also have a pervasive significance in the everyday consciousness of Malaysians.

At the same time, the state has used these divisions to maintain a certain form of political stability in the country. This is manifested in the fragile framework of the 'Alliance Formula', which collapsed temporarily in 1969 and had to be reconstructed into the *Barisan Nasional*. In doing so, the state tries to ensure that class struggle and communal conflict do not tear the society apart. In this sense it has recognized, shaped and perpetuated these divisions, and it is this which explains the particular form of communalism in Malaysia.

The Malaysian Marxists who merely assert the 'objective class position' of the Malay and non-Malay labouring masses, fail to appreciate that national oppression is a particular political form of class oppression in the present period. As we shall see in the Conclusion, there are those among the 'Progressives' who give grudging support to the state policies that restrict the democratic rights of the non-Malays to their own language, culture and education, for the sake of an abstract unity. It is precisely the defence of the democratic right of nationals to their own language and culture which will expose the real nature of class exploitation, rather than its suppression. Otherwise, it only serves the state's intention of fuelling Malay chauvinism (*bumiputraism*).

The Malaysian State and the Politics of Imperialist Domination

In contrast to the above approaches, this book's principal thesis is that dependent capitalism in Malaysia is incapable of generating capitalist development on the European model, in which allegiance to the state of the petty bourgeoisie and an important section of the working class could be gained by economic concession. The basis for bourgeois democracy—that is to say a political consensus under the dominance of the bourgeoisie—has instead had to resort principally to repression and communalism, or more precisely, repression through communalism.

The denial of democratic rights to the non-Malay population is the mechanism whereby the Malaysian ruling class seeks to maintain the loyalty of the Malay masses to a state that, despite its rhetoric, is unable to secure the advances for the masses to which they aspire, precisely because of its dependent relation to metropolitan capital.

Today, the democratic struggle is the principal component of the anti-imperialist struggle. It is a fundamental misconception to suppose that the struggle for democracy can divert the proletariat from the socialist revolution, or somehow obscure it. As Lenin himself put it:[15]

> Whoever does not recognise and champion the equality of nations and languages and does not fight against all national oppression or inequality, is not a Marxist; he is not even a democrat!

1. Pre-Colonial Malay Society: Historical Background

This survey of pre-colonial Malay society is not a detailed account of Malayan history, its intention is to try to establish the essential features of indigenous Malay society at the time of British colonization toward the latter half of the 19th Century. It also facilitates an examination of the nature of communal relations between the Malays and the immigrants of Chinese and Indian origin, since the Chinese had been mining and trading in the Malay states for at least a century before then.

The traditional Malay (feudal) social and political institutions prior to their transformation and cooption into the colonial and neo-colonial state ideological apparatus have to be appreciated in order to understand their current role in the Malaysian state's communalist strategy. These feudal institutions, especially the religious ones, have had a decisive ideological effect on the Malay masses; they have always operated in such a way as to introduce contradictions among the people.

An understanding of the nature of pre-capitalist societies also helps illuminate the specificity of capitalism, and thus the character and mechanisms of imperialist domination of the Malayan economy and society. It can then be seen that pre-capitalist societies have as much 'logic' about them as capitalist ones, and that beneath the court history of the intrigues of sultans and chiefs there is concealed the history of the subject classes. After all, these traditional modes of production could only reproduce themselves through the continual expropriation of the surplus produced by the peasantry. Contradictions are engendered in all class societies, and it is important to see how the colonial power used these to its advantage.

Who Was Here First?

Political practices based on 'ethnology', or 'race', is still prominent today whether in the service of the colonial state or the Malaysian state. Not surprisingly, the rhetorical question 'Who was here first?' is still employed in order to deprive ethnic minorities of their political rights. This question has been all too familiar in communalist politics in Malaya/Malaysia since the colonial period. It is, of course, an attempt to present the history of the people in terms of their 'racial' origins (and in this, pluralists are culpable), rather than as the product of their struggles. Consequently, it is claimed the non-Malay immigrants are not entitled to an equal share of the national cake because they are not the *bumiputra*; the immigrant worker is thus treated as a commodity par excellence in the capitalist economy.

If this argument is developed to its logical conclusion, then supreme political status should be accorded to the aborigines of the peninsula, the Orang Asli. The autochthons of the Malay peninsula comprised various groups classified as Negrito or Senoi, consisting of hunters and gatherers who subsisted along the coast, or nomadic tribes who depended on slash-and-burn cultivation in the clearings of the interior jungle.

The first Malay settlements clustered along river valleys on the mainland, and the Orang Asli were forced to move inland. There was some contact between the early Malays and the *sakai* (slave) as the Orang Asli were referred to by the Malays.[1] These ethnic Malay groups can be said to belong variously to the Deutero-Malay group, part of the Indonesian mongoloid peoples. They were thought to have moved southwards from Yunnan in south-west China some 3,000 years ago.[2]

In pre-colonial Malay society, a Malay 'national' identity did not exist. Most of the riverine settlements were insular, being separated by jungle, swamp, or mountain, and the chief means of transport was by river or sea. The composition of the Malay population itself was by no means homogeneous. Most of the Negri Sembilan Malays were of Minangkabau (Sumatran) origin, with their distinct socio-political system based on matrilineage. In the other states, in addition to local-born Malays and Minangkabau settlers there were Bugis (from the Celebes), Korinchi, Rawa, Mandiling, Batak (from Sumatra), Javanese and Achehnese, as well as Arabs. Usually, each of these different cultural groups set up separate settlements, as they were considered to be *anak dagang* (foreigners) distinct from the local-born *anak negeri*. Differences were defined not only in cultural terms, but also according to how each group fitted into the local class structure. The Bugis, for example, tended to form the large retinue of warriors around the chiefs or sultans, and to monopolize trade, while the local born Malays were mostly peasants who produced the surplus for their rulers.

This situation had significant implications for political suppression of the peasantry. The chief could always count on his retinue of foreign warriors to intimidate his subjects or to quell an uprising. Civil war was a constant feature in the uncertain conditions of the time and often the chiefs' strength was comparable to, or even greater than the sultans'. To understand this state of affairs, an examination of the character of the traditional mode of production is necessary.

The Malay Feudal Mode of Production

The development of the Malay feudal system by the 19th Century cannot be seen simply as the result of the internal developments of the social formation. External factors already had a significant influence on the contradictions within the local society.

Subsistence farming was the main preoccupation of the *kampong*; the surplus generated was minimal since there was no incentive on the part of the peasantry to increase their productivity:

> ...the authorities, Sultan, State Officer, local headman or 'anak raja', whoever had the power or might... helped themselves to any produce that they thought worth having whenever they felt able and inclined.[3]

Administratively it was more convenient for the chief to rule his subjects if they were concentrated in groups rather than dispersed over a wide area. Concentrated settlement also had some advantages for the peasantry because such farming practices as pest and weed control, construction of ditches, boundaries and defences, required co-operation (*gotong royong*). Constant harassment of the peasantry by rival chiefs and other potentates meant that there were benefits to be derived from having a lord and protector during those troubled times. In part this was the reason for the loyalty that the rulers expected and received from their subject peasantry. But whenever wars or oppression proved unbearable, flight was always a way out, as is clear from this peasant's lament:

> In former days, there was nothing to eat, there being a dearth of buffaloes, the planting of padi was difficult, and no one could be certain he would not have to flee on the morrow.[4]

Consequently, the peasantry grew such crops as coffee, tobacco, sago, bananas, maize, tapioca, sugar cane, pepper, gambier (for tanning and dyeing), and, of course, rice, all of which could be harvested annually. Some tree crops: sugar palm, areca, betel and coconut, for example, as well as fruit trees were also grown for their own consumption. Housing was in thatched, make-shift structures with few, usually portable household utensils. The only source of meagre income was the sale of cash crops or surplus foodstuffs, and sometimes, rice, to the Chinese miners. Forest products, notably rattan, *gutta percha*, bamboo, *damar* (wood resin) were also collected for export. There was no wage labour since the main object of production was consumption of use values, rather than the search for profit. Owing to the political subjugation of the peasants by Malay rulers, the chiefs could demand free labour from the peasantry under a corvee system known as *kerah*. Full-time craftsmen and artisans were rare for they existed only under the patronage of the aristocracy.

During the pre-colonial period, customary rules applied to the acquisition, use and disposal of land. According to these, although supreme rights to the 'negeri' (state) land were vested in the Sultan, every peasant in the community had the right to make use of land, as long as it was not cultivated by someone else and the exactions were paid to the Sultan, chief or other authority. The concept of proprietary rights developed from the original notion of usufructuary rights in areas of longer settlement.

Basically this was the level of development of the productive forces in Malay feudal society prior to colonialism. The minimal surplus meant that very few settlements were self-sufficient; produce and other commodities had to be transported by river and this partly explains why the early Malay settlements were found along rivers. The further goods had to travel inland the more toll stations they had to pass through; the alluvial soil to be found at the river estuaries was more fertile than that inland.

The typical Malay society described by Gullick[5] pertained to 19th Century conditions, but to a large extent it is the same today: a *kampong* varied in size from five to 100 or more dwellings, but around 40 was considered to comprise a *kampong* large enough to have its own *penghulu* (headman), mosque, and mosque officials. A district (*daerah*) would comprise of a few *kampongs* with a total population of about 1,000 people. The district chief normally resided in the largest *kampong*, and his authority depended on his district's size and potential, thus the tin mining districts of Perak had powerful chiefs. Revenue from trade passing through his *kampong* also contributed to a chief's power. Essential for the reproduction of the whole society, however, was the availability of land for rice cultivation.

Within the *kampong* itself, there were usually one or more kinship groups, identifiable by their separate homesteads as well as various forms of economic co-operation. The different groups in the village also tended to be related through intermarriage. Kinship relations followed the matrilineal pattern, although generally, inheritance of the headmanship was based on patrilineal descent. It was not necessary for the *penghulu* to belong to the aristocratic class, but usually he was one of the wealthier members of the society and had the support of the chief in the district, although formal appointment of the *penghulu* was supposed to have the Sultan's seal of approval (*surat kuasa*). As we shall see below, the sultan's power in relation to the chiefs was more apparent than real at that time.

The *penghulu*'s duties included maintaining law and order; providing corvee labour from his *kampong*; raising a defence levy or whatever was desired by the district chief; and handing over criminals to the chief. Islam had been established as the state religion since the 15th Century, and religious ideology was crucial to the feudal domination, with the mosque's *imam* as an important functionary in the political structure of the *kampong*. Nevertheless, religion in pre-colonial Malay society did not dominate the peasantry as does the contemporary state. Islamic law was not exercised at the expense of *adat* (local Malay customs), and religious leaders were often from among the people of their *kampong*.[6]

A degree of centralized authority had been established since the Malacca Sultanate became prominent in the 15th Century, and there were separate royal and chiefly lineages of hereditary succession. The degree of centralization varied from state to state, but for years the Malay communities of Perak and Selangor were subjected to political rule modelled after the Malacca Sultanate. The sultans and chiefs exercised their authority on a territorial basis and their authority was handed down through the patrilineal descent.[7]

The class system in traditional Malay society was thus marked by a distinct ruling class and a peasant subject class, and bound by political and ideological ties to the *raja* or sultan. The ruling class commanded power in every sense of the word—political, economic, religious, legal, military; upward social mobility into that class was unthinkable. The apex of the hierarchy was the sultan of the state; he appointed the chiefs, who in turn were aristocrats with their own chiefly lineage. The different forms of expropriation of surplus labour included the peasantry's performance of corvee labour, and taxation of produce and trade. By the 19th Century the rulers' received a lucrative income from: export duty on tin; landowner's royalty; import and excise duties on liquor and gambling; and shares of the tin mines profits.

In the chief's retinue, there were 'debt slaves' (*abdi* or *hamba*) and 'debt bondsmen' (*orang berhutang*); the status of the latter was higher than that of the former but they were no more than chattels. 'Debt bondswomen' were also kept for the sexual gratification of the chiefs' warriors. In addition to courtly chores, debt bondsmen were required to do agricultural work and the food produced was for the maintenance of the chief's household; that is, this surplus was used to keep the non-productive section of the community, the military and political personnel. No attempt was made, however, to organize the production of a large marketable surplus by the bondsmen. As we noted above, in general the Malay peasantry did not produce a large surplus, for to do so was to invite confiscation by the chief. Slaves and bondsmen were usually Orang Asli or Bataks from Sumatra who were non-Muslims, and thus the Islamic rule that Muslims should not be enslaved by other Muslims was circumvented.

Contradictions in the Malay Society

Historians of pre-colonial Malaya have tended to concentrate on the inherent weakness in the sultanate at the time in relation to the chiefdoms within each state. Some chiefs were much wealthier than the sultan and in a position to flout the royal wishes. Challenges to the throne were less frequent only because for much of the time the chiefs were also in rivalry amongst themselves. The contradictions inherent in the Malay traditional social formation occasioned by the periodic succession struggles and court intrigues involving the chiefs, provided the various European colonial powers with the opportunity to gain a foothold in the Malay states.

Chiefly power derived from the wealth that could be extracted from the subjects in the district. It was thus in the chief's interest to have as big a surplus as possible from the population so that they could be taxed accordingly. Since, as we have already noted, there was little intensive cultivation by the peasantry, that surplus could only be obtained through a more populous district. Increased revenue in turn enabled a chief to maintain a larger retinue to back up his power. The location of the lucrative mines in the outlying districts of the chiefs' was a crucial factor contributing to their relative strength vis-á-vis that of the sultan.

Theoretically, the sultan of the state was entitled to a portion of the state's revenue. In relation to actual royal power, however, this was not easy to enforce for it was not feasible to collect taxes in the outlying districts. As a result, the sultan was deprived of a valuable source of revenue from tin, which had become a vital commodity by the 19th Century. In the circumstances, disproportionate power accrued to the chiefs, who were enabled to wield strong influences in the struggles for succession.

By the time the colonial powers arrived this feature of the sultanates in the Malay states had become almost legendary. There was no rationalized system of succession to the throne, it automatically passed to the late sultan's son or brother. The ruling class was thus a rather closed and homogeneous group. Limiting the choice of succession to one lineage produced its own problems, for within one generation collateral branches had developed. Without a strict rule of primogeniture there were always more candidates than could be accommodated. Consequently, the group in power tended to form political alliances through intermarriage in an attempt to form an inner circle around the throne.[8]

External influences also accentuated the contradictions within the local society. The Malay peninsula lay at the crossroads of the east-west trade routes. Indian, Arab, and Chinese traders had been stopping over at the coastal ports for centuries. Until the 15th Century, the Malay peninsula lay on the outskirts of various kingdoms centred elsewhere in the Archipelago. As early as the 3rd Century AD, there were Hindu states in the northern part of the peninsula centred in Annam, Indo-China, and the Indian Coromandel coast,[9] from which Indian influence spread through the peninsula. The north-eastern part of the country had reputedly been a gold deposit centre for years and those states had been paying a gold tribute (*bunga emas*) to the Siamese king. Langkasuka, located on the east coast of what is now southern Thailand, was perhaps the most important kingdom to influence the east coast states; it existed over 1,000 years and even extended its control to the west coast.

During the 7th Century, the west coast of the peninsula fell under the control of the Sumatran Buddhist kingdom of Sri Vijaya; essentially a maritime power, it controlled all the strategic bases along the Straits of Malacca, from Acheh in the north of Sumatra to Tumasik (present-day Singapore) in the south. In the 14th Century, Sri Vijaya was overwhelmed by the Javanese kingdom of Majapahit. The strong Majapahit culture, a blend of Indian Hinduism and an equally strong indigenous culture, soon influenced Malay society. The old Malay chief adopted the title *Raja*, an authority with renewed 'divine right'. These Hindu influences, especially those surrounding the throne, survive to the present day together with the animism of the Malay masses.

In 1400, the Malacca Sultanate was founded by a Malay prince from Tumasik. This was the beginning of an indigenous system of political units that was to be established in the Malay states. The sultanates that followed derived their aspirations and traditions from this heroic period. The *Sejarah Melayu*, or Malay Annals, written in the 16th Century include legends and fables which have served to transmit the values and traditions of the ruling class.

In the Malay sultanates, the political system of the earlier Indonesian kingdoms was reproduced and rationalized. Malacca, situated strategically on the Straits, quickly grew as a trade centre. It was never free from the ambitions of Majapahit and Siam and when Cheng Ho's fleet arrived, Sultan Parameswara of Malacca willingly pledged allegiance to the Ming Emperor in return for protection; tribute and trade missions were then sent to China. Among the traders who stopped over at Malacca were the Arabs who not only brought commodities, but Islam as well. The Muslim religion had been established in the Archipelago at least a few centuries before the growth of Malacca. At Pasai in northern Sumatra there was an important Muslim state in the 13th Century, but not until the Malacca Sultan's conversion did Islam spread throughout the peninsula. From the 15th Century much of the Islamic influence emanated from Gujerat in India; Sufi missionaries too, played a large part in converting south-east Asia to Islamism.

During the 15th Century, the Malacca Sultanate under Tun Perak expanded its influence into the other states: Pahang, Trengganu and Kedah were taken out of Siamese suzerainty which was replaced with Muslim sultans. Johore and the surrounding islands were likewise brought under the expanding Sultanate and these

Malay states became fiefs of the Sultan of Malacca and the Malacca aristocracy.

European Mercantilism

The Malacca Sultanate existed for a comparatively short time considering the influence it had. In 1511, the capture of Malacca by the Portuguese signalled the beginning of Western influence and the consequent irrevocable change in the nature of the indigenous society. From this point, it is essential that any analysis of the local society takes into account the world economy and the state of development of Western capitalism. The purpose of the European traders was very different from that of previous traders whose concern was to be on the right side of the rulers rather than conquest and political control.

The mercantilist period of Western capitalism, between the 16th and 18th Centuries, marked a distinct phase in the relationship between the European powers and their colonies. The major trading nations (Spain, Portugal, Holland, France and England) built up worldwide colonial empires, frequently involving armed conflict among themselves. This stage, however, was quite distinct from the later imperialist stage toward the end of the 19th Century. During the mercantilist phase the colonial system had limited ends, namely, to protect the property and interests of their own merchants involved in the colonial trade—mainly monopolistic trading companies. This entailed excluding merchants of rival foreign powers and securing the best terms of trade for themselves; the mercantilists' main aim was to amass as much treasure as possible. New trade routes had to be found when the existing ones became monopolies of their rivals; navigation laws were enacted to confine trade to an individual country's own ships so that the strength of its navy could be maintained.

In this phase of colonialism only coastal ports and trading posts were affected since the merchant capitalists had little interest in penetrating into the interior of a country. The Europeans relied mainly upon their local or other Asian counterparts to obtain products from the hinterland. This reliance on a local intermediary (a role increasingly played by the Chinese) was the beginning of antagonism between the local Malays, and the 'middlemen' who became a link in the chain of exploitation. Before the advent of the Europeans, the Asian traders transacted with the Malays on a barter basis, and in the Malacca Sultanate generally, there was cultural and communal tolerance.[10]

Throughout their century of domination, the Portuguese never controlled the east-west trade because their Malacca outpost was too isolated from their other stations in Goa and the Moluccas. For much of the time they were on the defensive against the deposed Malacca sultans who had set up their capital in Johore, as well as

Acheh, and the Dutch. The 16th Century saw a three-cornered struggle between Acheh of north Sumatra, the Portuguese at Malacca, and the Malay sultans at Johore and Perak. At various times, the Achehnese succeeded in exercising control over Perak and Johore. The former had grown into a powerful kingdom and controlled the India trade. The demise of Malacca was accelerated by Muslim traders becoming attracted to Acheh, especially when port exactions at Malacca were becoming rather exorbitant.

The Dutch and the English made their appearance in the Archipelago at the turn of the 16th Century. In 1596, the Dutch managed to secure a base in Bantam, Java, the English too, set up a small station there, but at the time their interests were mainly confined to India. This left the Dutch as the only other European power contending with the Portuguese. But between 1540 and 1640 Acheh rather than the Dutch called the tune. In the first half of the 17th Century, Acheh exercised complete suzerainty over the Malay peninsula when it totally plundered not only Johore but also Pahang, Kedah and Perak. Not until 1640 were the Dutch strong enough, with the help of Johore, to take Malacca from the Portuguese.

But by this time, Malacca had lost much of its importance as a trading post. The spice trade, as well as the India-China trade, had been diverted elsewhere. Tin was becoming an important commodity of the peninsula because of the scarcity of silver bullion for the colonial trade, but most of the tin-producing states were vassals of Acheh. The Dutch made some futile attempts to rechannel this trade and shipping through Malacca, but gradually its port became redundant. Above all, the coercive nature of European administration drove many Chinese merchants away from Malacca.[11]

The rest of the 17th Century saw a power vacuum in the area with the decline of Acheh, while the Dutch lacked the means to enforce their will. The Johore Sultanate reasserted itself along the Sumatran rivers that had once been part of the Malacca Sultanate, in Siak, Indragiri, and Jambi. Around this time the Minangkabau people from West Sumatra migrated to the Malay peninsula; they were rice-growing peasants organized in small communities with a social system based on matrilineage.

The Bugis dominated the 18th Century. They were a seafaring people, traders and adventurers from the Celebes who had traded in the region for centuries. After the Dutch took over their main port of Macassar in 1667, the Bugis began to colonize settlements elsewhere in the Archipelago. They were extremely well organized in loose associations and had little contact with their own homeland. The usual court intrigues in the Malay states provided them with a convenient method of entrenching themselves in the sultanates. In Johore, Bugis managed to secure the highest positions in the nobility under Daeng Parani. His nephew, Raja Luma, even succeeded in becoming the first Sultan of Selangor in 1745. But as early as 1681 there had been a Bugis settlement at the mouth of the Selangor river threatening Kedah to the north.

The Bugis ruled from Rhio (islands to the south of Singapore), subjecting the rest of the peninsula to their power. Rhio became the most important commercial centre of the region, especially for the tin trade. In 1784, when the continual conflict with the Dutch ended in defeat for the Bugis, Rhio became a Dutch outpost. But by this time, the Dutch were a declining European power,[12] and at the end of the 18th Century, when the Dutch East India Company collapsed, the Bugis began once more to assume their former position.

When the British arrived south from Penang, there was a Bugis *Temenggong* (minister) in Singapore and his grandson, Abu Bakar, was Sultan of Johore; the Bugis had left their mark on the ruling houses in the Malay states. In all these states, the immigrants from the surrounding areas spread over a number of localities, living on mining and agriculture. This scattering of settlements further contributed to the decentralization of political control.

Summary

Pre-colonial Malay society could be characterized as feudal. Surplus was extracted from the peasantry through a non-economic exaction—a produce tax and corvee labour under the *kerah* system. Slavery and 'debt bondage' were in evidence especially in the aristocratic households. Under the local conditions of sparse population and ample cultivable land as well as scant incentive for increased production due to the fear of confiscation of the surplus by the overlord, there was little or no differentiation of the peasantry.

In these feudal conditions, Islamic religious ideology was as essential a part of political domination, as was the symbolic significance of sultans and the aristocracy for the Malay peasantry. As we shall see in the next chapter, these feudal institutions were not eradicated when the colonial power introduced capitalism into the traditional social formation. This also had implications, not least for the success of the state's communalist ideology and the perception of class contradictions in the rural sector.

The pre-colonial social formation entailed contradictions that were internal to the Malay feudal mode of production, but were exacerbated by external factors. As a trade centre the Malay peninsula was as old as the east-west silk and spice trade. Contradictions manifested by the frequent succession struggles as well as the fragmentary political units, were exploited by the various European colonial powers including the British.

The nature of relations between the Malays and the Chinese and other Asian traders and tin miners did not take on a communalistic form prior to colonialism. Chinese miners were often partners with Malay chiefs in economic ventures as well as allies in the constant civil wars between rulers. These Asians had been trading on a barter basis with the Malay states and there is evidence to indicate that relations between the local Malays and the traders were good, and even that a fair degree of assimilation had developed. Asian merchants took on the role of intermediaries only when European mercantilism began to dominate trade at Malacca and elsewhere on the peninsula. As a consequence of them a serving as a link in the chain of exploitation, contradictions between Asian merchants and the Malays assumed antagonistic dimensions.

2. The Impact of British Colonialism on Class Formation and Communalism

The division of Malayan society on a communal basis—between the Malays on the one hand, and the people of Chinese and Indian origin on the other—has its roots in British colonization of Malaya in the third quarter of the 19th Century. Not to see this as the centre-piece of colonial rule is at least part of the obfuscation of the phenomenon by pluralist and other social scientists. In this chapter, the impact of capitalism on the traditional mode of production will be examined. The fierce resistance of the Malay peasantry to British intervention at the outset, in no small way contributed to the strategy of the colonial state, in which the coopting of the traditional Malay ruling class into the state has been crucial. At the same time, not only were there political and ideological reasons for the colonial power to 'preserve' the Malay peasantry's *kampong* social structure, it also accorded with the economic requirements of Western imperialism.

The resultant massive immigration drive saw the growth of the Malayan working class and its emergence as the spearhead of the conscious struggle against imperialism. As that struggle grew, the communalist strategy of the colonial state evolved accordingly.

From Mercantilism to Imperialism

We shall first examine the evolution of British colonial policy which culminated in direct intervention in 1874. By the 18th Century, the British East India Company had grown into a powerful commercial concern[1] and its merchant capitalist backers in London were an important force in Parliament; it even had its own private army in the East. Prior to that time, the British had been primarily interested in India and especially in protecting the China tea trade. Moreover, the Malay Archipelago was recognized as specifically a Dutch sphere of influence and that diplomatically it would be unwise to enter into conflict at the time. The Dutch, reciprocally, did not interfere in India, while in Europe, Holland served as a useful buffer against France.

Toward the end of the 18th Century, however, it became increasingly essential to secure commodities that could be traded for

China tea. Silver bullion was found to be too expensive for this purpose, especially when the supply was exhausted owing to Spain joining France against the English in the war of 1779-85. Tin and spices from the Archipelago were seen as the answer, and the British began seeking a base in the area which would enable them to procure these commodities.

In 1786, after many expeditions had failed, Francis Light, a trader in the service of the East India Company, led a small force into the island of Penang which was offered to the British by the Sultan of Kedah in return for protection against Siam. The port quickly grew and became an important centre for trans-shipment of Indian piece goods and opium and a collecting point for tin and spices. A settlement of immigrants mushroomed around Georgetown. Besides commerce, the Malay, Chinese, Indian and European planters took to the cultivation of various spices such as pepper, gambier, nutmeg, and of sugar and coffee. By 1860, the Chinese population in Penang rapidly expanded from 3,000 in 1794 to around 28,000 (nearly half the total population); by 1840, the Indian population had also grown to almost 10,000.[2]

Despite Penang's growth, it never attained the vital role in the China trade that was envisaged for it. This was mainly because the Company discovered that the ideal commodity to exchange for the China tea was opium, which was cheap, and easy to grow and ship from India. As we know, China was soon paying out more in silver bullion than she was receiving in opium. With the new lease of life found in their old, highly profitable colonies of India and China, the British again postponed involving themselves in the Malay states. This phase of colonialism was marked, as we noted, by reliance on unequal exchange rather than coercion. This is not to say that coercion or 'gunship diplomacy' was not used to secure monopolies or unequal treaties with the local Malay rulers. At Penang, Light followed the practice of the Dutch and the Malay chiefs by appointing 'Kapitans' to uphold law and order in the respective settler communities. The British administrator, of course, held overall jurisdiction; British law was instituted in Penang in 1808.

It is important to bear in mind the context of British non-interventionist policy at this stage. By the 19th Century, Britain alone among the colonial powers was in a position to extend her interests and intensify the exploitation of the backward areas of the world. France had lost the Napoleonic Wars, while Spain and Holland had also become second-rate powers. British industrial capital had risen to a position of dominance, and the textile, mining, and metallurgical industries, which spearheaded the industrial revolution, were dependent for their prosperity and growth on the export market. The British industrial capitalists, being far ahead of their competitors had little to fear from free competition. The mercantile system, fettered by elaborate restrictions and regulations was felt to be incompatible with the freedom of capital to expand. Colonial policy, even aside from the cost of maintaining the Empire, thus came under attack from the 'Free Trade Party'. In Britain itself, the repeal of the Corn Laws reflected the struggle between the landed class and the ascendant bourgeoisie.[3]

The liberal policy was also an attempt by the British industrial capitalists to curtail the wealth and power of the merchant class. The Regulation Act of 1773 and Pitt's India Act were specifically aimed at securing state control over the colonies; ostensibly intended to check oppressive Company laws, the Acts were necessary for the next stage of the exploitation.

The Napoleonic Wars in the early 19th Century had no less repercussions in the East. After the French had established a revolutionary republic in the Netherlands in 1795, a new threat was posed to the British by all the Dutch possessions in the East, and to protect their India-China trade, the British captured Malacca that same year. They then moved further eastward to take the Moluccas in 1796. Throughout the war, Penang and Malacca served as calling points for British ships travelling between China and India. The French base at Mauritius was captured in 1810 and in 1811 the Dutch threat was removed when Java also fell to the British.

The moment that the Sunda Straits between Java and Sumatra was cleared, it was no longer necessary for the India-China trade to go through the Straits of Malacca, with the result that the importance of Penang waned in relation to Batavia (Jakarta). But after the war with France, in an effort to bolster the Dutch against any further European threat, Java, Celebes, Moluccas, Malacca, and various other outposts in Sumatra reverted to the Dutch. The British kept the strategic points at Mauritius, Ceylon and the Cape. By 1818, the Dutch had regained their former strength in the Archipelago.

The British bourgeoisie emerged from the war with France ready to consolidate a world monopoly for the products of their factories, and consequently viewed the Dutch threat in the East with alarm; they thus decided to try to secure full control of the Straits of Malacca. Raffles was sent to locate a position and in 1819, he opted for Singapore. He signed a treaty with the Temenggong of Johore, who ruled the island, for a factory to be established there; this treaty, however, had to be ratified by the Sultan of Johore who was the overlord. Complications arose out of the usual quarrels over succession, the gist of which was that the Temenggong was opposed to the prevailing Sultan, who also happened to be under Dutch control. Hussein, a contender for the throne who had been bypassed, was brought to Singapore by Raffles and recognized as the Sultan of Johore-Rhio. That same year, in return for $5,000 annually, Hussein ratified the treaty with the British. That was the manner by which Raffles 'founded' Singapore.

Singapore's phenomenal growth as an entrepot port is by now

legendary. Settlers, mostly Chinese from around the area and from China, began arriving in huge numbers. From an island peopled by about 150 Malays in 1819, its population by 1860 was almost 75,000, of which 85 per cent were Chinese and Indian.[4] The Dutch felt threatened by this, and a compromise was duly arrived at. By the Anglo-Dutch Treaty of 1824, the Dutch ceded Malacca and the remaining outposts in India in return for Bencoolen in Sumatra. Singapore was recognized as British and the right of free passage for all vessels through the British ports at Penang and Singapore was maintained. By this treaty the Johore-Rhio Empire was formally broken up.

At Penang, British relations with the Sultan of Kedah were soured. The Treaty of Cession in 1786 between the Sultan of Kedah and Light had not been successfully concluded, and the British still had not settled the payment due to the Sultan. There was continual harassment by the Sultan who called upon the aid of Lanuns, and they cut off Penang's food supply, which had been dependent on Kedah. The British gained the upper hand, however, and in 1800, secured from the Sultan Province Wellesley on the mainland opposite Penang harbour. The intention was that the Province would be used to grow food for the population in Penang, and also, to clear the area of pirates; but not until 1821, when the Malays from Linggi were fleeing from the Siamese, did the Province really begin to grow.

The dawn of the 19th Century saw the Siamese trying to regain suzerainty over the northern Malay states of Kedah, Perak, Selangor, Kelantan, and Trengganu, all of which had been sending annual tribute of the *bunga emas* to the King of Siam for years. The Siamese attacked Kedah in 1821 and were about to take Perak and Selangor when the British decided to act—previously they had tried to coax the Siamese into some kind of trading relationship. Flouting London's 'liberalized' colonial policy, Fullerton, the Governor at Penang, used 'gunboat diplomacy' to prevent the Siamese from carrying out their intention, and in a face-saving agreement, the Siamese were dissuaded from acting upon any further ambitions in the Malay states. The British also used a combination of force and a palace coup (once again backing their own candidate to the throne) to dislodge the Siamese surrogates in power at the Perak court, in order to establish British influence in the Malay states.

Of the three 'Straits Settlements' (Penang, Malacca, Singapore), Singapore became the most important. Its population grew with the trade boom. It became the main entrepot centre in the Archipelago for Straits produce: Indian cloth and opium, China tea and porcelain, and above all, British iron and manufactured goods. The British Agency Houses, which survive to the present day, were established from those early days and represented the main merchants managing the trade. Many were British private merchants who came to the East after the East India Company had lost its monopoly.[5] Much of the retail trade depended upon a comprador class, mainly Chinese and Indian, who were also the main source of revenue for the colonial administration, which was obtained through taxation of the Chinese gambling activities and opium. In 1805, almost 60 per cent of the total revenue of Penang accrued from these two sources alone.[6] Chinese farmers who began to cultivate pepper and gambier in Singapore soon moved into Johore for fresh land, and by 1830, pepper had become Singapore's main export.

The British had their first taste of Malay resistance when they tried to exact tribute from the small inland state of Naning, off Malacca. The first British force sent there was defeated by the local Minangkabaus, but the Naning War (1831-32) ended when the British sent in a large expedition. The British, in fact, had no right of tribute over Naning—these rights were taken over from the Dutch but those relating to Naning had lapsed long before.[7]

After the costly Naning War, the Colonial Office's directive on non-intervention had more strictly to be adhered to by the local colonial administrators, and in the period up to 1874, this policy was maintained. The period saw a great upsurge of tin mining by Chinese immigrants; in 1830, 15-20,000 Chinese miners and traders were in the country. The discovery of tin at Larut, in Perak, brought a huge influx of Chinese in 1850. Similar discoveries at Klang (Selangor) and Sungei Ujong (Negri Sembilan) brought even more Chinese miners. By 1874, there were an estimated 40,000 Chinese at Larut and 15,000 at Sungei Ujong.[8]

The Chinese were organized in tightly-knit clans, and secret societies provided an important institutional cohesive factor for political order. Labourers were recruited in China and sent to specific mines in Malaya. The 'Kapitans', who were entrepreneurs as well as overseers of the labourers, began to build up considerable power. They frequently played a strategic role in the conflicts between the rival Malay rulers by supporting and financing one against the other. The rival secret societies themselves were constantly feuding over the lucrative mines and territory. With the involvement of the Chinese miners and Straits merchants, the conflict between the Malay rulers took on a very different dimension from those previously applying.

Traditionally, tin had been extracted by the Malays by means of the *dulang* (panning) method, but it had been merely a peripheral occupation. The Chinese used the 'open-cast' method with mechanical pumps which enabled them to work the deeper and richer deposits, and they soon became the main suppliers of tin to the British. In the Straits Settlements (SS), Indian immigrants too had begun to settle in increasing numbers as traders, moneylenders and labourers. By 1871, the immigrant population in the Settlements was as large as that of the Malays as Table 2.1 shows.

Table 2.1
Composition of Population in the Straits Settlements, 1871

	Penang	Singapore	Malacca	Total
Chinese	36,561	54,572	13,482	104,615
Indians	18,611	11,501	3,278	33,390
Malays	75,216	26,141	58,098	159,453
Europeans	433	1,946	50	2,429
Eurasians	2,409	2,951	2,850	8,210
Total	133,230	97,111	77,756	308,097

Figures include immigrants from Indonesia, especially to Singapore.

Source: Ooi Jin Bee, *Peninsula Malaysia*, Table 5.2

British Intervention—Malay Resistance

In the final quarter of the 19th Century, British colonial policy in the Malay states, as elsewhere in the world, changed to one of direct intervention. Capitalism had developed into its highest stage, according to Lenin's analysis.[9]

Among the contributory factors necessitating this change of policy were: the need for raw materials and cheaper sources of labour; markets for British manufactured goods; and class struggle, leading to a decline in the rate of profit, at the metropolitan centre itself.[10] Monopoly capitalism had emerged out of competitive capitalism, and the other imperialist countries, especially Germany and the USA, had attained a position which enabled them to challenge Britain's industrial supremacy. Monopoly capital, in seeking to eliminate cut-throat competition on the home market, now it developed on a world scale.

In the imperialist countries' race to carve up the world Britain took formal control of the Malay states through the Pangkor Treaty in 1874; this marked the beginning of total domination of the traditional mode of production by the capitalist mode. British interests were no longer confined only to the coastal ports but surged inland. The opening of the Suez Canal in 1869 and the advent of the steamship had enhanced the importance of the Straits of Malacca. Above all, the British were pre-empting any move by Bismarck's Germany to take control of the Malay states. This was much in line with the Straits Settlements' traders' and merchants' desire for the Colonial Office to intervene and protect their interests in the Malay states.[11]

The European merchants and settlers began to take a keen interest in the potential for cash crop cultivation in the Malay states. They had advanced capital to Chinese merchants in the Straits Settlements during the mid-19th Century so that the latter could in turn finance the gambier and pepper plantations in Johore under the *kangchu* system;[12] but capital investment could be made more productive only if the planters had permanent titles to the land.

Until that time, the Chinese cultivators had grown only crops receiving minimal care and yielding quick returns with relatively small capital investment, practising a more or less shifting cultivation system. More stable conditions were necessary to the mining interests in order to ensure a steady supply for the burgeoning tin industry.

Britain's first opportunity for intervention was once again provided by the succession struggles in Perak:

> [The Larut Wars] were used as one of the pretexts for British intervention in Perak in 1874... the threat to the trade of Penang during 1872-3 provided one excuse for this change of policy.[13]

The British backed a challenger to the throne, the Mentri of Larut, against Raja Abdullah. The ensuing strife was complicated by cross-alliances with the rival secret societies, the Ghee Hin and the Hai San.

By way of the Pangkor Treaty, Andrew Clark (Governor of the Straits Settlements) managed to secure the acceptance of a British Resident in Perak who would 'advise the sultan on all matters of importance other than those affecting the Muslim religion'.[14] Similarly in Selangor, during the squabbles between rival Malay potentates and their Chinese mine-owner allies the British managed to have their own Resident accepted. In Negri Sembilan, the British supported a chief against his rivals and induced him to accept a Resident at Sungei Ujong, one of the nine 'states' of Negri Sembilan.

British intervention met with immediate resistance from the Malay peasantry. There was intense hatred of British rule, especially the new tax and revenue laws. The Perak Wars began when the first British Resident was killed in the uprising led by Chief Maharaja Lela in 1875. Reinforcements had to be sent from India and Hong Kong before the uprising could be put down. In 1877, villages in which suspected sympathizers of the rebels lived were burnt down and the leaders hanged.[15] In Selangor, the British Resident antagonized not only the Malays but the Chinese as well, the subsequent uprising was, however, put down. The Negri Sembilan War against the British and their client, Dato Klana, was led by Yam Tuan Antah, and massive reinforcements of Gurkha and Arab troops and artillery were deployed to put down this resistance. The other 'states' of Negri Sembilan, however, were not prepared to accept a British Resident, and he was confined to Sungei Ujong. At the conclusion of the Negri Sembilan War, the British were quite convinced that they had taught the Malays 'such a lesson as will eventually satisfy other native states of our supremacy....'[16]

Pahang was not rich in tin like the West coast states but it had very valuable trade with Singapore. The usual dispute over the throne there had existed since the Civil War of 1857-63 involving Johore and Siam. Britain's opportunity came in 1887 when their candidate, Wan Ahmad, was persuaded to accept a British 'Agent' in return for recognizing him as Sultan. The Pahang Rebellion broke out soon after the Residential System was extended there. This was the historic resistance led by Bahman, a peasant who had already distinguished himself in the Selangor War.[17] In 1891, a campaign of civil disobedience was mounted in which the people in Pahang defied all state regulations. The Rebellion lasted four years and for the most part it involved guerrilla warfare on the part of the Malays. Although the Rebellion was suppressed, the leaders, among whom were To' Gajah and Mat Kilau, were never caught but were given sanctuary by the people in Kelantan and Trengganu.

The west coast states of Perak, Selangor, Pahang and Negri Sembilan were federated in 1896 with Swettenham as Resident-General. This resulted in an even more highly centralized administration and took away whatever previous powers the states had. Until then, the northern states had been recognized as falling within Siamese sphere of influence. Toward the close of the 19th Century, the British decided to encroach on these states as well because of the growing incursion by the other imperialist powers. The Germans were negotiating with the Siamese for a naval base at Langkawi, just north of Penang, while the Siamese themselves were becoming more assertive in their control of Kelantan and Trengganu; this, itself, conflicted with British interests in those states—in 1900, the British firm, Duff Development Co. had sovereign rights over half of Kelantan.[18]

The British managed to have 'Advisers' accepted in Kelantan and Trengganu in 1902, but this was inadequate for their purpose. The opportunity for greater control arose during the realignment of imperialist forces at the time. The British signed an *Entente Cordiale* ending hostilities with the French in 1904 and they divided their specific spheres of influence in South-East Asia. It was also an opportunity for the Siamese to establish a *modus vivendi* with the French and British. The result was the Anglo-Siamese Treaty of 1907 whereby the Siamese transferred their rights and claims over Kelantan, Trengganu, Kedah and Perlis to the British. The Treaty did not include the Malay states to the north in the Kra peninsula.[19]

The British could impose their rule in these northern states only with great caution, for they contained the bulk of the fiercely independent Malay population; they had, however, intervened in the dynastic crisis in the Kelantan royal family.[20] In 1915, a peasant rebellion broke out at Pasir Puteh, led by Haji Mat Hassan, popularly known as To' Janggut. The Kelantan Rising was, above all, a reaction to the newly introduced land regulation. The District Office, a colonial institution, was sacked and the bungalows and property of the European planters burned and looted. Troops had to be despatched from Singapore and, in the words of the Chief Police Officer, they were '...a little barbarous and killed some innocent "klings" [Indians] whom they took to be mutineers'.[21] To'

Janggut was killed in action and his body hung upside down at the Kota Bahru town *padang* (square) for several days as a lesson to the rebels. There was also trouble at Pasir Mas and Ulu Kelantan.

The Trengganu Rebellion of 1928 was even more serious. The peasants there were organized and led by one Haji Abdul Rahman and yet another To' Janggut. They were totally opposed to the Sultan's acceptance of British control. The peasants defied the authorities by refusing to pay land rent and ignoring the other controls on their economic activities. At Kuala Brang they took over the government office but were dispersed further downstream at Kuala Trengganu. The second To' Janggut was killed in action and the British reestablished their authority only when reinforcements arrived from the capital.

Kedah, Perlis, Kelantan and Trengganu remained outside the 'Federated Malay States' (FMS) and were known as the 'Unfederated Malay States' (UMS). Instead of Residents they had 'Advisers' whose powers were narrowly circumscribed. Johore was the last state to be brought under British rule, in 1909, when the Sultan was induced to accept an Adviser.

In just about every state where the British established their rule, there was strong Malay resistance. In these struggles, the Malay peasantry played a major part since they were opposed to the new impositions on their livelihood by the colonial state. (These state policies will be examined later in this chapter.) This gives the lie to the usual assertions that the British were everywhere welcomed as the bearers of 'progress' or that colonialism itself was a 'civilising mission'.[22] The deep hatred for colonialism and the aspiration for independence can be attested to in studies of the rebellions.[23] The methods used by the colonialists against the insurgents, such as the razing of whole villages, and rounding up the people in 'strategic hamlets',[24] were to foreshadow the methods employed during the 'Emergency'. The British managed to prevail over the resistance less because of their military superiority than through their harnessing of the help of rival Malay factions. M. Amin's assessment of the resistance is worth pondering over:

> Armed Malay resistance gives the lie to the view, very effectively used by the British, that the anti-imperialist struggle in Malaya was confined solely to the non-Malay, i.e. mainly Chinese population. In fact the national liberation struggles of the 1940s and early 1950s can be seen as a continuation of the armed struggle first launched against the British colonialism by the patriotic Malay forces. The content of the Malay resistance was anti-imperialist, but it was characterised by spontaneity. With the development of the capitalist economy and the birth of the working class, the anti-imperialist struggle was gradually transformed into conscious struggle....[25]

The British Colonial State and the Malay Ruling Class

The fierce Malay resistance to British rule, as well as the cost involved for direct administration, led the colonial power to change its method of rule. Instead of using primarily alien police and army to maintain law and order, the British relied on the chiefs and *penghulus* to administer at the ground level. The Governor's despatch in 1893 stated: 'To unify and classify the government service of these states, great care must be taken to leave full scope for the employment of natives, especially the native aristocracy.'[26] The effect of this was to subordinate the feudal class relations in Malay peasant society to colonial domination. Local chiefs and aristocrats were turned into loyal vassals of the British who could assure them of protection against their rivals and rebellious subjects. The traditionally weak sultans were thenceforth revitalized, especially with the new state revenue imposed by the British.

Direct British political and administrative control masqueraded under the supposed 'advice' the Malay rulers had requested. The Malay aristocracy were first relegated to the minor roles of rural administration, while Europeans filled the executive ranks in all departments. In this respect, the colonial power was concerned to maintain:

> ...the special position of the Malay ruling class in relation both to the other Malays and other 'Asiatics', with the creation early in the new century of a junior administrative cadre drawn almost entirely from the younger generation of Malay aristocrats.[27]

The sultans were propped up by real as well as ritual authority within Malay society through the centralization of power within each state and the corresponding emasculation of the chiefs' authority. But even though the sultans had little say in the public policies which they rubber-stamped, the British Residents were careful to create an impression of seeking consultation with them, especially with relation to state matters and those affecting Malay customs and religion. This cannot be seen as necessitated by political expediency alone, but rather, as an essential part of British communalist strategy:

> To assure Malays that their traditional way of life was not threatened. Likewise, the safeguarding and defence of Islam gave the Malays a psychological assurance that the country was still theirs, despite the influx of immigrants.[28]

It is also for this reason that religion became inseparably bound up with communalism in Malaya. The increased status of 'Malay religion and customs' in the charge of the Malay rulers was meant to compensate for the loss of sovereignty. Constitutional and administrative changes were thus made to introduce Islam as the official religion:

> The preservation and reinforcement of the traditional bases of

authority and social organization implicit in British policy, and progressive centralization, combined to fashion a more authoritarian form of religious administration than that the peninsula had known before.[29]

The Rulers and their State Councils began to assume a greater responsibility for religious matters and a whole new hierarchy of religious officials—*ulama, imams, kathis*—functioned in the royal court and in the *kampongs*.

The Malay rulers were provided with personal allowances, and with increments as the state grew, as well as elaborate palaces and a privy purse at state expense. At the same time, the British left the subsidiary conferment of rank, title, and allowances within the royal courts themselves to the sultans and their advisers. This, of course, was to give the impression of 'observing Malay custom'. The rulers and senior chiefs alone held the privileged seats in the State Councils set up as advisory bodies to assist the Residents. These were basically sounding boards for local feeling regarding British policies, and to lend legitimacy to the policies through the aristocratic association. The Councils dealt with such business as mining leases, tariff regulation, taxation, public works, and local jurisprudence. With the abolition of debt-bondage, they also decided upon claims for compensation by the chiefs and their dependants. As the administrative load increased, however, the Councils were gradually reduced to rubber-stamping relatively minor state business, especially after the federal system was established in 1895.

With the stated intention of British administrative control to utilize the traditional Malay ruling class in local administration, the *penghulus* became the linchpins. They were given a moderate salary for the administrative charge of their *mukim* (the equivalent of the British parish), and entrusted with keeping the peace and enforcing government regulations. As the state regulations abounded, so did the duties of the *penghulus* and the British Residents saw in indirect rule a great benefit:

> A word of praise is due to the penghulus; many of them are old men accustomed to the old regime of the Malay rajas, but the energy and interest these officers display in their multifarious and responsible duties is remarkable. A penghulu is expected to administer and explain to the Malays in his mukim such intricate laws as the Land and Mining Enactments, the Procedure Codes and the Forest and Timber Rules. By no class of officer is the Government better served...[30]

This form of indirect rule served the British perfectly because the *penghulus* were part of the traditional social fabric of the *kampong* and in most cases they also had kinship and landholding ties with the local Malay community. As such, the impact of colonial impositions were absorbed by this system.

Amongst the traditional Malay ruling class, the British found the most difficulty in allocating administrative authority to the chiefs. With their direct line of traditional authority taken over by the District Officer, the chiefs became merely 'native magistrates' or 'judges' and assistants to the Residents on Malay questions.

The Malayan Civil Service, by the close of the 19th Century was, however, a strictly European preserve and was giving rise to some concern: 'If India were officered with Europeans on the same scale as the Malay states, it would be necessary for India to considerably retrench salaries.'[31] Consequently, in accordance with the policy to educate 'the sons of the higher order of natives'[32] the rulers were persuaded to send their sons to be educated for the purpose of the administration of and indoctrination into the British way of thinking. Places were reserved for Malays 'of good birth' in 'Government English Schools', which were to be found in all the main towns. These half-hearted measures, however, were inadequate to meet British requirements for administrative expertise or growing demands by the Malay ruling class for more Malay officers in the Administration. Thus a more purposeful colonial policy was elaborated which, as Roff puts it:

> ...was based on the old but designed unashamedly to create from the traditional élite a new class of colonial civil servants whose association with the British might, on the one hand, satisfy the myth of continued Malay sovereignty, and on the other hand, serve as a bulwark against possible encroachment from the residual non-Malay population in the future.[33]

In 1905, the Kuala Kangsar Malay College was created for this expressed purpose, and run along the lines of an English public school.

While the Malay ruling class was being groomed to participate in the colonial state, British educational policy toward the Malay masses was quite different. They received only a smattering of education in local schools, for as the Resident Birch remarked: 'It is very satisfactory to know that this system does not over-educate the boys... [who] almost all follow the avocations of their parents or relations, chiefly in agricultural pursuits.'[34] The minimum qualification for clerical work was a good knowledge of the English language and it is revealing that in Perak, in 1903, out of 2,900 boys who finished local schooling, only one found employment as a clerk.[35] We shall see later how this accorded with the colonial state's policy of confining the Malay peasantry to the subsistence sector. In Perak, in 1895, for example, only 1.25 per cent of the state revenue was devoted to education.[36]

This policy in respect of the Malay peasantry was further accentuated by the fact that all the Government English Schools were in the main towns, while the countryside's commitment to Islam meant that the mission schools were forbidden there. In contrast to colonial policy elsewhere, Christian missionaries were forbidden to proselytize among the Malays since this would conflict with British communalist strategy. Instead, Islamic education was stimulated and encouraged in the local schools. This succeeded in further segregating the masses and facilitating their susceptibility to communalist propaganda. In the 1901 Census of the Federation of Malay States (FMS), Malays made up less than 10 per cent of the total population of Kuala Lumpur, Taiping and Ipoh.[37]

The colonial power thus guided the traditional Malay ruling class into the Administration, ostensibly with the aim of 'promoting the special position of the Malays', meanwhile other nationals, Chinese and Indian, were excluded from administrative and political office. This was justified by the High Commissioner, in response to a request by the Malayan-born Indian community for a share in the administrative appointments in 1936, in the following way:

> This is the sixth country in which I have served, and I do not know of any country in which what I might call a foreigner—that is to say, a native not a native of the country or an Englishman—has ever been appointed to an administrative post.[38]

This illustrates the official categorization of the settled and permanently domiciled Chinese and Indians as 'foreigners'. By 1930, the proportion of Chinese born and resident in the country had reached 30 per cent, while the male:female ratio had improved from fewer than 2.10 in 1911 to nearly 5:10 in 1931.[39]

It has been argued that if the British had given equal opportunities to the Chinese and Indians it would have provoked Malay opposition and that 'the essential British role in Malaya as arbitrator and adjudicator within the plural society was to a large extent dependent upon preserving the distinctions between the separate communities.'[40] This is the classic pluralist view that ignores the fact that the segregation of the masses was the creation of the colonial power. Roff's own conclusion is all the more baffling considering he had correctly observed the intentions of the colonial power.

That the colonial state was not primarily concerned with the distinctions between immigrants and non-immigrants, but rather with the communalistic distinction, is evident from the fact that legal status as 'Malays' was automatically conferred upon the many Sumatran, Javanese, and other Indonesians who, encouraged by the colonial state itself, migrated to the Malay states. The religious criterion became the decisive one for citizenship. By creating a stereotype of the 'unassimilable aliens', the colonial government could, moreover, justify spending nothing on integrating the Indians and Chinese into Malayan society. Although this criterion was applied to the Indians, the stereotype was created more with the Chinese in mind than with the Indians, doubtless owing to the preponderance of the Chinese in the non-Malay population, but the attempt at division is quite clear.

During the 1920s, the colonial state enacted some changes to the General Clerical Service which were intended to reflect its so-called 'pro-Malay' policy. This was partly dictated by force of circumstances: until that time, the specialized services of the bureaucracy (railways, post, medical, public works) were mainly occupied by non-Malays; the Malays comprising only 10 per cent of the personnel in these services because of the scarcity of qualified staff during the initial years of colonialism. The British had mainly contracted English-educated Jaffna Tamils and other Indians to fill these positions. During the slump of 1921 and a crisis in state finances, however, there was a call for retrenchment of the overseas staff and that the Malays be equipped 'to take their proper place in the administrative and commercial life of these states'.[41]

These measures were accordingly adopted by the Retrenchment Commission and the Residents of the Federation of Malay States were all in agreement. This policy was also intended to woo the Unfederated Malay States (UMS), by demonstrating to them that the British were fulfilling their 'obligations' to the Malays. Thus the regulation was implemented for preferences to be given to the Malays in the subordinate ranks of the government services, and English schools began to be opened in the rural areas too. Soon the number of Malays enrolled in English schools in the FMS increased from around 700 in 1923 to 2,500 in 1933. Largely owing to this policy a Malay petty bourgeoisie was to grow up within the state bureaucracy; it became the class most susceptible to the communalist ideology of the state. This class, however, must be distinguished from the Malay ruling class: aristocratic, landowning, and occupying the highest echelon of the state apparatus.

The Colonial State and the Malay Peasantry

The British colonial state's attitude toward the Malay peasantry may seem paradoxical in the light of the capitalist state's role in proletarianizing the peasantry elsewhere.[42] This, we shall see, was not dictated by political expediency and ideological intent alone; there were sound economic reasons for preserving the Malay petty commodity sector. The decision to resort to large scale immigration of Chinese and Indian wage labour for capitalist exploitation in the urban and plantation sectors, has led to the particular class configuration in Malaya and shaped the state's communalist strategy since. The magnanimous image of British colonial rule frequently portrayed in pluralist accounts[43] will further be shown as false.

Upon the imposition of colonial rule, the British wasted no time in opening up the closed internal market of the Malay states. Land legislation (the Torrens System) was instituted to regulate land usage, fix tenure, register titles, and to control free alienation of land, which had been the norm. Tax and revenue laws soon followed and a generalized money economy was introduced.[44] As the plantation economy got under way and the infrastructure was established Indian immigrant labour was imported to work on the estates and to build roads, railways and other public works, while the Malay peasantry were to maintain their subsistence way of life in the *kampong* and be patronized as the *bumiputra*.

First, however, the ferocity of Malay resistance during the initial years of intervention had taught the British not to push the peasantry too far; a large degree of compulsion was required to get the jungle cleared and persuade the peasants to work in the plantations, since they were unlikely to abandon their subsistence lifestyle willingly.[45] This earned them the epithet that has been applied to all peasants in the Third World, namely, of being 'lazy and shiftless', this was the obverse of coaxing by the 'paternalistic' colonial master. This dual aspect of colonial attitude toward the Malay peasantry is best summed up by Roff:

> But in fairness it must be said that many Englishmen, as well as Malays, felt a genuine affection for the values and virtues inherent in Malay rural life and were reluctant to see it radically disturbed, holding that this was against the best interests as well as the wishes of the peasants themselves. Even where this was not so, it was widely, almost universally believed that the Malay, despite his charm, was indolent and shiftless and resistant to change and progress.[46]

Secondly, the Malay states had ample cultivable land for commercial use without the need to encroach upon the peasants' lands. This partly explains the absence of large scale peasant movements in Malaya other than those during the initial years of British intervention. This is not to say that within the Malay reservations themselves contradictions were not already being engendered through capitalist penetration of the rural sector, but nevertheless, they had not developed to the same degree as elsewhere in the Third World, where peasant uprisings were generated.

Immigrant labour from China and India was thus the ideal alternative for the British in Malaya. In these two British colonies, the local industry and agriculture had been disrupted by capitalism, and famine and war had further created 'surplus labour'. Abundant cheap Indian labour was not only available but the Indian labourers were considered to be 'docile by nature' and 'ideal' for plantation work.[47] Labour for the mines and factories was taken care of by the Chinese bosses themselves, and the colonial government had only to regulate the flow as it saw fit.

A further facet of this aspect of colonial policy, seemingly based on cold economic logic, emerged with the start of the rubber boom at the beginning of the 20th Century, when the colonial state sought to protect the European plantation interests from the competition of the Malay smallholders. Indeed, the Malay peasantry, far from 'lazy and shiftless', were quick to respond to the new economic opportunities in cash crop cultivation, rather than to stick to the deteriorating conditions of rice farming. As we shall see, they proved to be strong competitors against the plantation interests.

Not least in colonial reckoning, the all-important wage commodity—rice—was needed for the workers in the capitalist sector. The increased rice consumption was being met by imports from neighbouring countries, and rice imports alone constituted 35 per cent of total imports.[48] What better alternative but to encourage the peasantry to supply this necessity without seriously disrupting their lifestyle?

While the form of the traditional mode of production was conserved, it nevertheless lost its independence: it now functioned strictly in the interest of capitalist accumulation at the metropolitan centre. Colonial land policy was instrumental in creating the conditions for effecting this. First *ladang* (shifting) cultivation by the peasantry was restricted and the available fertile land was increasingly alienated to the mining and plantation interests. Compared to the plantation owners, heavier taxes were also borne by the peasantry.[49]

Despite the handicaps, peasant agriculture did develop, '... largely the result of spontaneous response to the growing demand for food products from the increasing population rather than through conscious government economic planning.'[50]

But the low price of rice was driving the Malay peasantry into market gardening or into wage labour or, especially during the rubber boom, into rubber production. The Malay peasants' lack of response to the colonial state's efforts to promote rice production led to the encouragement of immigrant peasant settlers from the surrounding Indonesian islands. This was only partially successful, however, for the Indonesian immigrants themselves were soon attracted to cash (mainly rubber) economy. Thus, in Perak by 1889, only 7,500 acres out of a total of 36,455 acres that had been alienated were being cultivated.[51]

The colonial government was, however, reluctant to allow the Chinese to cultivate padi. This was motivated by:

> ...the government's fear of political repercussions. The official opinion was that padi was a Malay preserve and the intrusion of the non-Malays could alienate Malay support for the British. Many officials were also opposed to the idea of building up a Chinese peasantry which would form a permanent population and compete with the Malays. (Lim,TG, 1977:187)

The Malay ruling class persistently put pressure on the British not to alienate land to the Chinese for padi cultivation.

Consequently, the Malay Reservations Enactment was passed in the Federal Council in 1913. This gave the Residents power to set aside specified areas of land (mainly rice lands) exclusively for Malay ownership, and also prohibited the mortgaging or leasing of Reservation land to non-Malays. In 1917, with the threat of rice shortage toward the end of the First World War, and the rapidity with which the Malay peasantry was turning to rubber rather than rice cultivation, the Rice Lands Enactment was passed. This restricted the cultivation of products other than rice in the Reservations.[52] Blame for the peasant land problem was laid upon the sale of land to the non-Malays, while the rapid alienation of land to the European interests and speculators was ignored. Most of these Reservation areas were unoccupied land in the interior where, '...not only were there few conflicting interests to be considered, but also the absence of a Malay population to take advantage of them.'[53] Additionally, there was insufficient suitable land for settlement, and inadequate provision for subsequent population increase or land needs.

Kept within the Reservations, land prices fell by as much as 50 per cent, and Malay peasant landowners petitioned to be excluded from the Reservations because their land could no longer be used as collateral for credit.[54] These conditions substantially contributed toward creating a class of wealthy Malay landowners who were in a position to purchase land free from outside competition, at prices well below the market level. They could also charge higher interest rates and impose stiffer conditions on loans, and accept Malay debtors' land as collateral.[55] Islamic laws prohibit usury, but there are many ways of circumventing them, for example: usufructuary loan (*gadai*) to the creditor; usufructuary mortgage (*jual janji*) whereby proprietary right is pledged, while the creditor also possesses the usufruct of the land. No actual transfer of money takes place in either case, while debt repayment is disguised as land sale.[56]

The Reservation laws did not, of course, frustrate the European capitalist concerns, although many applications for land by non-Malays who were settling in Malaya were turned down solely for communalist considerations:

> In some areas, non-Malay land applicants were rejected by officers although there were no Malay applicants for the land, and reservations were wilfully created to deny them of it.... In 1928, for example, in the midst of a lot of breast-beating about the protection of Malay land interests from the onslaught of Chinese intruders, the government reserved 75,000 acres of land for the Western oil palm industry....[57]

To boost rice production, the colonial state was forced to expend some funds on irrigating paddy land in Krian (the 'rice bowl' area) for the first time at the turn of the century. The Krian Irrigation Scheme was completed only in 1906, two decades after its conception. Far from being a generous gesture to the peasantry,

> ...the padi cultivators of Krian were dealt another blow by the official policy that the cost of any irrigation scheme would not be shouldered by the government alone... 'the natives are more appreciative of what is done for them by the government when they have to pay for it'....[58]

Consequently, the Krian peasantry had to pay an increase in taxation.

It was to be a further 26 years before any other infrastructural improvements in the rice growing sector were realized, that is, when the Drainage and Irrigation Department (DID) was established in 1932.

The 1918 harvest failure in India diverted most of the Burmese rice from Malaya, leading to shortage and price increase. The government-imposed rice control in mid-1919 lasted until 1921. The price of rice was subsidized by the state, but in essence it was a subsidy to the employers in the capitalist sector who otherwise would have had to increase wages to keep up with the subsistence level. The subsidy did not, however, absorb all the price increase and the remainder was borne by the masses. The rice price support scheme did attract some new rice growers but when rice imports were resumed in 1922, the paddy area once again shrank to its former acreage.

The decline in rubber prices provided the colonial government with another opportunity to promote rice cultivation. The severe discriminatory conditions placed on peasant rubber smallholders drove many into rice cultivation,[59] but when rubber prices rose again, rice output fell correspondingly. From 1920-25, local rice production accounted for only 38 per cent of total consumption; this declined to 28 per cent for the rest of the decade.[60] The 1923 Annual Report of the Federated Malay States shows that the colonial government was not unaware of the problems facing the peasant sector, although little was done to help them.

As rice consumption rose and by the time of the 1930s Depression the situation reached crisis point, the colonial state had to establish the Rice Cultivation Committee. Setting up of the DID had stabilized the area under paddy cultivation. It also had the effect of shifting the pattern of rice growing areas away from the traditional riverine settlements to the coastal plains. By 1939, the government managed to provide a measure of water conservancy to some 68 per cent of the paddy land in the Federated Malay States and the Straits Settlements.[61] In 1933, a Customs Duty was imposed on imported rice in order to fund these irrigation schemes; this increased the hardship of the masses who, were already badly hit by the Depression. Although yields in the irrigated areas increased, this was offset by constant or declining acreages elsewhere in the Federated Malay States. Thus Clive Kessler observed of the Kelantan peasantry:

> The intensification of Kelantanese agriculture benefited not the peasant but those who demanded a share of his produce; it stemmed from and contributed to the growing power of the central regime, and especially the chiefly aristocracy.[62]

The colonial government did little to ease the pressing problem of indebtedness of the peasantry to the Indian 'chettiars' and Chinese shopkeepers and middlemen. In 1911, according to Lim, TG (1977:84),in Krian alone, it was estimated that chetty loans to the peasantry amounted to $400,000. The peasants' padi supplies were tied down to Chinese millers, while their consumer needs also tied them to Chinese shopkeepers. These credit and marketing arrangements were clearly exploitative, but the government was reluctant to provide the needed rice mills, co-operative societies and drainage and irrigation works. The practice known locally as *padi ratus*, for example, placed the peasants at the mercy of the millers who gave them a much lower price for the rice than the market price.

The Rubber Smallholders

The peasantry had taken up smallholding rubber production from the industry's inception. In the rice growing areas, rubber constituted a peripheral occupation while elsewhere it was the main activity; rubber rapidly became the single most cultivated crop among the peasantry. Compared to rice, rubber had its attraction, especially during the rubber boom in the early 20th Century. The labour processes involved are quite different: the labour inputs are less once the trees have grown, and average gross earnings per acre are higher than for rice growing. The rubber trees are also less susceptible to climatic vicissitudes.

The discrimination against the rubber-producing peasantry, as has already been noted, was justified by the colonial government in terms of protecting the traditional way of life of the Malays. Between 1926 and 1930, about 55,000 acres only were granted to the peasantry compared to 174,000 acres granted to the estates.[63] Credit facilities were also easily accessible to the latter while the smallholders were considered a poor risk. Among other things, the government's distinction between 'smallholding' and 'estate' by using the 100-acre cut-off point as the object of regulations blurred the class difference and the smallholding peasants lost out. According to postwar figures, about 345,000 smallholdings were of less than 25 acres, and only 7,000 were more than 25 acres.[64]

The rubber smallholding peasantry suffered the most blatant discrimination during the restriction schemes that were introduced to solve the depressed price situation by means of restricting rubber exports. The first of these was the Stevenson Scheme in 1922: rubber holdings with production records (i.e. the plantations) were allocated quotas on the basis of their production performance during a common base year. But those without records (mainly the smallholders) were allocated quotas based on the 'Duncan' scale. The result was that the allowance for the peasantry tended to be underassessed, whereas the reverse was true of the estates' quota:

> Throughout the entire period of restriction, smallholders as a body received less than one half the average assessment of plantations although the evidence gathered by the government showed that the on plantations.[65]

The only respite for the peasantry during the period of restriction was to fall back on their other farm pursuits, while it has been noted that: 'It can be put to the credit of the Stevenson Plan that it saved many of the rubber companies from bankruptcy.'[66]

The discriminatory scheme reflected the extent to which the plantations' interests were represented in the colonial Administration; the scheme itself was overseen by a senior British officer in the Malayan Civil Service. The entire committee, except for one Malay, were representatives of the estates or the colonial state, while the peasant smallholders had no say in the committee, even though by 1934 they were accounting for 217,000 tons compared to the estates' 260,000 tons. At the end of the first period of restriction, the smallholders' share of production had shrunk to as little as 113,000 tons whereas the estate production had scarcely been curtailed at 246,000 tons.[67]

Mounting peasant discontent and violence led to the setting up of a committee which admitted the injustice done to the smallholders: 'The *Financial Times* of July 26 1948 pointed out that action taken by the International Rubber Regulation Scheme to restrict output of rubber smallholders may have caused in some degree the present disorders.'[68] An extract from a despatch to the Secretary of State at the Foreign Office brings this out clearly:

> [The scheme of 1934] reduced the output of the rubber in Malaya by means of a bill enacted by the then Conservative Government which enabled a committee sitting in London, composed of representatives of the larger Agency Houses to settle quarter by quarter exactly what the output of rubber should be.... You will not be surprised to learn, in order to keep the price of rubber up, that when war broke out the output allowed to all classes of rubber producers was 60 per cent of their pre-1934 capacity, and, what is even more astonishing, the quota was not raised to the full 100 per cent until the last quarter of 1940.... It cannot be held unreasonable that the smallholders in Malaya who had an acreage approximately equal to the plantations, have resented this control, particularly as it has since been ascertained by Bauer who was sent out from the LSE, that the IRRC was administered in such a way that the smallholders had no chance against the larger plantations....[69]

The allocation for the peasants was subsequently raised, and this served to defuse their resentment. Despite the discrimination, the smallholders manifested tremendous tenacity and capacity to survive, even when rubber prices were among the most volatile of raw materials. The restriction scheme of 1934, the International Regulation Scheme, was not dissimilar to the Stevenson Scheme except in so far as it was intended to cover the Dutch East Indies as well as the rest of the rubber producing world. It achieved market stabilization of a sort but once again largely at the expense of the smallholders. It has been estimated that under this scheme the losses inflicted on smallholders as a result of underassessment exceeded £10 million, and £30 million under the Stevenson Scheme.[70] Table 2.2 illustrates how this affected the smallholders.

Table 2.2
Annual Output of Rubber per Mature Acre of Malayan Estates and Smallholdings, 1930—40
(lb. to nearest 5 lb.)

Year	Estates	Smallholdings	Smallholdings as % of estates
1930	380	460	118
1931	375	445	119
1932	365	385	106
1933	355	465	131
1934	Regulation introduced during year.		
1935	295	240	81
1936	275	230	84
1937	375	330	88
1938	290	200	69
1939	290	200	69
1940	410	370	90

Source: P.T. Bauer, *The Rubber Industry*, p.97.

In addition to the International Regulation Scheme restrictions there was also a regulation forbidding new planting by the peasantry. The costs of replanting were, however, too great for the peasantry to undertake, particularly as the trees did not come to maturity for at least five years; moreover, there were no economies of scale to be reaped by the smallholders. The legislation was withdrawn only in 1947, but not until 1952 was the colonial government forced to undertake a replanting programme both for the estates and smallholders; this gesture was necessitated by the critical condition of the whole smallholding sector at that time (see chapter 5). Above all, it had been realized that the peasantry's low-cost production served to keep consumer prices down in the metropolis. The preservation of the petty commodity sector was also in line with the colonial state's communalist strategy. The 'Emergency' during the 1940s and 1950s was a hazardous period for the colonial state, and the concessions were part of the package to win the 'hearts and minds' of the peasantry. The Reservation Enactments largely succeeded in isolating the Malay peasantry from the non-Malay working class and the anti-colonial struggle. The *cordon sanitaire* operating upon *kampong* social relations, maintained the ideological domination of the traditional Malay ruling class which permeated the rural institutions. That the Malay

(Islamic) way of life had to be protected against the corruption of the non-Malay aliens was impressed upon the peasantry. The economic well-being of the rich Chinese was simply the obverse of the 'communist subversive' non-Malay workers. In short they all represented the same evil: 'materialism'.

But in the other parts of the *mukim* outside the Reservations, alienation of land by the planting companies and other local interests was under way at a phenomenal pace, and by 1940, most Reservations had reached maximum development,[71] but Malays continued to acquire land outside the Reservations mainly for rubber growing. In 1940 also, relaxation of the confinement of the Malay masses to the Reservations began. Land ownership was transferred almost immediately upon being alienated, and the economically dominant groups, mainly European interests, tended to gain most. Speculation was rife, and prime holdings, adjoining plantations or astriding roads, were bought up by foreign interests.

In the ensuing years, this contradictory process of the state desperate to cultivate the Malay petty commodity peasant sector, while at the same time unable to halt the forces of differentiation continued. The Enactments did serve as a countervailing force to the factors differentiating the peasantry. The mixed economy of most *kampongs* also allowed the subsistence-based Malay farmers to spread the effects of market forces. As we shall see in Chapter 6, the peasantry in the rice sector tended to be more susceptible to the forces accentuating differentiation than were those in the rubber sector. In most parts of the country, the peasantry tended to diversify their agricultural activities. Thus segregated from the urban sector, the Malay peasants did not become allies of the working class, a point to which we shall now turn.

The Colonial Economy and the Growth of the Working Class

With the arrival of imperialist capital, the power of capital to develop generalized commodity production in areas still under pre-capitalist relations of production was demonstrated for the first time. Initially, British capital invested in tin, which had been by far the most important product of the Malay states since the early 19th Century. Until 1913, Chinese tin producers accounted for at least three-quarters of the total output. Chinese workers had been recruited for the mines by the *towkays* (Chinese bosses) since the industry began. Many came as indentured labour with no intention of staying permanently, but the obligatio%to repay the cost of the passage to the employer, and the cycle of debts contracted as a result of the terrible working conditions, ensured that many never became free labourers. With the active connivance of the steamship companies the trade in the human cargo reached appalling levels of degradation. Between 1895 to 1927, six million Chinese went to Malaya. When European capital led to the expansion of the tin mining industry in the early 20th Century the stream of immigrant labour from South China increased rapidly. It was thus, quite unnecessary for the colonial state to use legislative or coercive means to induce the Malay peasantry to provide labour power for the mines.

By the turn of the century, British mining firms such as Osborne and Chappel, and what was to become Gopeng Consolidated, were established in 1902 and 1892 respectively. Tin was the essential raw material for the West's canning industry, but it was largely with the introduction of the dredge, which facilitated large-scale mining, that foreign capital began to dominate the tin mining industry; only the Western firms could afford this heavily mechanized method of production. The local, labour-intensive methods of mining were soon either dwarfed or destroyed, as Table 2.3 illustrates. In 1910, European mining agencies produced 20 per cent of the total tin output, but by 1940, their share had risen to 80 per cent.[72] Characteristic of monopoly capital, ownership and control were highly concentrated: in 1939, more than half the European output was controlled by Anglo-Oriental (Malaya) Ltd, a subsidiary of London Tin Corporation. For many years it has been one of the main suppliers of the world's tin, with substantial stake in the other tin producing countries, Bolivia and Nigeria.

Table 2.3
Percentage of Total Output of Tin by Methods used

	1928	1937	1954
Dredging	30.2	48.2	52.2
Gravel-pump	45.1	38.2	37.4
Hydraulic	8.4	4.3	2.3
Opencast	6.4	4.0	2.2
Lode	5.6	3.8	3.7
Dulang washing	1.8	1.3	1.8
Others	2.5	0.2	0.4
Total	*100.0*	*100.0*	*100.0*

Source: L.L. Fremor, *Report on the Mining Industry*, p.64, in Allen and Donnithorn, 1957.

Tin smelting also soon passed from Chinese to European control; Straits Trading Company established in 1887, built smelters in Perak and Negri Sembilan. In 1890, it moved to Singapore, and opened a smelter at Pulau Brani; another was built in Butterworth in 1902 and yet another in Liverpool in 1937. Straits Trading Company monopolized not only the tin of the peninsula, but of the surrounding area too. Eastern Smelting Company was the only Malayan competitor, but it was bought up by British capital in 1922, when it became part of Consolidated Tin Smelters.

The first European-financed plantations in the Malay states

concentrated on coffee growing. The colonial government undertook to clear the land, and a policy was devised to attract Western capital, while planters and loans were made available to investors. The interest in coffee was shortlived as a glut in the world market in the 1890s owing to overproduction in Brazil led to the diversion of investments into rubber. From then on, rubber became the mainstay of the Malayan economy alongside tin. The British Agency Houses played a management role in the varied forms of capital they handled and their activities were soon diversified into almost every branch of the economy.

The demand for rubber in the world market that was created by the growth of the automobile industry provided a spur for the Malayan rubber industry and as a result, rubber prices fluctuated with the fortunes of the US car industry. From 1900 to 1938, the US alone consumed half the world's output of rubber. The rubber boom promised large profits for investors, especially when wages could be kept low: projected profits were £35 per acre, and in 1910, dividends of around 225 per cent were paid.[73]

One of the earliest of the large plantation companies was Petaling Rubber Company, formed by Harrisons and Crosfield. Other Agency Houses with substantial interests in rubber were Guthrie and Sime Darby. These companies are still the main rubber producers in Malaysia today. Local capitalists, such as the Tan family of Malacca were also big plantation owners, as were rubber manufacturing concerns such as Dunlop, who had substantial interests from those early years. By 1914, Malaya was producing half the world's supply of rubber; the total acreage under rubber cultivation rose from 38,000 acres in 1905 to 2,250,000 acres by 1926.[74]

The urgent demand for rubber and tin thus provided the main impetus for the influx of capital into Malaya. Table 2.4 shows the estimates of Western investments during the early 20th Century. British capital's monopoly among the Western investors was as complete as could be expected of the colonizing power. The pattern of British investments in Malaya compared to those in her other colonies, however, showed a strong contrast: whereas two-thirds of all British overseas investments were in foreign government and municipal bonds, public utilities and railways, in Malaya 93 per cent of British investments were in plantations and mines (see Table 2.5). That much of the state finances for public utilities and infrastructure was raised almost wholly from local revenue is an indication of the wealth of Malaya. The different components of British direct investments in Malaya for successive years (see Table 2.6) show the preponderance of investments in the plantation and mining sectors.

The early plantations were manned by mainly indentured immigrant labour from South India. The labourers would sign a contract in India to work at a particular estate in Malaya for from

Table 2.4   Western Investments in Malaya, 1914-37 (US $ million)

Year	Direct Investments	Rentier Investments[1] (mainly govt. securities)	Total
1914	150	44	194
1930	447	113	560
1937	372[2]	83	455[3]

Notes: 1 Small size of government debt in relation to entrepreneurial investments can be explained by the modest role of the state in economic activities in Malaya, e.g. railways were built out of current revenue and by 1937, many loans had been redeemed.
2 About two-thirds was in rubber, and one-sixth in tin.
3 About 70% of the total investment was British.
Source: Allen and Donnithorn, 1957:200

Table 2.5   Estimated Distribution of British Overseas Investments in Selected Countries, 1930

Countries	Proportion of Investments in		Total[3]	
	Govt. Bonds (%)[1]	Others (%)[2]	(£m)	(%)
USA	—	100.0	200	5.9
Latin America	89.6	10.4	694	20.5
Canada and Newfoundland	76.7	23.3	446	13.2
Australia and New Zealand	89.6	10.4	617	18.2
South Africa	62.9	37.1	224	6.6
Europe	68.6	31.4	245	7.2
India and Ceylon	79.3	20.7	458	13.5
Others	59.4	40.6	260	7.7
Other British colonies	72.4	27.6	134	4.0
Malaya	7.4	92.6	108	3.2
Total	70.9	29.1	3,386	100.0

Notes: 1   Includes public utilities and railways.
2   Represents direct investments in mining, plantations, and manufacturing.
3   Total represents about 85% of all long-term capital invested by Britain in 1930.

Source: The Royal Institute of International Affairs, *The Problem of International Investments, 1937*, 1965, p.143.

Table 2.6   Components of British Direct Investments in Malaya

Sectors	1930		1936		1965		1970	
	(£m)	(%)	(£m)	(%)	(£m)	(%)	(£m)	(%)
Agriculture	92	85.2	94.1	80.5	95.6	66.4	112.5	61.6
Mining	8	7.4	13.1	11.2	10.4	7.2	15.6	8.5
Distribution	-	-	-	-	15.0	10.4	27.8	15.2
Manufacture	-	-	-	-	19.8	13.8	19.2	10.5
Others	8	7.4	9.7	8.3	3.2	2.2	7.7	4.2
Total	108	100.0	116.9	100.0	144.0	100.0	182.8	100.0

Note: Investment figures do not include banking, insurance, oil.
Source: J.A. Saham, Role of British investment in the development of the Malaysian economy, Ph'D thesis, Hull.

Table 2.7
Variation of Wage Rates on Estates

Year	Average Price of Rubber (cents/lb.)	Wage Rates (cents/day)
1922	20	40
1925	120	45
1930	20	40
1933	10	32
1937	32	50

Source: K.G. Tregonning, 1964, p.166.

three to five years. Indian labour was opted for, once Malay labour had been ruled out for a number of reasons, including the facts that: African labour was out of the question as slavery had been abolished in the British Empire in 1833; Javanese labour was difficult to import because of Dutch restrictive emigration policy.[75] The South Indian Tamils were thus considered 'ideal': they were already familiar with plantation conditions and with British rule. Additionally, they were supposedly good workers who at the same time were 'not too ambitious, and easily managed',[76] and lacked the enterprise to attempt to rise above their station, as the Chinese were allegedly inclined to do. Indian immigration was also considered to be a shrewd political measure to counterbalance the numbers of Chinese in Malaya, in line with one aspect of the colonial state's communalist strategy:

> [Governor Weld was anxious] ...for political reasons that the great preponderance of the Chinese over any one race in some of the native states under our Administration should be counterbalanced as much as possible by the influx of Indian and other nationalities.[77]

Wages were often below subsistence level and the workers' living conditions were appalling, even during boom years (see Table 2.7). The plantation workers invariably incurred debts at the estate store, which meant that in order to pay them they had to sign on for further service. When the rubber boom took off, labourers were recruited through the *kangany* system: the estate employer would send a foreman back to his native village in India and he would receive a free passage and a commission for each worker he recruited.[78] The plantation workers were employed on a monthly basis and lived in dilapidated filthy *bangsals* or labour lines (huts). The hardship they endured was such that Malaya was seen as '...a death trap yawning to engulf the surplus population of India'.[79]

Malaya's raw materials, rubber and tin, were always at the

mercy of the world commodity market. The first disaster struck the tin industry in 1929 when the Depression set in: tin prices fell from £284 a ton in 1926 to £120 in 1931. During such crises, the colonial state's economic interests were clearly demonstrated. The employers decided to solve or regulate the crisis by cutting down production; correspondingly the state refused any further applications for mining land. The Tin Producers Council, representing producers from the main tin-producing countries and dominated by the London Tin Corporation, duly called for compulsory restriction of output. Restriction was renewed on and off up to 1941 and a buffer stock of tin was also created to cushion the effects of fluctuating prices. Restriction created much unemployment and hit the local mining firms hardest, all of which induced Silcock to note:

> On the whole, it seems probable that the interests of Malaya as a low cost producer gained little if anything from the scheme, and that its adoption and renewal were mainly the result of pressure from the large group of companies that has extensive high cost holdings in Bolivia and Nigeria, in addition to its Malayan holdings.[80]

During the Depression, wages fell sharply as Table 2.7 shows. At the same time, estate employment fell from 258,780 in 1929 to 125,600 in 1932.[81] The labour laws provided barely any protection for the Indian estate worker. The Labour Ordinance of 1892, supposedly for protecting the workers, provoked protests from the planters and was abrogated. Sugar planters also protested against the abolition of penal clauses which were intended to punish the labourers who absconded from the *kangany* arrangement.[82]

The great demand for labour at the height of the rubber boom led the colonial government to step in and take an active role in recruiting labour, since the *kangany* system could scarcely meet the demand. The Indian Immigration Fund was established by means of a levy on the estates; camps were then set up in South India and assisted immigration got under way. A steamship subsidy was granted to the shipping firms, the administrative machinery was set up to assist recruitment, and in India, all emigration restrictions were withdrawn in 1897. Under such conditions of recruitment and employment, the immigrant workers were entirely at the mercy of the employers. Even the feudal social relations of the workers' home village were transposed into the new situation of the Malayan plantation, a purely capitalist enterprise. For example, the European planter had to be regarded as *peria dorai*, or, 'lord and master'.[83] This is an instance of the capitalist mode utilizing pre-capitalist relations of production for reproducing variable capital:

> African slave labour had built up the West Indian plantations and the Indian indentured labourer performed the same function for the British plantations in Malaya. The system was but a euphemism for slavery. It is said that nearly a million South Indians died in the process.[84]

The British attitude toward Indian immigration was echoed in the South African Sir Thomas Hyslop's oft-quoted remark: 'We want Indians as indentured labourers but not as free men.'[85]

The consequence of all this was the Indian plantation workers' relative isolation from the labour movement owing to their insular existence in the estates; but as we shall see, once they became unionized, they were among the most militant of the Malayan proletariat.

As if the degrading working conditions were not enough, in the event of a downturn in the economic conditions, the immigrants were simply shipped back like the commodities they had come to produce, without the rights of citizenship having been accorded to them. The intention of this policy, as we have indicated, was to fuel Malay chauvinism and *bumiputraism* rather than for economic considerations, for the immigrants were portrayed as alien bounty seekers of the commercial sector with no patriotic feeling for the *tanah ayer* (fatherland). Through the years this ideological means to cushion the impact of the recession was used against the workers, together with anti-labour laws. In 1908, South Indians provided 43,500 out of a total of 57,000 rubber estate workers; by 1918, the figure for Indian labour had reached 139,500.[86]

As the colonial economy expanded and socialized production became widespread, the bonds of the indenture system began to slacken and the Chinese workers spread to sectors other than mining. By the 1930s, the great influx of Chinese and Indian immigrants had changed the entire social structure of Malaya. Table 2.8 illustrates the pattern of immigration in the first decades of the 20th Century. The volume of immigrants can be compared to the development and growth of the main exports of Malaya, shown in Table 2.9. The flow of migration, however, is not reflected in Table 2.9. For example, between 1860-1957, four million Indians entered the country, while 2.8 million left and 1.2 million appear to have been wiped out by disease, snake bites, exhaustion, malnutrition, and so on.[87]

The distribution of the different nationals in the population was directly related to the degree of foreign economic penetration. Thus, the Straits Settlements and the west coast states contained fewer Malays than the east coast and central northern parts of Malaya. From the beginning, any hope of a class-conscious movement developing among the workers and peasants across communal lines was discouraged by the division of labour. Segregation was enhanced by a sort of 'cultural involution' within each community, and the colonial state catered neither for the social, cultural nor political needs of the masses (not to mention the economic needs), a process that served to provide the climate for communalism.

The non-Malays especially, had to rely on self-help and the philanthropy of the wealthy classes in their respective communities,

Table 2.8
Composition of Population of Malaya and Singapore, 1911-38
(in thousands)

	1911	1921	1931	1938
Malays	1,438	1,651	1,962	2,211
Chinese	917	1,175	1,709	2,220
Indians	267	472	624	744
Europeans	11	15	18	28
Eurasians	11	13	16	18
Others	29	33	56	58
Total	2,673	3,359	4,385	5,279

Source: Malayan Year Book, 1939.

Table 2.9
Value of Chief Exports from Malaya, 1906-54
(million Straits Dollars)[1]

Year	Rubber	Tin	Pineapple	Coconut	Palm-Oil	Total[2]
1906	11	89	3	9	—	293
1912	28	107	3	17	—	357
1920	280	128	7	52	—	879
1925	763	175	8	35	—	1,282
1929	440	182	9	36	1	925
1932	80	56	8	22	1	323
1937	489	190	9	31	7	897
1947	787	109	—	29	23	1,295
1950	2,455	479	12	144	37	3,961
1953	1,232	391	20	103	38	2,897

Notes: 1 Figures to and including 1920 refer to SS only.
     2 Includes others.

Source: ECAFE Economic Surveys of Asia and the Far East.

and this contributed to the perpetuation of the system of patronage that has become the hallmark of the main political parties, the Malayan Chinese Association (MCA), the Malayan Indian Congress (MIC), as well as United Malays National Organisation (UMNO). The colonial power's reluctance to incur what it saw as unnecessary expenditure was rationalized thus: 'British colonial administrators were so impressed by the high level of communal organisation among Malayan Chinese that they left them virtually alone to manage their own affairs.'[88] As we saw, the 'special position of the Malays' was of no value to the Malay peasantry, though it served the ideological purpose of denying political rights to the non-

Malays.

The communalist intent of the colonial state is clearly revealed by the fact that the majority of the Malays who had settled in Malaya were also immigrants from elsewhere in the Archipelago. The Minangkabaus and the Bugis in particular, are relatively recent immigrants. The Malayan Census Report of 1931 pointed out that:

> Only a negligible fraction of the Malay population consists of descendants of pre-19th century immigrants... more than half of it has less than 50 years' prescriptive right to the title 'owners of the soil'. The Malays are in fact merely immigrants of generally longer standing than the other migrant races represented in the peninsula and are in no sense an autochthonous population.[89]

As capitalism developed, social relations within the different communities were transformed accordingly. Within the Chinese community, the Triad societies and guilds under which most of the Chinese workers had been indentured, began to lose their restrictive hold. Despite the criminal aspect of these secret societies, the colonial government had relied on them to keep the Chinese community under control. The British officer, Pickering, thus wrote: 'If secret societies were abolished, we should have no check at all on the thousands of disorderly class of Chinese.'[90] Soon, however, the colonial government substituted the secret societies for the Chinese Dialect Associations (*hui guans*), and set up the Chinese Advisory Board to act as intermediary between the state and the Chinese masses. These were clearly dominated by the rich comprador elements in the merchant class. They performed charitable functions and provided education and culture for the Chinese community.

The ready availability of cheap labour power meant that the workers had little bargaining power, nor did the colonial government provide any form of social security during recessions; employers were requested to spread the work during slack periods, failing that, the workers were simply repatriated. The Societies Ordinance of 1889 led to the eclipse of the Triads, and by 1920, their hold on the Chinese masses had distinctly lessened. With the new and varied forms of production, freer movement of labour became possible. Openings now existed not only in the tin and rubber industries, but also at the harbour, the municipality, railways, mills, iron workings and foundries, as well as all manner of small industries in the towns. Consequently, the paternalistic relationship between the worker and employer began to be replaced by the contractual one. This of course applied to a lesser extent in the smaller firms.

A radicalization of the working class in Malaya was facilitated partly by oppressive labour conditions, and partly by anti-colonial nationalist movements in countries from which the immigrants had come. In China, the anti-imperialist movement was gathering strength as the Western powers and Japan carved up China. Chinese reformists and revolutionaries, including Dr Sun Yat Sen, relied for support upon the overseas Chinese, and they made several visits to Malaya for that purpose. The political education of the Chinese masses grew from these struggles in China, and too, they were to fire their own struggle in Malaya in the years to come.

The Chinese nationalists managed to obtain the financial support of the local Chinese bourgeoisie in order to start modern Chinese schools in Malaya for the education of the masses. In this campaign, the task of propaganda and socialization was performed mainly by dedicated activists and militants, especially among school teachers.[91] By 1906, there were already six big Chinese schools in the main towns of Malaya and Singapore. Dr Sun was a greater influence than the other reformists, and he established contacts not only with the *towkays* and secret societies, but also with the labouring masses. Branches of the 'Kuomintang' and 'Reading Societies' were set up in most towns; the revolutionary paper, *Chung Hsin*, was first published in 1907. Soon after the founding of the Republic of China in 1911, Chinese education underwent further expansion, and by 1920, there were at least one or more Chinese schools in every town in Malaya; more than 40 in Singapore; and more than 30 in Penang. All of these were established within the Chinese community without government assistance, for by 1914, education accounted only for 1.1% of the total federal expenditure.[92]

The Chinese schools were to become important institutions for the inculcation of a radical anti-colonial sentiment among the masses. This was the case, especially after the Second World War, when the commercial bourgeoisie lost its influence over the non-Malay masses to the Communist Party of Malaya (CPM). The years after the First World War saw some intense protest struggles against imperialist attempts to dismember China. School children often played an active part in these, but they provoked some measure of control by the colonial state over the Chinese schools through the Education Bill in 1920.

With the prevailing political climate, secret unregistered labour unions came into existence, notably the Pineapple Cutters Association in 1908. In 1927, the Nanyang General Labour Union (GLU), formed in Singapore in 1925, claimed affiliation with 42 Malayan Labour Unions and a membership of 5,000. Numerous strikes were called at the time, by such groups as the Chinese fitters' in 1926-7; the Singapore Traction Company workers' in 1927, and the Singapore shoemakers' in 1928. In 1929, in the Kinta tin mining district alone, employee organizations claimed a membership of 11,600 in 1929.[93]

As we have noted, because of the relatively isolated conditions of the plantations, Indian workers were slower to organize. By 1927, however, a number of social and professional associations of clerical, administrative and technical staff (with largely Indian membership) as well as an Estate Asiatic Staff Association, had been formed. These did serve as a catalyst for Indian workers' organization. From the 1930s, the independence struggle in India began to arouse the Indian masses, as the Chinese had been roused by anti-imperialist struggles in China. In the plantations, the British employers and planters had imposed a further division: the estate managers were mainly North Indians and non-Tamil speaking who considered themselves a race apart from the labourers. This divide-and-rule policy was also applied when Sikhs were recruited for the public and private police forces, especially in the officer ranks; this was to have implications for the struggles ahead, as was shall see in the next chapter. Education of the Indian workers' children was left in the hands of the estate employers.

The Depression in the early 1930s marked a turning point in the attitudes of the immigrant Chinese and Indians regarding their status in Malaya. Through force of circumstance, familiarity with the new situation and for other reasons, they began to regard Malaya as their home. At the time, labour was in a weak position because of the Depression and the halting of free immigration by the Immigration Restriction Ordinance in 1930. Consequently, the sex ratio levelled out and birth rates of the non-Malays shot up. Gradually with greater mobility of labour and unionization, the workers began to acquire a better bargaining position, and the 1930s saw the beginning of a period of intense class struggles, the development of which has to be understood in the light of the divisions that existed among the labouring masses.

Thus, by 1931, the working class was deeply segregated, with Tamils predominating in the rubber industry, and the Chinese in the tin and ancillary industries (see Table 2.10). The Malays, for reasons already noted, did not constitute a substantial part of the working class, although Roff notes the first Malay trade union in 1894, the *Club Kapitan-kapitan dan Injinir-injinir Melayu*, formed by Malay seamen and engineers.[94] Thus it was that the communalist strategy was erected upon this material basis of a segregated labour force, a point largely obfuscated by pluralists and other social scientists. An example of the attempts to maintain a divided labour force is provided by the *Selangor Journal*, a publication of English plantation owners:

> To secure your independence, work with Javanese and Tamils, and, if you have sufficient experience, also with Malays and Chinese; you can then always play the one against the other.... In case of a strike, you will never be left without labour, and the coolies of one nationality will think twice before they make their terms, if they know that you are in a position that you can do without them.[95]

This communalist ideology fed upon the separateness of the peasantry in relation to the diversified working class. It was a

Table 2.10
Ethnic Composition of Labour Force in the Two Major Industries in the FMS, 1931[1]

	Rubber	*Tin*
Malays	27,618	543
Chinese	100,989	70,704
Indians	131,099	4,622
Total	*259,706*	*75,869*

Note: 1 In the Unfederated Malay States, there were some 1,000 tin miners and 100,000 rubber workers—61,374 Chinese and 34,776 Malays.

Source: V. Purcell, *Chinese in Malaya*, pp.239-40.

division not only of occupation, but of geographical and socializing space. For the masses as a whole, therefore:

> ...the chances of communicating and interacting among themselves (were) limited, and their separation and ignorance of one another's way of life... led to the formation of stereotypes and prejudices. In other words, although the lower classes of the various races are in almost the same economic position, differences and racial antipathy (were) widespread among them, and these prevented the recognition of a common fate and destiny.[96]

The (Non-Malay) Commercial Bourgeoisie

The colonial economy changed the character of trade that had previously existed in the Malay states and Straits Settlements, and with it the various strata of the non-Malay (mainly Chinese) commercial bourgeoisie. The relationship between them and the British colonial state corresponded to their relationship vis-à-vis the masses. Because of the nature of class formation and communalism that we have noted so far, their relationship to the masses was mainly with the non-Malay working class and less to the Malay peasantry. We have also seen how the Malays were actively discouraged from commercial activities that could have given them the skill and opportunity to organize the masses and thereby threaten the colonial power. Instead, this task was left to an 'alien' community.

The spread of non-Malay commerce consequent upon the imposition of colonial rule, was simply an extension of the activities of non-Malay merchant capital based in the Straits Settlements, which concentrated on the export of raw materials and the import of British-manufactured goods. This tended to be the preserve of English-educated comprador bourgeoisie, while a parallel stratum of (usually vernacular-educated) commercial bourgeoisie carried on the import of foodstuffs from China for the rapidly growing Chinese population. Thus, within the Chinese community itself, colonial policies favouring the comprador class were giving rise to violent conflicts, which have variously been interpreted as 'cultural divisions' within the Chinese society, secret society wars, and so on, but P.P. Lee, for example, has shown them to have deeper, socio-economic reasons.[97]

In the Straits Settlements, the merchant class was most fully established at Singapore. By the time the British had come to dominate the economy, the Teochew merchants were already well established in the rice (from Siam) and remittance (to China) business, and also in financing gambier and pepper cultivation. After 1819, the British 'Freetraders' began to wrest control of this profitable business from the Teochew merchants and used the Malacca Hokkiens (who were well-established at Malacca and spoke English and Malay equally well) as a bridgehead. Government regulations on taxation, land, and so on, basically worked to benefit the European merchants so that most of the revenue was raised from tax on opium farming and gambling, the Chinese being the main consumers. The European free-traders were hardly taxed at all.

Soon the Chinese merchants were reduced to the role of the intermediary between the metropolitan interests and the local population. Outside of this formal arrangement, however, these non-Malay local merchants were left very much to their own devices to get what they could from the local trade. In this they displayed their legendary enterprise, the attribute paralleled by the *dukawallah* of Africa.[98] But the Chinese merchants became totally dependent on the Europeans both for capital and goods, and thus lost the autonomy they had when trade was merely complementing domestic consumption in the peninsula.

An examination of the structure of the Chinese commercial bourgeoisie is important for an understanding of the nature of class alliances in the struggles ahead and the strategy of the British colonial state. To minimize risks the European Agents naturally wanted to deal with that stratum of Chinese merchants which had the financial means. They found this comprador class in the so-called 'Malacca Chinese', who, culturally, were different from the newly-arrived Chinese settlers. This upper stratum of the Chinese merchants consisted of the wholesalers who also had monopoly rights on opium, drinking and gambling, of which the most lucrative was opium. The rents for opium rights were so high that only the richest of the Chinese had the capital to afford them.[99] These 'Malacca Chinese' were thus in the colonial state's favour, and they were made the unofficial administrators of the Chinese community, as 'Kapitans China' or as Justices of the Peace.

The second stratum of merchants comprised the retailers:

shopkeepers, who were dependent upon the wholesalers but not directly involved with the metropolitan class. They included the merchants who had been established before colonial rule and who later lost out to the comprador class, since there were greater financial rewards in the colonial trade than in gambier and pepper.[100] The Teochew merchants' monopoly of the rice trade from Siam was destroyed when the British took over Chinese monopolies in Siam, after the Bowring Treaty in 1855;[101] they also took over the junk traffic from Siam to Singapore, and the remittance business. Reduced to playing the role of 'middlemen', especially in the rural areas, this stratum of merchants soon became the target of communalist propaganda by the various Malay elements. They were portrayed, predictably, as the 'blood-suckers' of the Malay peasants, and held up as evidence of the 'Chinese domination of the economy'. Government officials also:

> emphasized to the peasants that Chinese middlemen producers were responsible for their poverty, and appeals were made to the racial loyalties of the peasants to eliminate this class of traders. (Lim, T G, 1977:199)

The third stratum includes those in crafts: carpenters, boat, ship, and house builders who were dependent on the expanding entrepot economy and the urban sector. The lowest was the 'informal sector', for example, casual labourers, rickshaw drivers, street vendors, domestic servants, dock and station porters.

The dialectal specialization in the different trades was, and generally still is, a feature of the Chinese commercial class in almost every town in Malaya. Social organization was based on common territorial origins in China (*hui guans* or associations), and the local community was usually linked on a clan or lineage basis. Only later were the Chinese in Malaya to become aware of their 'national' identity, through the nationalist movement in China as well as the communalist policies of the colonial state. The stratum of commercial bourgeoisie which began to dominate the *hui guans*, and thus to have more influence over the Chinese masses, was the 'Chinese' group rather than the English-educated upper stratum of 'Malacca Chinese', the direct beneficiary of the metropolitan bourgeoisie.

As the Malayan economy grew and new opportunities became available with the huge influx of immigrants, mercantile activity was no longer confined to the straight exchange of local produce for European goods. Services for enterprises in the distribution sphere were called for. The Chinese Chamber of Commerce was formed in 1906 by the most prominent of the various dialectal leaders. It is the organization par excellence of the Chinese commercial bourgeoisie.

In the 1920s and 1930s, as tin and rubber prices slumped owing to the Depression, many Chinese merchants were ruined, but this led to their obtaining some degree of autonomy from the colonial economy. They were still dependent on the import-export trade, but they now began to seek other, more secure avenues for investment in the local economy, such as real estate; light consumer industries (oil milling, cement, transport, food manufacture, sawmills, timber, tailoring, outfitting, contracting, printing, publishing, building, rubber milling, tobacco, hardware, iron foundry, fish business, medicinal products, among others); and pawnbroking. In Singapore, the service occupations were also derived from the activities of the overseas Chinese elsewhere in the Archipelago.

In 1903, one of the first Chinese banks—the Kwong Yik Bank —was started by Wong Ah Fook, a planter, merchant and contractor. The Teochew merchants also started the Sze Hai Tong Bank, while in 1912 the Hokkiens opened the Chinese Commercial Bank, the Ho Hong Bank in 1917, and the Overseas Chinese Bank in 1919. In the 1930s, during the Depression, the three Hokkien banks merged to form the Overseas Chinese Banking Corporation (OCBC), which is now the largest local banking group in the country.[102]

With the development of Chinese banking, their capital rapidly reached a high degree of concentration, because only those with large financial resources could survive the competition of foreign capital. The feudal relations in the Malay states were a considerable constraint on internal market expansion and the home market was mainly supplied by British imports. This explains the minimal expansion of Chinese industrial capital and the rather overblown lending and commercial sector. Domestic industrial capitalists thus tended to be the large commercial bourgeoisie.

In 1937, the extent of the Chinese bourgeoisie's holdings was estimated at approximately $200 million (£40 million) compared to foreign investments of $454.5 million (£90 million), of which 70 per cent was British.[103] From a command of 64 per cent of the tin mined in the Federated Malay States, in comparison with the European proportion of 36 per cent in 1920, the proportion mined by the Chinese bourgeoisie had dropped to 33 per cent by 1938.[104] Chinese capital in the rubber plantations in 1931 can be seen in Table 2.11, which shows 12.5 per cent ownership in the Federated Malay States and Straits Settlements, compared to 84 per cent foreign ownership and 2.3 per cent Indian ownership.

In addition to the tin and rubber industries, Chinese capital was invested in many of the secondary industries, especially the pineapple industry which, in 1938, accounted for 1.2 per cent of Malaya's export trade. Market gardening and pig and poultry rearing were also an exclusively Chinese preserve. They also dominated the building and the skilled artisan trades; tailoring and cobbling; logging and timber; and land development.

We shall look later at the class alliances of the rich, upper

Table 2.11
Ownership of Rubber Estates of 100 Acres and Over, by Ethnicity, 1931

	Foreign (No./Acres)	Chinese (No./Acres)	Indian (No./Acres)	Malay (No./Acres)	Total (No./Acres)
FMS	665/821,049	299/ 92,389	119/26,927	23/4,883	1,106/ 945,248
SS	87/146,809	162/ 52,864	34/ 9,910	9/1,834	292/ 214,417
Total	*752/967,858*	*461/145,253*	*153/36,837*	*32/6,717*	*1,398/1,159,665*

Source: *Malayan Rubber Statistics Handbook* (Singapore), 1932, p.15.

stratum of the Chinese bourgeoisie in subsequent Malayan politics. At this stage, it needs only to be pointed out how the colonial state singled out the most well-to-do in the Chinese community as the leaders, and instituted the system of patronage that went along with this leadership. Thus, even when the 'Malacca Chinese' no longer had a monopoly of the local economy, they were still retained by the British as the advisers on Chinese matters, which can be interpreted only as yet another instance of the colonial state's communalist strategy. By contrast, the lower strata of the Chinese commercial bourgeoisie, who were less dependent on the colonial economy and could not count on the protection of the colonial state, were, in the years ahead, involved in the anti-colonial struggles of the masses.

The Indian Commercial Bourgeoisie

Like their Chinese counterpart, the Indian commercial bourgeoisie followed in the wake of the influx of Indian labourers in order to service the circulation sphere. They came, for example, as merchants, bankers, money lenders, shopkeepers, peddlars, contractors, and generally were of higher caste than the Tamil labourers. Among them were Hindu and Muslim traders from the Malabar and Coromandel coasts of South India, and textile merchants from Sind and the Punjab. They exhibited a degree of regional preference: the North Indians settled in Singapore; South Indian Muslims in Penang; and Chettiars in Kuala Lumpur, and they were organised in the Chambers of Commerce.

Among the Indian commercial bourgeoisie, the Chettiar moneylenders made the biggest impact on the economy, providing credit to European entrepreneurs, Chinese businessmen, Indian petty traders, the Malay aristocracy, and most importantly, the Malay peasantry. Their relationship as creditors to the Malay peasantry has attracted the most attention to date. The peasantry mortgaged their land and property against the Chettiars' loans and consequently, with the capitalist penetration of the rural sector, more and more land passed into Chettiar hands. The Chettiars had a reputation for being able to 'lay a finger on the pulse of any man's business should they care to lay it' (Lim, T G, 1977:84). They bankedtheir money on call at 10 per cent and loaned at up to 36 per cent per annum or more. In 1930, the Chettiars placed the total loans they had made to peasants in the FMS at $100 (Lim, T G, 1977:200).

In the Federal Council in 1932, the Chettiars were criticized for their extortionist role.[105] Clearly, the colonial state had moved against them only in the face of mass protest. The Malay Reservations Enactment restricted the Chettiar credit relations with the Malay peasantry, but this legislation could be easily evaded by the use of a nominee to hold land on behalf of the Chettiar. When the question of landlessness among the peasantry became critical, in 1931, and the Malay rulers themselves were alarmed, the Small-holdings (Restriction of Sale) Bill was passed:[106] there was to be no order of sale for less than 25 acres of rural land without the consent of the Ruler-in-Council of the state. Chettiars all over the country protested that their vast investments were jeopardized, and during these exchanges it emerged that Chettiar loans to Malay smallholders in the Federal Malay State amounted to $125 million.[107] Except for a small concession, the government came down against the Chettiars, being concerned to manifest a readiness to protect the interests of the Malay peasantry from the Indian moneylender.[108] This led to the Malay Reservation Act of 1933 designed to tighten up on the previous Act. This new Act stipulated that no holding could be transferred, exchanged, leased, or otherwise disposed of to a non-Malay.

During these events, the Chettiars did not even get the support of the rest of the Indian community—much less of the Indian workers—since they had their own exclusive organizations and religious institutions. The colonial state did not fail to project the image of the heartless and exploitative Chettiar. In 1935, the 'Moneylenders Ordinance' was duly passed by the Straits Settle-ments Legislature in order further to curb the activities of the Chettiar.

Before that date, it was the moneylending activities that facilitated the increased Indian land ownership in Malaya. From the 1920s onwards, they also began to invest in rubber; not only the Chettiars, but retired government servants and Indian businessmen also invested in rubber. During the Depression, the forfeiture of mortgaged land saw further agglomeration of land into Chettiar hands before it was halted by the government (see Table 2.12).

Compared to its Chinese counterpart, the Indian commercial bourgeoisie's stake in the whole economy was not large. In 1938, Indian ownership of rubber estates stood at 87,795 acres, or 4 per cent of the total rubber acreage.[109] By 1935, there were two Indian (Chettiar) banks in Malaya, the Chettinad Bank and the Bank of Chettinad, which had branches in the main towns of Malaya. In the

Table 2.12
Land Owned and Held in Mortgage by Indians in the FMS (Acres)

Year	Land Owned	Land Held in Mortgage
1928	101,681	75,038
1938	152,843	65,970

Source: Proceedings of the Federal Council, FMS, 1939, B33.

early 20th Century, these Indians began to form Associations in most towns and districts to protect their interests, and their membership included the substantial numbers of Indians in state employment.[110] Consequently, the Indian Associations tended to be very loyal to the colonial authorities, and constantly fêted the officials. Patronage of government officials was sought after, and the leading members of the Indian community were occasionally rewarded with appointment to a government board, committee or council.[111]

Because of the diverse character of the Indian commercial and petty bourgeoisie, factionalism between these groups within the Associations was common. Needless to say, they had little contact with the Indian labourers in the estates and municipal depots:

> In fact, there was a self-conscious attempt to stand aloof from these people, to show the other communities of Malaya that they were different and could not be tainted with the same 'coolie' brush. These people would use the word 'coolie' in the same derogatory sense as the Europeans in Malaya.[112]

From very early on, as part of their communalist strategy, the British cultivated the upper strata of the Indian community; the state appointments with which, as has already been noted, they were from time to time rewarded, in turn were passports to economic opportunity.

As in the Chinese community, the Depression caused considerable hardship not only for the Indian working class, but also for the lower strata of the petty bourgeoisie. The setting up of Unemployment Relief Committees by the Indian Associations marked the beginning of a greater degree of self-help and mutual assistance in the Indian community.

Colonial Policies: Specific Effects on Communalism

In this section, certain specific communalist policies of British colonialism will be examined. Some of these have already been alluded to in earlier sections. Here, only the key policies in maintaining communalism will be considered: colonial education policy; the decentralization proposals; and the question of retrenchment in the state bureaucracy.

The British policy on education for the masses in the three communities ranged from token paternalism (toward the Malay peasantry) to complete neglect (of the Chinese); the Tamil labourers were presumed not to require any education at all. While the traditional Malay rulers' children were being taught in public school-type institutions to administer in English, their subordinates in the government services were competing for places in the 'Government English Schools'.

As we have seen (p.31) the rest of the Malay masses were given only a modicum of vernacular education, enough to make them 'better peasants and fishermen':

> The great object of education is to train a man to make his living. You can teach Malays so that they do not lose their skill and craft in fishing and jungle work. Teach them the dignity of manual labour, so that they do not all become 'kranis' [clerks] and I am sure you will not have the trouble which has arisen in India through over-education.[113]

Free Malay vernacular education was provided up to primary level, but there was no secondary education. In 1919, an attempt was made to stream Malay pupils into secondary classes in English schools and these were known as 'Special Malay Classes', but most of the English and mission schools were located in the urban areas, out of reach of the majority of the Malay masses.

As for the Chinese masses, the colonial authorities generally assumed that they could take care of themselves through self-help within the Chinese community. That is how Chinese schools came about, and the majority of the Chinese registered at these rather than the Government English Schools. The fees in the English schools were more than most of the people could afford, also, the migratory character of the Chinese population meant that most of the Chinese pupils were over-aged for admittance to these schools. But a stronger motivation than either of these factors, was the nationalist sentiment being created by the political struggles in mainland China, and this factor was instrumental in their choice of modern Chinese education rather than English, the language of the colonial master; this, in spite of the fact that employment prospects were higher for pupils who had gone through the English stream. Thus, in 1938, there were 26,974 Chinese pupils in government and aided English schools; but 49,271 in Chinese schools in the Federated Malay State and Straits Settlements, and a total of 91,534 pupils in all the Chinese schools throughout the peninsula.[114]

The socialization process involving Chinese pupils in English schools and that undergone by Chinese school pupils were in contradiction. Those in the latter schools were to different degrees influenced by the ideology of nationalism and democracy propagated by the radical school teachers at the grassroots, many of whom were from mainland China. In contrast, Chinese pupils in the English schools were taught English colonial values and a totally different ethos based on competition and liberal democracy. Of course, not all the English school Chinese pupils fell prey to the dominant ideology, many of them had enrolled only with an eye to better work prospects.

The Indian masses in the plantations, were left to their own devices. Unlike in the Chinese community, the leaders in the Indian Associations were a caste apart if not culturally alien to the Tamil workers. Consequently, the latter could not depend on the philanthropy of the rich Indians, nor did the plantation managers fulfil this need in any way. Not until 1900 were Tamil schools deemed necessary, as a means whereby to entice the Indian workers to stay in Malaya when labour was again in demand.[115] The Indian Labour Code of 1912 required all employers in the plantations to run schools for the workers. However, '...no interest was shown in the recruitment or training of teachers for Tamil schools; their mere existence satisfied the requirements of the Labour Code.'[116] In 1937, there were 548 Indian schools with an enrolment of 23,350 pupils.[117]

Thus, in pre-war Malaya, the colonial government had no clear-cut education policy, and the dearth of educational provisions reflected the lack of social provisions for the masses in all three communities. The effect of this was the retraction of all three national groups into their respective communities, already divided in the different sectors of labour. The labour segregation of the Malayan masses was thus reinforced by the necessity for self-help and association within each cultural group, while the Government English Schools served to socialize the well-to-do in all three national groups into the colonial ideology.

The other two issues arising out of British colonial policy during the 1930s are linked: the decentralization proposals, and the retrenchment of non-Malays (mainly Indians) from the lower ranks of the state bureaucracy. The contradictions inherent in colonial rule became clear in the 1930s, and emerged during the Depression.[118] They revolved around the central axis of British colonial strategy in Malaya, namely, erecting the edifice of 'protecting the special position of the Malays and Malay rulers'.

By the 1930s, two urgent problems had to be solved by the British: one economic, the other political, but both inextricably linked. Basically, it was the fact that the economic exploitation of the Malay states was being impeded by the fragmented system that hitherto existed: namely, the Federated Malay States, and the Unfederated Malay States, as well as the Straits Settlements. The Federated Malay States possessed the rich tin deposits and were the more highly developed of the Malay states. The Unfederated Malay States, on the other hand, had less in the way of raw materials needed by the colonial power, and supposedly had a greater degree of autonomy. Notwithstanding, the British never experienced any difficulty in getting their own way as Permanent Secretary Meade's remark referring to the Malay rulers exemplifies: '...those unhappy dummies will, of course, agree to anything that they are told to accept...'[119]

By the 1930s, however, Johore had become the largest rubber producer, and Kelantan and Perlis, the largest producers of rice; but all were still 'unfederated'. The urgency of the problem of self-sufficiency in rice had been faced already during the Depression and considered as too big a drain on Malaya's export earnings.[120] Some of the logical solutions to the problem were, however, considered politically inapt for preserving the communalist strategy:

> The least indication of trying to grant non-Malays access to padi fields to cultivate rice—something patently sensible in the circumstances of the depression-induced unemployment—provoked howls of 'giving Malaya away to the foreigner'...[121]

Self-sufficiency in rice could also have been realized by state expenditure on irrigation and drainage schemes to increase productivity; the colonial government's reluctance to take any constructive action arose as much out of neglect, as out of a disinclination to inject changes that would accentuate differentiation of the peasantry.

Consequently, the Clementi Administration proposed a scheme to rationalize the fragmented constitutional system of Malaya. It involved decentralization to the states first, to be followed by recentralization into a single administrative unit. The decentralization proposals were intended to create the impression that the British did respect the formal authority of the sultans; to centralize the Adminstration immediately might have provoked reaction from the Malay rulers (precisely what happened during the Malayan Union crisis after the war). The British had contemplated annexation in 1875, 1879, 1880 and 1895, but each time this option was rejected because the local colonial official felt that they already enjoyed relative freedom of action and preferred to avoid any unpleasantness with the Malays.[122]

It was in fact during the decentralization proposals in the early 1930s that the non-Malays in Malaya had the first taste of the communalist politics to come: the issues bound up with their citizenship, representation, and other political, social and economic rights as defined by the state. The proposals were seen by the Indian community as 'an accelerated move towards a pro-Malay policy',[123] but their views did not change a policy decided upon already. The Colonial Under-Secretary merely noted their views and assured them that their status as 'British subjects' in the Straits Settlements and 'British Protected Persons' in the Federated Malay States would be maintained.[124]

The question of nationality became the crux of the issue of

representation of the non-Malays in the administrative and technical services, as well as in the Legislative Council. In the Malay states, no non-Malay was eligible to become a citizen however long he was domiciled there. In 1936, the Indian member of the Federal Council pressed for the status of 'subjects of the Sultan' for all persons born in the Sultan's state, but the cynical reply of the High Commissioner has already been noted (p.32). Thus, all the non-Malays who had been born and bred in a country which was the only one they had known, still found themselves with 'alien' status. While the Government made concessions to non-Malays in the medical and technical services (purely because there were inadequate qualified Malay personnel), it would not allow non-Malays to be admitted into the Malay Administrative Service, the state apparatus.[125]

Even on the question of representation of the non-Malays in the State and Federal Council (these were invariably drawn from the rich and selected members of the various communities), the colonial state did not hesitate to attempt to divide each community. For instance, when the Indian member, Veerasamy, was appointed to the Federal Council, the High Commissioner made it a point to stress that he was selected to represent Hindu interests and that, since most Ceylonese were also Hindus, the government reserved the right to appoint a Ceylonese to this position:

> It appears to have been the Government's intention to divest the newly-appointed member of any claim to represent the Indian community as a whole, and correspondingly to disillusion the Indian community of any belief that they were represented as a community on the Council. The Indians saw in this move an attempt to divide the community on religious grounds.[126]

The decentralization proposals did not resolve the contradictions of British colonialism—the problems inherent in the system were merely recognized. The solutions were postponed until after the Second World War, when the colonial power was forced to come to terms with the demands for Independence. In this, as we shall see, the colonial state relied on its well-proven communalist strategy.

3. The Anti-Colonial Movement

The workers' struggles in Malaya began with the progressive unionization from the 1930s onwards and reached their peak of intensity between 1948 to 1960, during the 'Emergency'. The colonial state perceived that the real threat to Western imperialist interests in Malaya lay in the working-class anti-colonial movement. Its communalist strategy had stood it in good stead thus far, and this strategy was consistently pursued and refined throughout its campaign of repression against the working class and its allies among sections of the petty bourgeoisie.

By isolating the mainly non-Malay working class from the Malay peasantry, the British colonial state ensured that the unity around the proletariat would not arise. At the same time, the traditional Malay rulers' ideological domination over the peasantry also shielded them from the influences of the radical Malay petty bourgeoisie.

The defeat of the workers' movement enabled the colonial power to effect the changeover to a neo-colony by handing over the political reins of government to the traditional Malay ruling class and to its non-Malay bourgeois allies. The communalist politics that overshadowed the Independence manoeuvres will be examined in the next chapter.

The Making of the Radical Labour Movement

The first labour unions were necessarily formed in secret and, because of the employers' hostility and the general isolation of the workers, were unregistered and illegal. Stenson has noted that one of the few unions registered under the Societies Ordinance was, for example, the Pineapple Cutters Association, in 1908, but it was again deregistered in 1913.[1] Gradually, however, the factors impeding the organization of the workers were overcome.

The first sections of the working class to be unionized were those in the new capitalist enterprises associated with raw materials processing: saw mills, rubber, and pineapple factories, tin smelters, coal mines; and engineering works, railways and traction companies. The workers in these enterprises were predominantly

Chinese, but some were Indians and Malays. Unskilled workers were the first to be unionized. During the 1930s, with restricted immigration and with labour in a strong position, skilled tradesmen —tailors, barbers, brickmakers, engineering workers, 'night soil' carriers,[2] cigar rollers—also began to be unionized and to use their economic muscle to strike.

The protests over the conditions of indentured labour led to its abolition in 1913 and the passing of a Labour Code of 1912. This Code brought together all the labour laws that hitherto had been passed piecemeal in the State Council. There were provisions for length and validity of contracts; working hours; inspection of work place; the right of workers to initiate action against employers; as well as stiff punishment for labour offences. The only substantial change was that the worker was now 'free' and no longer bound by the indenture contract. The Labour Code embodied general conditions for all workers as well as separate sections for Indian and Chinese labour.

Further conditions and terms laid down by the government were contained in the Indian Emigration Act of 1922, governing the employment of Indian labour. This led to another Code in 1923, under which Indian labour could not be held to make contracts of more than one month's duration, and the minimum age for employment of Indian child labour was fixed at ten years.[3] The implementation of the law, however, fell far short of its professed intention, and the planters' representatives on the Federal Council made it clear that they did not expect the Labour Department to apply the Code strictly, especially with regards education, health, and land allotments for the workers.[4]

Labour was in a weak position as long as the colonial government could conserve low wage rates by controlling the labour supply through immigration controls. Free mobility of labour meant little while there was a constant supply of labour and concerted action by the employers to keep wages down. Planters in the estates had their own methods of maintaining low wages, such as running their own estate stores which in turn determined the workers' cost of living. They also employed divisive tactics such as contracting higher paid Chinese labour on piece rates.[5]

The 4th May movement and the 1911 Revolution in China, with the corollary of the 'Campaign for National Salvation' in Malaya, had a great impact upon the political consciousness of the Chinese masses in Malaya. It was as much a campaign for the defence of workers' rights as it was a nationalist struggle. As the trend toward unionization (see pp.50-1) continued, the government decided to reverse its former policy of refusing to register trade guilds under the Societies Ordinance on the grounds that they were subversive; from 1928, therefore, trade guilds were henceforth to be registered.[6]

The overseas nationalist movement of the Indians in Malaya

was neither as pervasive nor intense as that of the Malayan Chinese, nor did it have strong economic and social institutions to build upon. The Indian workers themselves were divided along caste lines and by cultural differences; for example, Tamil and Telegu workers sometimes clashed.[7] Nevertheless, by the 1920s, there were occasional stoppages of work, and such social and professional associations as, in 1927, the Estate Asiatic Staff Association, were being formed by Indian clerical, administrative, and technical staffs.

The Depression was a period of acute misery for the masses, but it also brought changes that led to rapid unionization of the workers. Free immigration came to an end partly owing to the demand for its curtailment by the Malay rulers, who resented the encroachment of Chinese and Indians on the land and business opportunities. The Immigration Restriction Ordinance was passed in August 1930 and the Aliens Ordinance in April 1933; these had explicitly communalist intent. In 1938, under pressure from the Congress Party, the Government of India banned emigration to Malaya.

When tin and rubber recovered from the Depression and prices rose again,[8] labour unrest broke out in response to the rising cost of living. It was at this point in 1930 that the Communist Party of Malaya (CPM) was formed and began to lead and organize the workers' struggles. The General Labour Union (GLU) became one of its most important united front organizations. The Malayan GLU was subsequently formed in 1934. The following year there were two important strikes, one at the coal mines in Batu Arang and the other at the Singapore Traction Company, the city's largest bus transport company. These strikes were particularly significant in that the labour force involved in both comprised all three national groups, and tremendous solidarity was shown throughout the strikes. At the Batu Arang collieries, there was even an attempt to set up a soviet, with its own government and militia.[9] There was a similar display of working class unity at the Penang waterfront, the Central Railway Workshop, and the Tanjong Pagar Labour Company in 1938.

In the mid-1930s, the skilled artisans had as many grievances as the workers and were among the first to respond to the new situation. In September 1936, the Chinese cutters at the Singapore and Johore Bahru pineapple factories sparked off a series of strikes that involved skilled as well as unskilled labour. It spread to building workers, night soil carriers, and traction workers. Because labour was in short supply, employers were forced to grant concessions. These strikes were concentrated mainly in Singapore, but by 1937, they had spread to Selangor, Negri Sembilan, Malacca, Johore, and Pahang. During the recession, between 1937 and 1939, wage cuts and redundancies again led to a strike at the Singapore Traction Company in 1938.

Within the Indian working class too, political conditions in Malaya as well as in India began to give rise to a new consciousness. As Hindu reform groups and the Indian press emerged, so did the Central Indian Association of Malaya (CIAM), formed in 1936 in response to overtly discriminatory policies of the British.[10] This was composed mainly of the professional and merchant classes, but nevertheless, it created some framework for association and bargaining and it did attempt to intercede on behalf of the Indian estate workers. The CIAM's protest to the government of India about reductions of the wages of Indian labourers by the planters was partly responsible for the ban on emigration from India.

Industrial disputes within the Indian labouring sector soon began to increase. From 1937, Indian stevedores and godown workers at Penang Harbour were very active in agitating over wages and conditions there. Strikes were also called by cigar rollers and petroleum workers in 1937. Toward the end of the 1930s, the nationalist fervour in India began to affect the Indians in Malaya too. In 1937 Nehru visited Malaya and encouraged Indians to defend their interests by forming unions. There were other visits by such Indian political leaders as Pandit Kunzru in 1938, and Gopalan in 1939. That same year, the Johore Indian Labour Association was formed. In Selangor, the Indian dock workers at Port Swettenham and Klang were organized and the Indian Associations at Kajang and Kuala Langat revitalized. An 'uplift' campaign was carried out amongst the Indians who were indignant about their conditions—a task was performed by *kanganys* as well as school teachers.[11]

In 1941, there was serious unrest at estates in Klang, led by radical labour leaders who:

> ...looked upon their struggles as not merely industrial but also as a political struggle against British imperialism. The British disingenuously used Indian troops to fire on strikers, creating bad feelings among Indians.[12]

It led to a declaration of state of emergency. By then, the clerical and administrative workers in the government services, who had suffered during the retrenchment of the Depression period, were also unionized.[13] Trade union legislation was extremely restrictive: for example, the Trade Union Bill of 1939 made no provision for legalized picketing.

Towards the end of the 1930s, political developments in China began to influence the Chinese masses in Malaya to an even greater extent. After the outbreak of the Sino-Japanese War of 1937, 'Overseas Chinese Anti-Japanese National Salvation Associations' were formed all over Malaya and Singapore. These became yet another important united front organization for the CPM, although they were also patronized by sections of the Chinese bourgeoisie. The workers' strikes extended into the 1940s.

The Radical Malay Petty Bourgeoisie

Among the Malay population, it was the radicalized section of the petty bourgeoisie that took the lead in the anti-colonial struggle. Even though in the end they failed to gain the mass support of the Malay peasantry, their importance was that they were the only Malay anti-colonial force. To examine its growth is as important for an appreciation of its specific mode of formation as for an understanding of the workings of communalism in Malaya.

The radical Malay intelligentsia who came into their own in the 1930s were different from the reformist religious 'modernists' who were the first critics of the traditional Malay status quo to emerge from within the Malay community itself. The latter were mostly Arabic-educated, students who had returned from the Middle East and came from small commercial and petty bourgeois backgrounds. They had opposed the established state religious authorities for their watered-down versions of Islam,[14] and blamed the social and economic backwardness of the Malay masses on this factor. Underlying their fundamentalist assertions was a dislike of the domination of the commercial sector by the foreign as well as non-Malay interests. The protest against the *orang asing* (foreigner) was, and still is, strongest in the urban areas rather than in the rural districts. The reforms they demanded, such as the setting up of co-operatives that would eliminate the non-Malay middleman, accorded well with their Islamic fundamentalist views against usury.

In order to disseminate their views, *Kaum Muda* (Modernist Group, as the reformists were referred to, as opposed to the *Kaum Tua*, the Traditionalists), started their newspaper, *Al Imam*, in 1906. But unlike their Indonesian counterpart they never succeeded in elaborating a nationalism that could rally the mass support of the Malays, and this modernist minority was soon crushed by the Establishment religious bureaucracy. It was left to the Malay vernacular-educated intelligentsia, mainly teachers and journalists, to take up the banner of anti-colonial nationalism.

By 1920, the number of Malay vernacular schools in Malaya had increased to 757, with an enrolment of 46,000.[15] Most of the state's meagre expenditure went to Malay vernacular education while the non-Malays were left to their own devices. The Sultan Idris Training College (SITC) at Tanjong Malim was opened in 1922, and it was a key institution in the creation of the Malay vernacular-educated intelligentsia. In contrast to the Kuala Kangsar Malay College, which was exclusively designed to groom the sons of the Malay rulers, the SITC students were mainly culled from the village vernacular schools, and thus some of them were from peasant backgrounds. Nevertheless, the SITC was yet another elite-producing institution, run on the lines of an English public school.

During the 1920s, SITC students were greatly influenced by

the Indonesian nationalist movement through their wide reading of the local vernacular and Indonesian literature and newspapers. Graduates from SITC were, moreover, forced to confront the issues affecting the Malay peasantry, since there were few opportunities for employment (as we have noted, government business was conducted in English) except to teach in the *kampong* vernacular schools. For them, the self-confidence, vibrance, and radical character of Indonesian intellectual and political life was a source of inspiration in their aim to combat the fatalism and 'all-round poverty of the Malays'.[16] The 34 new vernacular newspapers and periodicals that were started in Malaya between 1920 and 1930 indicated the growing nationalist awareness.

In 1938, Ibrahim Yaacob, assistant editor of *Majlis*, along with a number of other young nationalists formed the *Kesatuan Melayu Muda* (KMM) (Young Malay Union), which 'neither professed loyalty to the sultans and the British nor spoke of non-cooperation, but worked to promote nationalist feelings and teachings among its members, whose strength lay in the lower classes'.[17] The KMM espoused a strong anti-colonial stand as well as opposition to the 'bourgeois feudalist' traditional elite.[18] Some liaison took place between the KMM and the CPM, but nothing substantial. The radical Malay intelligentsia, however, failed to harness the mass support of the peasantry, who were ensconced within the feudal social relations of the traditional Malay rural society. The Malay rulers were later to distort the question of anti-colonial nationalism into one of Malay communalism to suit their purpose.

In addition to its anti-colonial nationalism, the radical Malay intelligentsia also aspired to a 'Pan-Malayanism': a political union of Malaya and Indonesia into a greater 'Malaysia Raya'. This idea, which formed an essential ingredient of Malay nationalism was later to be encouraged by the Japanese during their war-time occupation of South-East Asia. It was, however, an idea that the British were eager to suppress.

The ineffectiveness of the KMM before the war was as much owing to its close surveillance by the colonial authorities as to its organizational shortcomings and failure to win over the mass support of the Malay peasantry. The peasantry's aversion toward anything *siasat* (political, equated with 'government business' and best left well alone) was one obstacle:

> The term 'politics' was understood by the Malays to mean 'treason'. It was in the nature of our people to be wholly loyal and submissive to the government, to the authorities, to the Rulers... any unfamiliar movement was feared by them.[19]

Another obstacle was the perpetuation of this view backed by intimidation:

> ...the fact widely known in the 1930s, that the British were employing

agents to hunt down persons plotting to subvert the present order.[20]

Ibrahim Yaacob and many of his comrades in the KMM were arrested by the Police Special Branch in 1941 and were in Changi Prison until their release by the Japanese in 1942.

The Japanese Occupation: Brutal Communalism

The three years of Japanese occupation (1942-45) provided a baptism in politics for the masses in Malaya, but it also had untold repercussions for their unity, partly because the similarity of imperialist rule was augmented by the lack of pretence on the part of Japanese fascism, which adopted blatant communalist measures during its rule.

The humiliating rout of the British by the Japanese shattered the racist myth of white supremacy that had been part of colonial ideology; this served to imbue the masses in all the communities with greater self-confidence in the anti-colonial struggle after the war. The experience of resistance against the Japanese was also an invaluable test of the masses' ability for armed struggle and organization. Throughout the Occupation, the Allies relied on the efforts of the Malayan Peoples Anti-Japanese Army (MPAJA), organized by the CPM. The organization of the resistance forces and the co-operation with the Allies was acceded to by the British only at the very last moment of the invasion because they were reluctant to accord legitimacy to the CPM, which was not only the main threat to British imperialism, but also had a preponderance of Chinese membership:

> The political danger that lay in using the (MPAJA) lay in the strength that this would lend to a post-war claim for equality of status in Malaya for the Chinese.[21]

This would, after all, dispel the image created by communalist propaganda of the unpatriotic 'alien' Chinese, but in the end, the British had to come to terms with the fact that, at the time, the CPM was the only organization in Malaya both capable of and willing to oppose Japanese fascism.

The Japanese set about exploiting the communal differences among the people. The Chinese were singled out for the most severe treatment mainly because they were the suspected communists. This was also partly a retaliation by the Japanese for what they had received at the hands of the Chinese guerrillas during the Manchurian campaigns. Between 17 February and 3 March 1942, more than 5,000 Chinese were systematically massacred in Singapore.[22] The *kempetai* (Japanese equivalent of the SS) generally assumed that high school students, harbour workers, and Hainanese were all communists. The literature on the Japanese atrocities against the Chinese is plentiful and well-documented.[23]

The treatment of the Malays was hostile at first, but the

Japanese saw the advantages of preserving the formal authority of the Malay rulers and maintaining the communalist strategy that sustained them.[24] Malay was adopted as the common language for the entire Japanese Command in South-East Asia. The Malay police force was also useful for Japanese purposes to command the obedience of non-Malays and to fight the guerrillas. During the war, the Japanese actively sponsored the idea of *Malaysia Raya* by initiating KRIS (*Kesatuan Rakyat Indonesia Semenanjung*: Union of Indonesian and Peninsular Peoples), which was led by Dr Burhanuddin, Ahmad Boestaman and others in the KMM.[25] Although the KMM was co-opted into the Japanese sponsored movement, it did not fit in with Japanese interests and was sympathetic to the resistance. However, as has already been observed, it cannot be denied that the period of Japanese occupation was significant for the development of Malay nationalism.

While the Indian masses were treated equally badly (thousands were sent to the 'Death Railway' in Burma), the Indian leaders' disaffection with British colonialism was channelled into the Indian Independence League (IIL) and the Indian National Army (INA). They were influenced by the Indian National Congress's refusal to help the British war effort in India. The INA was, however, never wholeheartedly supportive of the Japanese, and sections were also sympathetic to the resistance; the MPAJA managed to recruit from within the INA and IIL:

> A number of interviews I had with the estate labourers conveyed a distinct impression of the widespread sympathies that existed between estate workers and anti-Japanese guerrillas. In this region a large number of guerrillas were Indians, mostly ex-labourers from estates.[26]

When, in 1943, the INA was revitalized under Subhas Chandra Bose, who took the Indian nationalist campaign into the plantations as well, it evoked a strong response from the Indian workers; the war years thus effected some radical changes in the attitudes of the Indian workers in Malaya.

Under the Japanese, the economy was ruthlessly pillaged to assist the Japanese war effort. Trade unions were prohibited and labour was organized into Labour Service Corps and sent wherever it was needed—as far as Burma, Thailand, and Java. For ordinary people, it was a time of great hardship, with soaring inflation and food scarcity. Chinese refugees who had fled ahead of the advancing Japanese army into Singapore were sent back to the countryside in the mainland to grow food. Unwittingly, this was to work in favour of the guerrillas in the resistance for these Chinese became vital courier links as well as providers of food. The numbers of Chinese 'squatters' (as these refugee farmers were called) grew during the Occupation. They concentrated mainly on market-gardening and have since been the main source of food for the urban population, supplying rice, vegetables, pigs and poultry. The shortage of food and consumer goods during the war served as an impetus for growing food locally and for the handicraft industry.[27]

The traditional leadership of the bourgeoisie in the Chinese community was eclipsed by the organizing role of the MPAJA and its civilian wing, the MPAJU (Malayan Peoples Anti-Japanese Union) which was formed with the specific task of building an underground mass base; both of these were organized by the CPM state committees. The task of the civilian wing was to collect funds, food, clothing and other material support for the guerrillas, but far more important was the political work of building the mass base. This aim was not difficult to achieve amongst the Chinese masses who bore the brunt of the Japanese brutality. During that time, many of the *towkays* (rich Chinese bosses) had either fled to India or were lying low in the towns; some were outright collaborators. Only the MPAJA provided consistent resistance against the Japanese, uniting and organizing the people. Spencer Chapman, a British officer who was in the 'stay-behind' force with the resistance, recalls how, as the guerrillas passed through the outlying *kampongs*, the villagers brought their legal and domestic problems to the guerrilla leader for him to settle since: 'The guerrillas stood for them as the one representative of law and order in the Japanese-occupied Malaya.'[28]

The recognition of MPAJA's moral authority during the war is also attested to by others:

> The 'communists' in Malaya were therefore a hidden force of moral power. The public looked upon them as the invisible army which held in check the oppressors of the people. It is openly admitted that but for the 'communists', the Japanese police would have made life impossible, and the informers and blackmailers would have turned life into a nightmare.[29]

The MPAJA dealt with traitors and informers, issued instructions, levied taxes, and settled disputes. The majority of the guerrillas were rural workers, squatter farmers, rubber tappers, mine labourers, and urban workers, as well as members of the petty bourgeoisie. These were mainly Chinese, though by no means entirely Chinese, as state propaganda has suggested, there were also Indians and Malays within their ranks. For example, there were sufficient Malays to warrant the construction of mosques in the guerrilla bases.[30] The war years also provided opportunities for cross-communal co-operation. The MPAJA thus had links with the *Ashkar Melayu Setia* (Loyal Malay Army) in Perak, and with *Wataniah* in Pahang, and with the KMM.[31]

The MPAJA suffered from many constraints in the war effort. There was poor communication between the guerrilla groups, but they managed to establish a courier system. There was a total absence of external communication and supplies until the first contacts with Force 136 in May 1943.[32] Not least, the MPAJA suffered a serious setback when over 100 guerrilla commanders, state committee members, and members of the Central Committee of the CPM itself were ambushed at the Batu Caves in September 1942.[33]

Perhaps the most serious consequence of the Japanese Occupation and the culmination of the years of colonial rule, was the bloody communal riots just after the war. These began as retaliation by some resistance groups against primarily Malay collaborators and the police. In fact, in Johore 'the Japanese had actively fomented trouble between the Malays and the Chinese'.[34] Consequently, there were bloody clashes and casualties in Batu Pahat. These sporadic outbursts of retaliation and counter-retaliation spread throughout the country, notably at Padang Lebar, Negri Sembilan, Pahang, and Perak. These were the first serious clashes of a communal character which would become part of the everyday consciousness of the various communities affecting subsequent inter-communal relations.

The Post-War Workers' Struggles

Both before and during the war, the British Colonial Office had been deliberating about post-war Malayan strategy. A new basis had to be found for British imperialism which would break away from the unsatisfactory colonial set-up that had existed until then (partly discussed on pp.61-2).

> When the British return to the ⅜Malay½ States, the least that will be hoped for from them is a new and refreshing attitude towards their problems. A return to the old order would not be consonant with the modern trend of political thought.[35]

Until then, the British were not prepared to contemplate demands for democratic representation, most loudly voiced by the workers and the radical petty bourgeoisie. The buttressing of the feudal Malay rulers was, as has been stressed, the colonial power's strong card in its communalist strategy:

> The Sultans are not an anachronism: they are a buffer between us and political developments such as have taken place in Ceylon, a buffer also between us and the Chinese.[36]

In July 1943, the Colonial Office and the War Office jointly set up a Malayan Planning Unit (MPU) to formulate plans for post-war Malaya. To find an alternative to the 'Old Guard' colonialists in the prevailing class structure of Malaya in order to facilitate the transition to a neo-colonial situation was crucial for British imperialism. Self-government was the order of the day, but at the same time the vital interests in the tin and rubber industries and other Western investments had to be secure.

The MPU had consulted the British owners of Malayan tin and rubber assets. The state of the post-war British economy meant that the British were even more concerned than ever to secure their major dollar earners: rubber and tin. In 1945, Britain was bankrupt; she had liquidated £1.1 billion of her overseas investments and acquired an external debt of £3.4 million.[37] Of the total world output in 1948, Malaya produced 45.8 per cent of the rubber and 28.1 per cent of tin. These provided more in terms of gold and dollar reserves for Britain than was afforded by the entire export drive over the same period.[38] The dominant position of the US after the war allowed it to buy cheap rubber and tin from Britain as a condition for its aid; this, in turn, meant depressed wages for the Malayan workers. But before examining post-war British colonial strategy, it is necessary to consider the class forces as soon as the war ended.

Immediately upon the Japanese surrender, and until the re-occupation of Malaysia by the British a few months later in September 1945, the MPAJA was the sole force in control of the country. Inland towns were taken over by MPAJA units and they were the administering authority throughout the peninsula. However, it vacillated over taking power and missed the opportunity to be rid of British colonialism.[39] The CPM leadership was indecisive,[40] but the Party had counted on laying the ground work for taking power at a later date through extending its mass work in the open united front activities. Among other things, the support of the Malay peasantry for the mass struggle against colonialism was still lacking. But the ensuing three years up to the 'Emergency' were to demonstrate the limitations of the constitutional means of struggle for national liberation.

When the British returned to Malaya, the CPM (Communist Party of Malaya) was legalized, since it had been the main ally of the British Military Command during the war. The CPM made 'Eight Proposals and Six Suggestions' to the British Military Administration, calling for democratic freedoms and representative institutions leading to self-government. At the same time, the Peoples' Committees, established by the MPAJA in the towns and villages, were extended to incorporate all the national groups. Other front organizations were formed, including Women's Associations and the New Democratic League; but of these, the GLU (General Labour Unions) were still the most important. They were based on district rather than on occupation, and so embraced all trades and industries and, more importantly, transcended communal divisions.

The strength of the workers' organizations was demonstrated in October 1946 when the CPM called a series of lightning strikes at the Sentul workshops, Batu Arang collieries, Lumut, Taiping, Ipoh, Parit Buntar, Sungei Siput, Raub, Kuala Lipis, all MPAJA strongholds.[41] The strikes also extended to Singapore. Post-war economic conditions largely facilitated the formation of workers' organizations: 'The demands put forward by labour spring not from any ordered political doctrines but from a genuine feeling of distress.'[42] Under the British Military Administration, the rice shortage was exacerbated by graft and corruption, price manipulation and inefficiency.[43] The socio-economic conditions were reflected in July 1947 in the 'Report of the Wages Commission' by the economist T.H. Silcock, Chairman of the Commission: '...disappointment and disillusionment, shortages of supplies, lack of houses and amenities, high prices, low wages, and the foment of new political ideas.'[44]

The extent of the degradation was not merely owing to the economic conditions. Stenson has referred to strike demands at the time which included such provision for basic human dignity as, the right of estate workers to mount their bicycles from the place of work itself. Apparently, normally they had to push their cycles until they had passed the planter's house before they could mount.[45] The workers qualified their strike demands with the reminder that: 'The real wage we are demanding today is much less than the real wage we were given in 1939.'[46] And even the *Straits Times* admitted that the workers' demands were reasonable.[47]

To meet the challenge of the workers, the British Military Administration worked hand in glove with the employers, planters, and Agency Houses. In March 1946, the United Planting Association of Malaya (UPAM) urged the government to enforce the pre-war Societies Ordinance in order to control the unions. The mass struggles that followed forced the Administration to regard the workers' demands more seriously. The basic demands put forward by the GLU in October 1945 called for: the abolition of the contract of employment; an eight-hour day and six-day week; equal pay, regardless of sex or colour; and social insurance and compensation. The process of unionization continued to spread rapidly, and the strength of the unions was demonstrated to the workers as much as the employers. In December 1945, 18,000 municipal workers, rubber factory and brewery workers, bus and taxi drivers, as well as engineering workers were on strike. In 1946, an attempt by the British Military Administration to harass the workers by arresting a MPAJA militant, Soong Kwang, led to 'the biggest stoppage of work since the reoccupation'.[48]

Unionization had advanced more in Singapore than in the mainland, but by 1946, it had proceeded apace there too. A Pan-Malayan GLU (PMGLU) was formed in February 1946 and all sections of the working class were encouraged to join it. There was another show of force by the unions on 15 February, the anniversary of the fall of Singapore. Seventeen people were killed in demonstrations in Johore.[49] When a national trade union organization had been realized, Malay clerical workers and Indian plantation workers unions became some of the most militant. The postwar labour shortages had begun to attract more Malays into wage labour in the urban sector than previously; this was particularly evident at the Sentul workshops of the Malayan Railways. The Indian workers were no longer content to accept pre-war labour conditions, they formed the *Thondar Padai* (Youth Corps), which heralded a new militancy among the Indian workers who had borne the brunt of much of the wage restraining measures.

But most importantly, the PMGLU provided a co-ordinating body for labour which helped to break the 'divide-and-rule' tactics of the British, already noted, by putting forward collective demands. Its weekly paper, *Vanguard*, was printed in four languages and broadsheets, strike bulletins and other information were also distributed. In addition, the PMGLU concerned itself with local problems and rendered assistance such as strike relief, sympathy strikes, as well as protection against victimization. By April 1947, the PMGLU membership was 263,598, more than half the total labour force in Malaya, and 85 per cent of all the unions.[50]

The wave of strikes continued into 1947. In March that year, dockers and tin smelters struck in Penang and thereby paralyzed the works. In subsequent months, strikes in Singapore continued unabated, while on the mainland, railway and estate workers also came out:

> The labour situation on rubber estates still gives grounds for uneasiness. There have been on average 27 strikes a week for the last seven weeks and the prospects for the immediate future do not appear to be bright.[51]

In most cases the workers won their demands for increased wages and better conditions.[52] No longer were they prepared to suffer the indignities and paternalism of the preceding years. Stenson notes a strike by Chinese and Indian hospital workers because they objected to being referred to as 'boy'. Elsewhere in Penang, municipal workers demanded the removal of the designation for 'Coolie Lines Road'.[53]

The British Military Administration used all the means it could muster to break the strikes, including the use of Japanese prisoners-of-war as well as British troops. It even recruited a Ceylonese military labour force, and in reversal of previous policy, began to use Malays to replace strikers.[54] Left-wing newspapers were closed down and their editors imprisoned on charges of sedition.[55] The post-war Labour Government's policy of fostering 'responsible' trade unionism was another method employed to combat the workers' militancy.[56] The local colonial administrators and employers began to call for a return to the paternalism of the pre-war days.[57] But during the post-war period, the British could not ban trade unions as it would have contravened the 1940 Ordinance and risked international condemnation.

The Politics of Communalism

After the war, the clamour for self-government by all the oppressed, colonial peoples had to be faced by the imperialist countries. The British in Malaya had to solve the problem of how to hand over political power and simultaneously keep its economic interests intact. But as we have seen, the only credible and consistent force leading the nationalist movement was that rooted in a militant left-wing working class. In the Malay community, the nationalist forces, led by the radical petty bourgeoisie, were similarly anti-colonial. Consequently, it was essential for British imperialism to find an alternative to these class forces. The Constitutional talks after the war represented the limit of the colonial state's communalist strategy; namely, the 'institutionalization' of communalism in the country.

Immediately after the war, the Malay rulers were (in the eyes of the British) tainted with having collaborated with the Japanese.[58] Moreover, the Malay nationalist forces were increasingly influenced by the idea of *Nusantara*, or union with Indonesia.[59] Even elements within the English-educated Malays in London were caught up by the idea:

> The ultimate goal after which the Malays in Malaya and Indonesia are striving for is a federation of all Malay lands in SE Asia in the future.... In political outlook, the Malays in Malaya have come more and more under the influence of their brothers in Sumatra and Java.[60]

The 'Malayan Union' (MU) proposals were mainly intended to: transfer the sultans' jurisdiction to the British Crown and so remedy the pre-war situation; create a unitary state, but excluding Singapore; grant citizenship to the non-Malays. This last provision was the minimal condition for a liberal-democratic facade and could not have been excluded since the non-Malays had played such a significant role in the anti-Japanese resistance. The MU, however, was not intended to be a preliminary move to prepare Malaya for self-government. No elections were envisaged, as the administrative organs and legislature were to be filled by the Governor's nominees, with limited powers. It has been pointed out by K.H. Khong, that J. de V. Allen's view that the MU was meant to 'punish the Malays and reward the Chinese'[61] is mistaken, for the directive on overall policy in Malaya by the Cabinet Committee specifically stated that the changes should be subjected to 'special recognition of the political, economic, social interests of the Malay race'[63] Another proviso was that citizenship, as formulated in the MU proposals, did not confer any special rights or privileges on the non-Malays that they did not previously have.

The sultans in the nine states were not pleased with the MU proposals but found themselves in a difficult position because of the stain of collaboration during the war. By 21 December 1945, the British had concluded all the nine treaties with the sultans, taking advantage also of the confusion just after the war and the dearth of information. But the British had not envisaged the scale of opposition by the Malay rulers, who, when they had fully appreciated the implications of the MU, began to mobilize support against it among the Malays. The British had planned to:

> ...push the new Constitution through by shock tactics with the minimum of consultation or less. It was presumed that Malaya would be liberated, like Burma, with military force.[63]

The opposition to the MU was the first time the Malay rulers had attempted mass activity since colonization. Clearly they were eager to protect their feudal privileges which they felt were threatened by the new proposals. Among other things, the MU proposed to abolish the need for their formal assent to legislation; this would be the prerogative of the Governor's. The State Councils were similarly to be abolished.[64]

The Malay rulers protested through formal channels[65] and also announced the withdrawal of their signatures from the treaties they had recently signed. They then began a campaign against the MU within the Malay mass organizations that had sprung up. The propaganda they adopted was crudely communalistic and directed against the proposals for equal rights for the non-Malays.[66] An example of such Malay associations was the *Kesatuan Melayu Johore* (Johore Malay Association), led by Malay aristocrats and top Malay officials, including the *Mentri Besar* (Chief Minister) and the *Mufti* (the religious head after the Sultan).[67] It called for mass support to 'protect the privileges of the Malays'.[68] Onn Jaafar, son of a former *Mentri Besar* and a Malayan Civil Service officer, led the Malay movement in Johore, and in May 1946 formed the United Malay National Organization (UMNO).

In December 1945, the British confronted the first public demonstration by the conservative Malay forces when MacMichael, HM's representative for the Colonies, arrived in Kota Bahru to ratify the MU proposals. The demonstration of about 10,000 had slogans such as: 'Malaya belongs to the Malays. We don't want other races to be given the rights and privileges of the Malays'.[69] When the White Paper on the MU was published on 22 January 1946, protests by the conservative Malays grew fiercer, these were not so much against British rule as for the 'reinstatement of British justice'.[70] Some placards even read: 'Father protect us till we grow up'.[71]

A congress of 42 Malay organizations in March 1946 to coordinate action against the MU called upon all the Malay rulers to boycott the functions relating to the MU, including the Governor's installation ceremony, and for all appointees to boycott the Advisory Councils.[72] In this campaign, the Malay leaders relied on the support of the Malay petty bourgeoisie and the whole network of the traditional feudal authority system down to the *kampong* level.

It is though, unlikely that the Malay peasant masses were affected by the constitutional fracas, except for the bombardment of communalist propaganda. The British Military Administration's monthly report for February 1946 states: 'Opposition to the MU proposals is mainly confined to the upper and educated classes... the peasant generally speaking having no views on the subject at all.'[73] But it is clear that the British had misjudged the situation, for as J. de V. Allen put it: 'Even the most loyal Malay was not prepared to be annexed so late in the British Empire's day.'[74]

In the other sections of the Malay community, the radical intellectuals in the KMM (Union of Malay Youth) had formed the Malay Nationalist Party (MNP) in October 1945. Its chairman, Mokhtaruddin, was also a member of the CPM. In 1946, KMM had an estimated membership of 60,000.[75] In marked contrast to the conservative Malay Associations formed by the Malay aristocracy, the MNP's programme included:

(a) The right to self-determination of the Malayan people.
(b) The union of Malaya with equal rights for all races.
(c) Freedom of speech, press, meeting and religion.
(d) Improvement of the standard of living of the people.
(e) Improvement of the agricultural conditions and the abolition of land tax on agricultural land.
(f) Improvement of labour conditions and the establishment of trade union hours of work.
(g) Introduction of educational reforms on democratic lines, including free education and the establishment of national schools.
(h) The fostering of friendly relations between all races in Malaya.
(i) Support for the Indonesian Independence Movement.[76]

Because the MU was seen as an attempt to tighten British grip on Malaya further the MNP demanded an end to colonial rule. The Party did not see the non-Malays as representing a threat to the Malays at all, but maintained that the unity of all the peoples of the country was necessary for the democratic struggle to free Malaya from colonialism.[77] Instead, it saw the feudal remnants of the traditional Malay society as a major impediment in the development of the Malay *rakyat* (people).

Unfortunately, the MNP suffered from the same weakness as the KMM: it was too far removed from the peasant masses who remained bound to the feudal outlook and remained in obeisance to the traditional rulers. Peasant differentiation had not reached the extent necessary to attract the peasantry to ideas of republicanism and anti-colonialism. The dominant ideology of communalism held greater sway in the closed society in the *kampong*. The MNP had a revolutionary youth section called *Angkatan Pemuda Insaf* (API, means FIRE), or Organization of Youth for Justice; its chairman, Ahmad Boestaman, was arrested in April 1947.[78] API itself was declared illegal by the authorities that same year.

The CPM similarly opposed the MU on the grounds that there was no real democracy under it, nor, in substance, did citizenship for the non-Malays entail any legal rights:[79]

(a) There were no arrangements for election of representatives to the Legislative or Executive Councils. Instead of which, 'Advisory Councils' were set up, all appointees of the Governor. At the same time, members of the Executive Council were all British officials.

(b) Membership of the Advisory Council required a competent knowledge of English. The English-educated in Malaya at the time merely represented a small minority.

(c) There was 'not an odour of freedom' within the Advisory Council itself:

> The Governor alone shall be entitled to submit questions to the Advisory Councils for their advice. The Governor may act in opposition to the advice given to him by the members of the Advisory Council if he shall in any case consider it right to do so.[80]

Furthermore, all members of the Council held office only at the pleasure of the Governor and could be dismissed at any time.

(d) Singapore was to be a separate political unit despite its close historical, political, economic, and social ties with Malaya. The CPM saw this as an attempt by the British to use Singapore's economic hold over the mainland to control the politics of the MU without having to bear the responsibility. British imperialism was not yet ready to permit a similar process of 'liberalization' and self-government for Singapore, because of its economic potential and its radical labour movement which posed a threat to British interest.

The alternative proposals by the CPM were based on genuine democratic demands:[81]

(a) Singapore to be an integral part of Malaya.

(b) A National Assembly to be set up through universal suffrage.

(c) The right to vote for all Malayans over the age of 18 irrespective of sex, class, colour, political and religious beliefs.

(d) Freedom of residence, language, and education to be guaranteed in the Constitution.

(e) Legislative and Executive Councils to be appointed by the National Assembly. These bodies would have the right to veto any bill or enactment pertaining to Malaya passed by the British Government.

(f) Singapore would be governed by a Municipal Council and Mayor with powers over the administration of the city.

(g) The establishment of state councils, with members elected by universal suffrage.

But despite the protests from every quarter, the British proceeded with the inauguration of the MU on 1 April 1946. They had underestimated the reaction of the Malay rulers, for ultimately it was their support that was valued above that of any other class forces in Malaya. The support of the Malay rulers was the axis of British communalist strategy. On the day of Governor Gent's installation of office, there was a spectacle of 'tremendous crowds of wildly excited Malays'[82] descending upon the Railway Station Hotel in Kuala Lumpur (where the rulers were staying) to ensure that the rulers did not attend.

The fury of the Malay opposition to the MU forced the British to reappraise the situation, for the anti-MU mood of the conservative Malays was beginning to turn into an anti-British one. The possibility of a MU where 'no European would be able to travel or sleep without an armed guard... where no industrial machinery would be safe from sabotage... where blood will run and where business will suffer and decay...'[83] was becoming a reality, especially as the working class was already restive. There were thus few alternatives left except for the British to make a volte face. So Gent started immediate negotiations with the rulers behind the backs of all the other groups in the country. By May 1946, he was convinced that the MU had to be abandoned in favour of a 'Federation of Malaya'. The Colonial Office was at first not convinced by Gent's reversal, suggesting that he was 'weakening before the colonials'. His view was, however, soon confirmed by Malcolm MacDonald, the Governor-General designate.

Essentially, for the British to submit to the Malay rulers was a small concession to make, while at the same time, this episode served to perfect the communalist strategy. The rulers' main complaints had been the bullying manner with which MacMichael had secured the treaties with the Sultans, and the granting of citizenship rights to the non-Malays. Their only demand was for a return to the 1941 status quo, and they had no objection to the idea of a Federation of Malaya.[84] They did not challenge continued British rule and British economic, political, and military interests was thereby assured. That at least was made clear, for even during the heat of the MU crisis, the Sultans and UMNO leaders liaised freely with British officials. In fact, at the conclusion of the Pan-Malayan Malay Congress held to protest against the MU on 4 March 1946, the top British officials were all invited to the dinner and were even toasted.[85]

The Federation of Malaya proposals were thus drawn up in July 1946 by a working committee consisting of eight British officials, four Malays representing the rulers, and two UMNO representatives. The exclusion of all non-Malay interest groups demonstrated the communalist intent in these new proposals. Among the terms of reference was:

> That these states are Malay states ruled by Your Highnesses; the subjects of your Highnesses have no alternative allegiances or other country which they can regard as their homeland and they occupy a special position and possess rights which must be guarded.[86]

The formal authority of the Sultans over Malay customs and religion was to be maintained; Federal Legislative and Executive Councils were to be established with members appointed by the British High Commissioner.[87] The citizenship provisions for the non-Malays were to be tightened: instead of the five-year residential requirement under the MU, the Federation required 15 years of residence before citizenship could be conferred, and applicants were required to have an adequate knowledge of either the Malay or the English language, in neither of which were the majority of the non-Malay masses very proficient. Singapore was still to be excluded, nor was there any representative democracy, on the grounds that Malayans were not yet ready for it.

The communalist strategy of British imperialism was manifest in these secret negotiations with the Malay rulers and UMNO. The intention was not only to isolate the radical nationalist forces, but also to exclude from the proceedings the commercial and petty bourgeoisie in the non-Malay communities. Significantly, the Working Committee of the Federation proposals gave no progress reports to the public.

The new proposals, evoked a chorus of protest from the other political forces in Malaya, which had been excluded from the talks. The radical Malay intelligentsia and the working-class forces opposed the Federation's attempt to divide the masses and thus perpetuate colonial rule,[88] by means of not transferring democratic rights to the people. UMNO had been recommended by the colonial government as the organization through which nomination of Malay candidates to the Federal and State Councils should be channelled. The Chinese Chambers of Commerce opposed this on the grounds that the exclusion of Singapore would weaken the Chinese position. In fact, that this was a consideration in British communalist strategy cannot be ruled out, in addition the economic and strategic advantage of keeping Singapore out of the Federation. Similarly, the Malayan Indian Congress (MIC), formed in August 1946 by the Indian commercial bourgeoisie, opposed the Federation.

During this time, the Malayan Democratic Union (MDU), formed in December 1945, came into prominence. Led by the English-educated intelligentsia it became another united front organization in which the CPM worked. The MDU manifesto contained an eight-point programme of political and social reform:[89]

(a) Self-government for Malaya within the British Commonwealth.
(b) A Legislative Assembly of freely elected representatives of the people.
(c) Universal suffrage for all Malayan citizens over 21 years of age, irrespective of race, sex, religion or property.
(d) Freedom of speech, person, press and meeting.
(e) Educational reform, including free elementary, secondary, and technical education for all.

(f) A social security system including free medical services.
(g) Improved standard of living for all.
(h) Complete equality in employment regardless of colour.

It thus entirely favoured democratic order and self-determination for the Malayan people based on equality, and believed that the economic, political and communal problems that existed could be solved only when colonial rule was terminated.

The MDU began to co-ordinate a United Front of all the various sections of the people affected by the Federation proposals. All the major political parties condemned the conspiratorial manner in which the negotiations had been conducted between the British, the rulers and UMNO. Thus, the Council for Joint Action (CJA) was formed, comprising the MNP, MDU, Singapore FTUs, the Clerical Union, the Straits Chinese British Association,[90] MIC, Indian Chamber of Commerce, and the Ceylon Tamil Association. Their main counter-proposals were:[91]

(a) Singapore should be an integral part of Malaya.
(b) Self-government through a fully elected legislature.
(c) Equal citizenship rights for all who have made Malaya their home.

In the same month, the Council was extended into the Pan-Malayan Council of Joint Action (PMCJA) with the inclusion of the Pan-Malayan FTUs and the MPAJA Ex-Comrades Association. It immediately demanded that the British government repudiate all its negotiations with UMNO and the Malay rulers, and instead recognize the PMCJA as the representative body of all the communities in Malaya and with which it might negotiate the constitutional issue. The PMCJA then launched a mass campaign to oppose the proposals, with letters to the press, public meetings, mass rallies and demonstrations all over the country. The *Malaya Tribune* reported 'crowds of thousands' and described a demonstration in Penang as 'one of the biggest gatherings ever witnessed'.[92]

Shortly afterwards the MNP left the PMCJA to form a parallel Council of Joint Action called *Pusat Tenaga Rakyat* (better known by its acronym 'PUTERA'). This was necessitated by political expediency rather than differences with the PMCJA, because the conservative Malay newspapers were baiting the MNP for being 'stooges of the non-Malays'.[93] The largest organizations in PUTERA were the MNP and API. Together, the PMCJA-PUTERA coalition presented a 'Peoples' Constitutional Proposals' to the Secretary of State for the colonies in July 1947. Its main points were:[94]

(a) Automatic citizenship for all persons born in Malaya. Citizenship rights in any other country should be renounced for 'Melayu' citizenship.

(b) Persons not born in Malaya could acquire citizenship if: they are more than 18 years of age; are of good character; had resided in Malaya for eight out of the previous ten years; passed a simple test in Malay; and took the oath of allegiance.

(c) Equal rights and opportunities in political, economic, educational and cultural spheres regardless of race, creed and sex.

(d) Malay to be the official language but usage of other languages should be permitted.

(e) For the first nine years, not less than 55 per cent of the legislative representatives would be Malays.

(f) Singapore should be part of the Federation.

(g) All members of the Legislature to be elected by the citizens.

(h) Members of the Executive would be elected from among the members of the Legislature.

(i) A Council of Races to be set up with powers to delay any legislation for up to three years if it had racial implications.

(j) The Malay religion and customs should be under the control of institutions set up by the Malays.

(k) The Malay rulers to be retained as constitutional monarchs.

All these points were formulated with the view to win the broadest support. Thus point (k) was intended to take into account the fact that the Malay peasantry were still bound by a feudal outlook. PUTERA dropped its previous proposal for 'special provisions for the advancement and upliftment of the Malays' after the first point, calling for equal rights for all 'Melayu' citizens, had been adopted. 'Melayu' is of course the generic reference to the Malay. It showed a willingness on the part of the non-Malays in the PMCJA to accept the principle of assimilation, which was far removed from the prevailing communalist rhetoric.

The government refused to heed the storm of protest and the mass campaign that followed, maintaining that 'consultations with all sections of the population, particularly the non-Malays had been adequately carried out'.[95] It published the Revised Constitutional Proposals in July 1947, which in no way differed from the Draft Agreement. In the same month the Chinese Chambers of Commerce joined the PMCJA-PUTERA coalition after having failed to negotiate with the British on its own. From then on, the coalition began employing economic boycott or *hartal* to apply pressure on the government. A nation-wide *hartal* was called on 20 October 1947, the day of the opening of the British Parliament. Besides the boycott by local business, there was a general strike by the workers:

> Hundreds of thousands of dollars were lost by the government, industry and business today when the hartal kept labour away from the ports, rubber estates, tin mines, business houses and streets. Industry in Selangor almost entirely took a forced holiday.[96]

Similarly in Singapore, the *hartal* was:

...an impressive spectacle... with its miles of shuttered shops and its streets almost empty of traffic. The organizers of the hartal certainly made a proper job of it... succeeded in bringing about an almost complete shutdown.[97]

The Chinese bourgeoisie in the Chambers of Commerce were not consistent in their opposition to the colonial authorities. They constantly shifted their position and persisted in making their own representation to the government, appealing for a change of policy. The manner in which they performed differed strikingly from that in which the coalition performed its political task, which was always oriented toward the masses and accompanied by political education. Subsequently, the Chinese Chambers of Commerce accepted nominations to the Federal Legislative Council in February 1948, justifying their action by arguing that they would fight 'from within'. The Chinese bourgeoisie compromised with the colonial authorities, largely because of the threat posed by the radical workers' movement. As we shall see in the next section, the constitutional issue was being fought simultaneously as the workers' struggles on the economic front were reaching a climax, the prelude to the 'Emergency'.

Despite the overwhelming opposition to the Federation proposals, the colonial state refused to concede, confident that its communalist strategy would work and relying on the support of the Malay rulers and their social bases. The workers escalated their struggles when they realized that the British had no intention of granting the basic democratic rights. The authorities replied with even stronger repressive measures, reimposing the Societies Ordinance and the Banishment Ordinance.

By proposing the Federation of Malaya on those terms, the British craftily deflected the anti-colonial forces by putting the PMCJA on the defensive, that is, the non-Malays could merely demand citizenship rights instead of the more substantive demands for full independence and representative government. This, again, was because of the need to assuage the communalist slant in the colonial state strategy. The Governor-General, Malcolm MacDonald, described the PMCJA-PUTERA counter-proposals as 'idealistic and impractical'. Subsequent events and continued British intransigence were to convince the various parties in the coalition of the futility of the constitutional means of struggle against the colonial state. Nevertheless, the PMCJA and PUTERA won this tribute from such an unexpected source as the *Straits Times*:

...the first attempt to put Malayan party politics on a plane higher than that of rival racial interests and also the first attempt to build a political bridge between the non-Malay communities and the Malay race.[98]

Consequently, the coalition urged all parties to boycott the

Federal Legislative and State Councils, including the Singapore Legislature. The Singapore Constitutional proposals had proved to be no less of a sham: the elections were for six seats only out of the 22-man chamber; only British subjects could vote, which immediately excluded almost all the Malays living there; and above all, it was a blatant attempt to legitimatize the separation of Singapore from Malaya.

Prelude to the Revolt: Reaction

With the Constitutional crisis, the political lessons of the anti-colonial struggle added fuel to the labour movement. Industrial unrest occurred on an unprecedented scale between 1946 and 1948 and involved frequent clashes between police and workers. But by 1947, the colonial state and the employers had begun their offensive against the workers.

The methods used to defuse the militant labour unions were to set the precedent for similar repression up to the present day. The government first enforced the registration of all unions under the restrictive 1940 Societies Ordinance. This meant that the Registrar of Trade Unions could inspect the proceedings and accounts of the unions and so proscribe any links with non-registered unions; namely, the Pan-Malayan, and the Singapore GLUs, which were dominated by the CPM. The GLUs had refused to be registered on the grounds that the Act was too restrictive, and to comply would have meant a complete lack of freedom to act. Among the clauses of the Act, it was stipulated that government employees were not allowed to join unions of non-government employees, an obvious attempt to divide the labour force. Also, union funds were not permitted to be used for political purposes in the manner defined by the government. By March 1947, most of the affiliates of the PMGLU had been registered, and the government thus managed to maintain close supervision of their activities.

The labour movement had all along been much stronger in Singapore. In August 1946, the SGLU had reorganized itself into the SFTU, but was not required to register under the Ordinance. The PMGLU thought that it would do likewise by simply reorganizing itself formally into the PMFTU; but no sooner had it done this than the Registrar insisted that all its affiliates would have to register as well and all links with non-registered organizations severed, including subscription contributions to any federation. It was clear that the government was trying to isolate the weak unions.

At the same time, the government went about promoting 'sound' trade unionism, which meant simply the establishment of 'independent' trade unions to break up organized labour. In this project, it was only partially successful, and even this limited success was confined to white-collar workers. The FTUs were excluded from official consultative bodies, and before long, the SFTU and the PMFTU were given an ultimatum to reconstitute themselves before they could be reregistered. This was aimed at breaking up the radical trade union movement.

The repression thereafter was relentless. The *Straits Times* editorial of 17 March 1947 sounded this warning to the unions: 'This marks the beginning of that firmer handling of extremism and lawlessness in the Malayan labour movement for which employers of all races have been clamouring...'[99] Through the colonial state, the employers could implement whatever measures they desired to counter the strength of the unions. They had already formed associations to strengthen their position, for example the Malayan Mining Employers Association, and the Malayan Planting Industry Employers Association. Their interests were consolidated and represented in the Singapore Association and the Malayan Association. These Associations began to resist the workers' wage demands and to enforce strict conditions of employment and discipline.

After the wave of strikes in early 1947, reaction from the employers and the state followed swiftly. Between February and April of that year, the police were sent in to deal with workers in Kedah, where Indian estate workers had taken control of many estates. At Bedong estate, workers clashed with police, resulting in 21 workers injured and 66 arrested. The strike leader died a few days later at the hands of the police.[100] At the Dublin Estate, a workers' meeting addressed by an FTU official, was broken up by police killing a worker and wounding five others. Collusion between the police and the planters had been revealed by the *Democrat* newspaper on 28 February 1947. This was also later confirmed in the MIC Report, 'Findings of the Board of Inquiry into the Kedah Incidents'.[101] Estate managers began to enforce the Trespass Act against union officials, and striking rubber tappers were summarily dealt with. All known militants were victimized and isolated and jointly denounced as 'outside agitators'.

The 'Kedah Incidents' occurred at a time when the FTUs were mobilizing the Indian workers into a co-ordinated body to confront the UPAM (Planters Association). In March 1947, the Selangor Estate Workers' Union presented a collective demand for a 100 per cent wage increase for all Indian workers, war rehabilitation grant, sick pay, and the removal of trespass restrictions.[102] This was a significant attempt to bridge the divisions in the working class by bringing the wages of the Indian workers into line with the Chinese workers. The UPAM refused any concessions, arguing that the falling rubber prices would bankrupt the estates. Instead they decided to cut contract tapping rates (on which the Chinese tappers were dependant) by 20 per cent.[103] The various estate workers' unions then combined to form the Pan-Malayan Rubber Workers Council, but the Registrar refused to recognize it.

But estate workers were not the only section of the working class that faced state and employers' reaction. Dockers, mill workers, municipal workers, all faced cuts in wages. Mass dismissals were commonly used as a threat to strikers. Consequently, the number of strikes began to decrease noticeably, and the workers' actions reduced merely to defending themselves against the concerted reaction. The Willan judgement of October 1947, which ruled in favour of the estate owners' dismissal of three women tappers who had been on strike, became a licence, '...a legal right of all employers in similar circumstances, to refuse to take back strikers'.[104] This virtually questioned the right to strike itself. The court judgement also became the signal for the arrest of leading trade unionists, for example, Appadurai of the Penang FTU, and Vanivellu of the Kedah Federation of Rubber Workers Union.[105]

By the beginning of 1948, a climate of repression had been firmly established. The employers were as strong as they had been before the war. The unions were finding it increasingly difficult to send in pickets to support strikes. The FTU finances were drastically cut because of state surveillance of union accounts and proceedings, and they could afford fewer full-time organizers. The government could, furthermore, avail itself of the power of banishment to deport Chinese and Indian militants alike. The disarray in the labour movement coincided with the disaffection within the CPM leadership around this time, when the Secretary-General Lai Teck was unmasked as a double agent.[106] He absconded abroad with the Party funds.

In the middle of 1948, the workers' struggles approached a climax as a new wave of labour unrest broke out, involving estate workers, factory workers, dockers and miners in most of the west coast states and in Singapore. At Port Swettenham, 200 Malays were employed to break the strike there.[107] Elsewhere, employers used lock-outs and called in police to evict strikers. The case of the Chan Keng Swee Estate in Segamat, Johore, was particularly serious. The police were called in to evict the labour force which had been dismissed *in toto* by the new European management there. They refused to leave and occupied the estate. The police then baton-charged the workers and beat seven to death and injured ten others.[108] Raids were carried out in union premises throughout the country and union officials arrested or harassed.

The labour unrest became the excuse for the government to introduce amendments to the Trade Union Ordinance on 31 May 1948. Through this bill, it banned the PMFTU, the SFTU, as well as the State Union Federations. Federations of trade unions were no longer allowed except on a single occupation basis. The amendments also lay down conditions for the holding of trade union office, such as that of a minimum of three years' experience in a particular industry. It was virtually an emasculation of the whole labour movement, and the Malayan trade union movement to this day has not attained the strength it had during those post-war years.

The combined repression against the workers by the government and the employers both on the economic front and over the Constitutional issue left little option for them except to opt for open revolt. But the final decision for a showdown was pre-empted by the colonial state, which began an offensive against the workers itself soon after. On 4 June 1948, Gurkha troops were despatched to Johore and police leave in Kedah was cancelled. A few days later, the editor of the Communist Party daily, *Min Sheng Pao*, was arrested on a sedition charge. This was followed by the outlawing of the FTUs.

On 17 June, when three European planters were killed, the Governor-General declared a state of Emergency throughout Malaya. The Emergency Regulations were extended to Singapore on the 25 June. Under the Regulations, the CPM and the PMFTU were banned, and the police were given wide powers of arrest and detention. The authorities took advantage of this to raid union premises, and hundreds of political activists were arrested. By July, the number of strikes had dropped to a negligible figure as the unions were completely suppressed. From then on, employers were given a free hand to impose wage cuts, redundancies, and withdraw those concessions that had been won by the workers.

4. Class Conflict and the National Democratic Revolution

The declaration of State of Emergency in June 1948 marked the beginning of the armed struggle in the National Democratic Revolution, which was to last until 1960, when it was officially declared to be over. The failure by the working class (led by the CPM) to achieve the first stage of the national democratic revolution can be attributed to the lack of sufficient preparation for the armed struggle. Though, as has been pointed out, that decision was pre-empted by British imperialism. Despite the failings of the CPM, the armed struggle managed to tie down Western imperialist forces for many years and to entail counter-insurgency operations on a scale that was not exceeded until the Vietnam war.

We have examined the Colonial Office and Foreign Office documents of the period at the Public Records Office in London which became available with the lifting of the 30-year rule of secrecy. From these it has been possible to provide evidence of the thinking and calculation of Western imperialism for South-East Asia, but especially the importance laid on securing Malaya for economic, political and military-strategic interests. They show the priority accorded to defeating the anti-colonial forces spearheaded by the workers. The post-war period was also one of redividing the world by Western imperialism, which under the hegemony of the US, began to move toward an integration rather than division of interests. These records reveal the articulation of the whole Western imperialist, rather than solely British, interest in Malaya.

The atmosphere of repression during the 'Emergency' provided British imperialism with an opportunity to deflect the forces of revolt and effect the neo-colonial accommodation. The entire colonial strategy—especially the aftermath of the Malayan Union crisis—had convinced the British that the custodians of an Independent Malaya must be the traditional Malay rulers. This was in keeping with the communalist strategy of British rule followed since colonization. At the same time, the neo-colonial arrangement had to accommodate the upper strata of the non-Malay bourgeoisie, who were, and still are, a necessary link in the imperialist domination of the Malayan economy. The vacillating politics of this class, reflecting its narrow and limited material interests, was harnessed by the colonial state. The stark conditions during the 'Emergency' enabled the imperialist power to exploit sectional interests and thereby isolate the working class and the peasantry. Thus, the 'Alliance Formula' with all its contradictions was devised in the Independent Malaya. The reform measures conceded by the colonial power and grudgingly agreed to by the Malay rulers, were in many ways necessitated by the ferocity of the revolt. It alerted them to the dangers of pursuing too overt a policy of discrimination against the non-Malay masses.

The Imperialist Stake in Malaya

While World War I had unleashed the proletarian revolution in the Soviet Union, the end of the Second World War saw a tide of struggles for self-determination and for democracy throughout the colonies and semi-colonies. It was a time of great crisis for imperialism. The weakened European powers, including Britain, had to concede the new division of the world imposed by the US, which would open their erstwhile colonies to US exploitation. The Marshall Plan was the principal vehicle for achieving this, as indicated by a spokeman for the US monopolies:

> If you succeed in doing away with the Empire Preference and open up the Empire to US commerce, it may well be that we can afford to pay a couple of billion dollars for the privilege.'[1]

Similarly, the Atlantic Charter asserted US hegemony over the Western imperialist bloc. Point IV of the Charter stated:

> They will endeavour, with due respect to their existing obligations, to further the enjoyment by all states, great or small, victor or vanquished, of access on equal terms to trade and to the raw materials of the world which are needed for their economic prosperity.[2]

The vital importance of Malaya's raw materials was the main preoccupation of Western imperialism, and this is amply reflected in much of the Foreign Office communications and other documents of the period. This, and the concern with which it viewed the anti-imperialist movement is summed up neatly by Creech Jones, the Colonial Secretary in 1948:

> Malaya is far and away the biggest dollar earner in the Empire... when Malaya derives no tangible advantage whatsoever from staying within the Sterling Area. The effect is made worse when it is borne in mind that, apart from the question of War Damage Compensation, the Malayan Governments have had to shoulder the enormous burden of rehabilitation without any assistance from His Majesty's Government. Furthermore, there is at present a widespread feeling in Malaya—and I am not at all sure that it is not partly justified—that His Majesty's Government, by controlling the price of tin, has hitherto denied to the Malayan Governments and producers the benefits which should rightly be theirs... we have here the germ of a powerful

and dangerous secession movement in Malaya, which is the bulwark of our whole position in SE Asia and indeed in the whole of the Far East...[3]

This Colonial Office communication shows British imperialism's preoccupation not simply with the strategic importance of Malaya, but with that of the whole region. The facts and figures gathered by the Economic Intelligence Department of the Foreign Office reveal Malaya's overwhelming contribution, above that of all the British colonies, to Britain's dollar-earning capacity. (See Table 4.1) The main importers of Malayan raw materials, (rubber and tin) are tabulated in Table 4.2, in which it can be seen that the US tops the list. Thus, the extreme sensitivity of the British to any threat to UK as well as Western interests posed by the anti-colonial forces was solidly based:

> It would clearly be disastrous if Malaya were ever to meet the same fate as Burma. We should of course lose one of our principal dollar-earning sources. Worse than this, we should also lose one of the principal sources of vital raw materials, as a result of which the economy not only of the UK, but also of the US would suffer very severely... It seems to me that in the foreseeable future we shall be met with strong demands for constitutional developments in Malaya which we would be very rash to grant if there was the remotest risk of things developing badly'.[4]

As we shall see in later sections, the British were concerned that constitutional developments should proceed along the lines prescribed by the colonial government, and that the mantle of political power should pass into the hands of their protégés in the local ruling class. The scale and intensity of the repression during the Emergency showed that in Western imperialist reckoning, Malaya meant more than simply rubber and tin:

> We should regard SE Asia as a whole and devise a coherent policy for dealing with it over the whole region.... I feel that it is no exaggeration to say that this region has assumed a vast importance in the world-wide struggle between the democratic and communist causes, quite out of proportion to its industrial and political developments.... We

Table 4.1
Net Surplus of Main Dollar Earners of British Colonies, 1948

Colony	Net Surplus ($ million)
Malaya	172.0
Gold Coast	47.5
Gambia	24.5
Ceylon	23.0

Source: Economic Intelligence Department, FO, 13 April 1949; FO371/76049/5704.

Table 4.2
Main Importers of Malayan Raw Materials, 1948

Country	Value of Imports (US$million)	Total Imports (tons)
US	270.0	727,000
UK	65.0	186,000
France	14.0	84,000
Germany	17.0	49,000
Canada	—	42,600
Italy	9.0	21,000
Netherlands	7.5	13,000
Sweden	5.0	14,000
Belgium	5.5	12,000

Source: Economic Intelligence Department, FO, 13 April 1949; FO371/76049/5704.

think—as we feel sure that you do—that a deliberate and planned effort must be made to hold the communist advance in Asia beyond the boundaries of Pakistan, India, Tibet, Burma, IndoChina and the Philippines, and to keep it away from Siam, Malaya, Indonesia…. To do that we must have a constructive policy in which all the governments in these countries can cooperate as partners…. We need Asian equivalents to the Marshall Plan and the Atlantic Pact that should offer the Asian Governments and peoples economic, political, and if necessary, military aid in their resistance to communism…[5]

The need to rally the support of the US, and indeed the other Western countries, as well to maintain the boundaries of Western sphere of influence was recognized by the British:

To devise such a policy, all the governments concerned in the region should be invited to cooperate. In addition, the governments of the USA, Australia, and New Zealand should participate. The USA are particularly important because probably no Plan adequate on the economic and military side is possible without a large measure of help from them.[6]

That the problem was always posed in terms of Western imperialist, and not simply British interest is clear from the above communication. In fact, before the US determined its policy, the British Embassy in Washington was constantly encouraging the Americans to take on a bigger commitment in Asia. In particular, a columnist in the *Washington Post*, Stewart Alsop, had proposed some policies along those lines. The British Embassy was soon able to note that 'some new development of policy in the direction suggested by Stewart Alsop can no longer be excluded'.[7] It must be recalled that at the close of the 1940s, the US needed some persuasion to be involved in SE Asia, having just received a sharp blow from the Chinese Communists. A telegram to the Foreign Office from Sir G. Thompson in Bangkok indicates this: 'The Americans have hinted strongly that, having had their fingers burned in China, they are unwilling to risk burning them further in SE Asia...'[8]

Aware of this fact, the British nevertheless began to press the Americans to be involved in alternative ways, such as their dollar investments, if not military aid:

> To the British, SE Asia is a vital anti-communist bastion and buttress of their power in the Orient. Voluminous documentation to support this thesis, and the proposed dollar investment program to go with it, has been compiled recently under the direction of Moberly Esler ening, British Under-Secretary for Far Eastern Affairs, who is planning to join Foreign Secretary Bevin in Washington next Tuesday...[9]

There was never any doubt that 'combating communist influence' in SE Asia was always synonymous with protecting the interests of entrepreneurs in Malaya as well as the metropolis. Among the Foreign Office files was a well-savoured lecture by one Dr W.J. de Jonge, who was described as:

> ...a well-known figure in the rubber world... very politically-minded... his job is to agitate on behalf of the planters association.... His politics are right-wing.... He is intelligent and pro-British... he is trying to whip up interest in SE Asia as the scene of growing communist influence.[10]

The stress in Dr Jonge's lecture was on the strategic importance of Malaya for Western imperialist interest and not on its economic potential only:

> SE Asia can be regarded as one of the most important bases of the air corridor Europe-Asia-Australia; with the support of naval bases it can command the Indian Ocean and it places the industries of Central Siberia in an extremely precarious situation. SE Asia can furthermore present a serious obstacle to any attempt to dominate the respective oceans.... I just now showed the strategic importance of SE Asia as a supplier of indispensable raw materials for war, such as rubber and tin. I may add that the oil of the Far East, together with the oil of the Middle East, is urgently needed for meeting the needs of world consumption in 1951. SE Asia, this enormous sphere of political, economic, and strategic importance, is being very seriously threatened.[11]

This view was, after all, congruent with British thinking:

> But if Burma, Siam, and IndoChina all fell to the Communists, the foothold in the perimeter ring, especially Indonesia would be precarious. Moreover, Malaya would be dangerously threatened and the maintenance of our position in the South China Sea depends on the existence of bases there and at Hong Kong. Without these bases, the position in the perimeter countries, even if bolstered up by US aid would become militarily impossible.[12]

By 1948, the workers' struggles and the anti-colonial movement had reached such a point that British imperialism was determined to take the offensive. The Singapore Conference of HM Representatives on SE Asian and Far Eastern Affairs concluded: '...that SE Asia should be regarded as a region in which an emergency exists and that policy towards it should be pursued with a proper consequential note of urgency'.[13] The note of urgency was echoed in this communication from the Commonwealth Relations Officers to the Australian Government:

> The situation in SE Asia is immediately critical. In Burma, a third of the Army has defected to Communist forces. In Malaya, the trouble is not only local, but is instigated by Chinese Communists. In a word, the plain fact is that Malaya is the only place where we are actively fighting against Communism, and moreover it is a territory for which we are responsible. Clearly we cannot afford to lose Malaya to Communism.... We have recently had a further appeal from the Commander-in-Chief, Far East, strongly supported by the Commissioner-General, for assistance.... In the light of the above appreciation, Ministers have felt that immediate help should be sent to Malaya....[14]

The 'Emergency': 1948-60

With the imposition of the Emergency Regulations, the hitherto legal parties and organizations were proscribed. The main object of the colonial state's repression was, of course, the CPM (Communist Party of Malaya). With the victory of the Chinese Revolution in 1949, the authorities in Malaya were scrupulous about distinguishing between Communism in general and the CPM in particular. It was part of the propaganda policy to 'drive a wedge between the CPM and the CCP'.[15] This was in order to prevent the CCP from harnessing the support of the Malayan Chinese for the CPM:

> To emphasize that the Malayan movement has Moscow or Peking behind it is to build it up unnecessarily and to cause heart searching among local Chinese as to whether they are wise to oppose such powerful forces. For overseas consumption, that may well be the best line, but for our purposes it seems to me much better to concentrate on drawing every possible distinction between support for the Communist Government in China and Communism in Malaya.[16]

The above communication reveals the meticulousness of the colonial state in its propaganda to the point of designating the CPM. In another communication between the Colonial Office and the Foreign Office, there is a long discussion regarding whether the CPM-led liberation army should be referred to as the Malayan 'Races' Liberation Army, or, Malayan 'Nationals' Liberation Army. Some Colonial Office officials preferred the former since it preferred not to present the CPM as a national liberation army, while others, who were keen to prove the CPM's communist orthodoxy, preferred the latter since it more closely resembled the Chinese 'Peoples

Liberation Army'.[17] Again, when the question of the recognition of the newly founded People's Republic of China arose in 1949 at the height of the Emergency, the fear that it might inspire the Malayan masses again aroused the colonial government's anxiety:

> While it is desirable for the sake of world opinion to represent the war in Malaya as against the CPM and not merely against colonial unrest, publicity should avoid writing up International Communism in such terms as to make it seem a powerful bandwagon on to which people would be wise to jump.[18]

But while 'for overseas consumption' the armed struggle in Malaya was presented as being at the instigation of Moscow and Peking, it is clear from this telegram of High Commissioner Gurney's to the Secretary of State for the Colonies, that the British themselves knew the contrary: 'Communism in Malaya receives, so far as we know, no material support from either Moscow or China.'[19]

Within Malaya itself, the colonial authorities were wary of any development of the anti-imperialist forces. For example, when the Malaya Council of World Affairs was formed, Malcolm MacDonald, the Commissioner-General sent this despatch to the Foreign Office:

> The only way to deal with such initiatives in the field of regionalism is to show tolerance and at the same time seek to modify any 'anti-imperialist' tendencies that may show themselves.[20]

When it reached the Foreign Office, a sceptical T.S. Tull commented on the margin of the file: 'I do not see quite how M. MacDonald is going to be able to modify "anti-imperialist" tendencies...'[21] When Dr Burhanuddin of the MNP (Malay Nationalist Party) was elected President of the Council and Mr Thivy, the Indian nationalist radical was elected Vice-President, MacDonald received the following despatch:

> We do consider Mr Thivy's position is anomalous, if not slightly improper, and I should be grateful if you would inform me if at any time the Council gives trouble.[22]

The colonial state took advantage of the Emergency Regulations to either imprison or deport hundreds of political activists and trade unionists and by the end of 1948, more than 13,000 people had been accounted for by these means. Deportation was the favourite method used to deal with the militant masses, at least until the logistical problem got out of hand. Those deported to China were left to the mercy of Chiang Kai Shek's army. The numbers involved are revealed in the following despatch from the Colonial Office to the Foreign Office:

> You will appreciate that at the moment Chinese immigration into Malaya is extremely restricted. In fact, a net loss back to China of nearly 29,000 persons has been recorded in the months January to July 1949.[23]

At the very start of the Emergency, the British colonial government barely managed to get away with this drastic method of repression, as is clear from the following:

> ...propose to expel Chinese from Malaya at the rate of 2,000 a month. In normal conditions in China we would certainly have expected very vigorous representation from the Chinese government about the regulations.... However, the reactions of the ⅜Chinese½ Central Government, whose days are numbered, are not of great importance one way or another. It will almost certainly be replaced... I must say that I think that the absence of any check on the executive in this mass expulsion of residents of Malaya is unfortunate, and that in practice grave injustice is liable to be done to individuals. I should have thought it possible, by the exercise of ingenuity, to have provided for some sort of review of executive action in appropriate cases. Certainly, had such provision been made, the scope for propaganda against barbarous British injustices would have been less.... The fact is that Whitehall has been presented with a fait accompli.[24]

When this despatch reached the Foreign Secretary's office, the response was as smug as could be expected:

> The Regulations are a step in the right direction though possibly rather a drastic one. However, due no doubt to the Chinese government's preoccupation nearer home, I think we have got away with it this time... I think we should say nothing in our reply to the Colonial Office to suggest that we are in any way displeased.[25]

The methods used and atrocities committed by the British to extract information from villagers and suspects, or to strafe villages in search of 'CTs' ('Communist Terrorists', as the guerrillas were referred to by the authorities), anticipated later US activities in Vietnam.[26] The touchstone of the 'containment' policies of the British was the Briggs Plan of resettlement of the half million Chinese squatters, who were the vital supporters of the guerrillas, but to deport them proved to be too big a logistic problem. The 'Briggs Plan' involved moving them en masse into 'New Villages', which were no more than concentration camps with high barbed-wired fences, heavily-armed police guards, curfews, and other prohibitive regulations. This measure succeeded to some extent in monitoring guerrilla movement and the MNLA (Malayan National Liberation Army) were forced to retreat into the jungle interior to grow their own food. The duration of the national liberation war, however, testifies to the popularity of the people's war. The British had been expecting a swift victory:

> Situation in Malaya: In general, our reading of the situation is that it is necessary to take strong action as quickly as possible to stamp out the immediate danger. In the first place, it is important that the forces available for defences should not be locked up in Malaya for a long drawn out campaign.... The longer terrorism remains unchecked the greater the danger that its Communist supporters will be able to represent the terrorists as national heroes. Once this idea gained

ground, the effects on the strategic position in the whole of SE Asia might be incalculable.[27]

The Central Committee of the CPM launched the armed struggle only in December 1948: six months after the declaration of State of Emergency. The MNLA comprised no more than 10,000 active regulars, against which, British imperialism ranged 40,000 regular British and Commonwealth troops; 70,000 armed police personnel; 300,000 Malay Homeguards; including aircraft, artillery and naval support, '...perhaps the largest armed force in proportion to population ever used in a colonial war, testifying to the support the liberation movement gained and the degree of the suppressive effort.'[28] The US gave full support to the British, and among other things supplied arms and helicopters.[29] The Griffin Mission of 1950 also recommended that immediate aid should be given for: radio and similar communication technology for the police; road building and earthmoving equipment; teacher training for Chinese primary schools and the revision of Chinese textbooks.[30]

The revolutionary forces underestimated the British imperialist resolve to carry out a long war of attrition. The latter in turn did not fail to use communalist politics to isolate the guerrillas. Thus, although there were hundreds of Indian recruits in the MNLA and even a whole Malay regiment, the armed revolt was presented by the authorities as a strictly Chinese revolt. Malay guerrillas' role in the national liberation war was not insignificant, as this War Office Report of 1949 shows:

> The main centre of bandit activity has of late been the central Pahang area, where their attacks have been concentrated on the destruction of property. The major attacks in this area have usually been executed by Malay bandits, specially reinforced for the occasion by one or two Chinese gangs... Recent bandit movement and meetings of bandit leaders in this area have lent credence to the announcement by the CPM of the formation of a Tenth Regiment of the bandit army, composed entirely of Malays.[31]

As early as January 1949, the concern shown by the authorities regarding Malay recruitment into the MNLA was quite evident: '2(c) Malays. Unsatisfactory as more Malays appear to be joining the bandits. At the start there were very few. Deterioration is confined to certain areas'.[32] During the first few years of the Emergency, Sir Charles Boucher, the British GOC in Malaya, even thought that '...a dead Malay terrorist was worth seven or eight Chinese'.[33]

The large numbers of Malays detained (more than 1,000) soon after the Emergency was declared was not publicized, in accordance with the same communalist consideration.[34] Among them were most of the MNP leaders, Ahmad Boestaman and Ishak Haji Mohammed. Rashid Mydin is still a prominent MNLA leader. The 'New Villages' were also partly intended to sever any close contact the rural Chinese may have had with the Malay peasantry. The

British used the same tactic as did the Japanese during the Second World War: using mainly Malay security forces to fight the 'Chinese CTs'. The local Malay rulers played a not insignificant part in stressing communalism, especially by pointing out the incompatibility of Islam and Communism and warning the *kampong* folk against the erosion of traditional Malay loyalty. The anti-communist propaganda campaign was especially fierce in Pahang where the MNLA's Tenth Regiment was most active.

By 1950, the government was 'further from suppressing the communist revolt than the day it began'.[35] The expenditure on the Emergency alone had increased from M$24 million in 1948 to M$120 million in 1950, one-third of the total budget of the year.[36] Guerrilla attacks on police stations, rubber estates, and other economic targets increased from 82 in September 1948 to 558 in October 1950.[37] Nevertheless, these sporadic attacks never reached the extent of a major offensive, and by the mid-1950s, the authorities had managed to gain the upper hand.

The 'Alliance Formula' and Neo-colonial Politics

During the Emergency, it became the urgent task of British imperialism to cultivate the non-communist alternative to the Malayan nationalist movement. The colonial state ensured that the mantle of political power would pass to the local Malay ruling class. The traditional Malay rulers were easily co-opted since they had been groomed by the British since the early days of colonialism, but some accommodation still had to be found between them and the non-Malay bourgeoisie who form a decisive link in the chain of imperialist exploitation of the Malayan economy.

The shifting alliance of the upper stratum of the Chinese and Indian bourgeoisie has been noted, and the colonial government had not been slow to appoint some of its representatives to the legislative and other advisory bodies. We also saw how the CPM had eclipsed their traditional influence in the non-Malay communities during the war. With the Emergency Regulations and the banning of the CPM, the rich Chinese leaders with the help of the colonial authorities began to take advantage of the vacuum created in the leadership of the Chinese community. As early as 1948, the idea of a Malayan Chinese Association (MCA) as the counterpart of the UMNO (United Malay National Organization), had been conceived by Sir Henry Gurney, the British High Commissioner:

> I have recently had long and frank talks with the Chinese members of the Legislative Council and representatives of mining and rubber interests with a view to obtaining more active help from the Chinese against the terrorists.... Steps are now being taken by leading Chinese to form a MCA open to all who have made their home in the Federation with the object of cooperation with the government and with other communities in restoring peace and good order in this

country... I have mentioned this development to Dato Onn and am satisfied that it will be helping in forth-coming Malay-Chinese conversations on long-term problems... I intend to pursue these developments strongly since without the active help of the Chinese we cannot succeed. They are as you know notoriously inclined to lean toward whichever side frightens them more and at the moment this seems to be the government.[38]

This 'behind-the-scenes' plan is also borne out by MacDonald's telegram to the Secretary of State: '...the High Commissioner has played, behind the scenes, a decisive part.'[39]

Thus, on 27 February 1949, the MCA was formed sponsored by 16 Chinese businessmen who were also members of the Federal Council, dedicated to pro-British policies. The British High Commissioner himself openly stated that he wanted the MCA to be 'stronger than the CPM and to provide the Chinese with an alternative standard to communism'.[40] The MCA Constitution even provided Chinese members of the Legislative and Executive Councils with an automatic qualification to be officers of the Association. Throughout the remaining years of the Emergency, the colonial government secured the help of the MCA in the operation to remove Chinese squatters into the 'New Villages'. The MCA also helped to recruit Chinese members into the police and armed forces and carried out the government's anti-communist propaganda. In time, the MCA did succeed in winning over sections of the Chinese petty bourgeoisie through patronage and communalist appeal of 'fighting for Chinese rights *within* the government'.[41]

The hallmark of the MCA to date remains its use of patronage to create a social base in the Chinese community. During the 1950s the government allowed it to sponsor multi-million dollar 'Social Welfare' lotteries whereby it could render financial assistance in order to increase its influence. In addition to the lotteries, the upper stratum of the Chinese business class could use its economic muscle to bestow patronage regarding employment, charity, and social and cultural services within the Chinese community.

The next step in the political strategy of the colonial state was the establishment of the Communities Liaison Committee (CLC). This had made its debut in January 1949 as the 'Sino-Malay Goodwill Committee', an informal closed-door forum for the upper classes of all three communities. Dato Onn, leader of the UMNO, has been accredited with initiating its formation,[42] but the records (see Note 38) show that Sir Henry Gurney had initiated the idea. The Committee included five Malays and four Chinese, all members of the Legislative Council, including Tan Cheng Lock, and Yong Shook Lin of the MCA; later it was expanded to incorporate leaders of the Indian community. The CLC was actively patronized by the Governor-General, Malcolm MacDonald himself, who attended all the Committee meetings.[43] It was promoted as the 'multi-racial' neo-colonial alternative to the CPM.

The communal bargaining within the CLC predated the similar secret negotiations within the later Alliance National Council. While the agreements within these were presented as 'non-communal' solutions to the rest of the country:

> The Committee never developed a genuine non-communal approach to the problems confronting Malaya, it did demonstrate that significant communal compromise was more likely to emerge from semi-secret and 'off-the-record' negotiations conducted by communal leaders.[44]

From these negotiations, the bare bones of the 'Alliance Formula' began to take shape, rife with contradictions from its inception. Dato Onn had been won over to the British view that they had to accommodate the non-Malay upper class, especially when the Emergency was proving to be more than just a 'mopping-up' operation and it was evident that the majority of the non-Malay masses was on the side of the guerrillas:

> The lessons of the Emergency awoke the dominant Malayan politicians to the dangers of perpetuating an arrangement in which political power is concentrated in the hands of one racial group while another, almost of the same size, is left with perceptibly less access to that power.[45]

At the time, the crucial issues facing the non-Malays were those of citizenship. Onn had to try very hard to persuade the conservative elements in UMNO to relent on the citizenship question and to accept the CLC recommendations to reduce the residential requirement for citizenship for non-Malays from 15 to 10 years. It will be recalled that Dato Onn had led the first revolt over the British Malayan Union's proposals in 1946 to grant citizenship rights to the non-Malays. After a melodramatic resignation from the UMNO Presidency, Onn succeeded in getting the CLC recommendations accepted by UMNO.

The fragile limits of this 'Alliance Formula' were realized when Onn, through a fatal miscalculation, thought that the British-inspired 'nationalist' movement could be liberalized and expanded by opening up the UMNO membership to the non-Malays. The traditional Malay rulers in UMNO would not hear of this, and when Onn realized that another feigned resignation would be futile, he left UMNO to launch the Independence of Malaya Party (IMP) in June 1951. The IMP mainly attracted the upper strata of the petty bourgeoisie, the *Mentri Besars* (Chief Ministers) and the like.

Within the Malay community, Onn was accused of being a 'traitor to the Malays'.[46] Meanwhile, an ultra-communalist *Persatuan Melayu Semenanjung* (Peninsula Malay Union) had been formed to oppose Onn's policies. Similarly, a 'Malay Union of Singapore' was formed. Tungku Abdul Rahman, a prince from Kedah, who represented the dominant traditional Malay rulers, became the new President of UMNO. Until then, and indeed until the IMP had shown itself to be a spent force, there is no doubt that the British had cultivated Onn to represent what they had hoped would be seen as more liberal tendencies in the neo-colony that was being created.

From the beginning of the 1950s, the British colonial state began to introduce reforms in a gradualist fashion, in an attempt to detract from the anti-colonial movement's influence. First, a selective ministerial system was permitted to present a facade of local custodians taking over from the colonial power. Five Malaysians: Dato Onn (UMNO President until June 1951), Tengku Yaacob bin Sultan Hamid (brother of the Sultan of Kedah), Dato Mahmud bin Mat (*Mentri Besar* of Pahang), E.E. Thuraisingham (CLC Chairman), and Dr Lee Tiang King (another CLC member), were appointed by the High Commissioner to head the Departments of Home Affairs; Agriculture and Forestry; Lands, Mines and Communication; Education; and Health respectively. This was billed as: '...a sure and steady progress toward freedom and democracy'.[47]

Secondly, the colonial government had to make some concessions regarding the granting of citizenship rights to the non-Malays; this was one of the main demands of the nationalist movement. In 1950, only 500,000 Chinese and 230,000 Indians had Malayan citizenship:[48] a mere fifth of the total Chinese population despite the fact that by 1947, more than three-fifths of the Chinese and half the Indian population in Malaya were local-born.[49] In 1952, therefore, the colonial authorities made some amendments to the Federation of Malaya Agreement Ordinance. Instead of the 15-year residential requirement and the stipulation that both parents of the non-Malay would-be citizen must have been born in Malaya, the amendments permitted citizenship on the following terms:[50]

(a) A total of 10 out of the 12 preceding years of residence, including the 2 years immediately preceding the date of application. The applicant must be of good character; be proficient in Malay or English; and must intend to stay permanently.
(b) Citizens of the UK or British colony, or born in either of the SS [Straits Settlements].
(c) That person should have been born in any of the Malay states or that one of the parents was also born locally.

It can be seen that the British colonial state was reluctant to abandon its communalist strategy. The amendments fell far short of the demand for citizenship based on *jus soli* principle, whereby all who are born in the country can claim automatic right of citizenship; the conditions were also more stringent than those in the Malayan Union proposals of 1946. This, after all, was in accordance with the demands of the conservative Malay rulers, who refused to accept even basic bourgeois democracy, and especially equal political rights for the non-Malays.

Without doubt, the amendments did enable more Chinese and Indians to acquire Malayan citizenship. V. Purcell estimated that between 50 per cent to 60 per cent of the Chinese and 30 per cent of the Indians would have become eligible.[51] By the end of 1953, 1,157,000 Chinese and 255,000 Indians had become citizens, comparatively a slightly bigger fraction of the total numbers of non-Malays than under previous regulations.[52]

As K.H. Khong has pointed out,[53] by 1952 most of the UMNO leaders who had opposed citizenship for non-Malays had, in one way or another, been co-opted into the Administration, and appointed either as Ministers or Legislative Councillors, *Mentri Besars*, State Councillors, or members of various advisory boards. Furthermore, any protests or demonstrations were impossible while the Emergency Regulations were in force.

The next 'safe' reform introduced by the colonial power was elections to the Local Councils and Municipalities, but even at this level, no real democracy was permitted: the British High Commissioner had the power to revoke the elections as he saw fit; the *Mentri Besar* (appointed by the High Commissioner) could appoint up to one-third of the members; there was no fixed tenure of office, since the Ruler-in-Council could dissolve the Council as he deemed fit; and lastly, the Local Councils themselves had no autonomy, since everything needed ratification by the High Commissioner or the State Government.

The Kuala Lumpur Municipal Council Elections in February 1952 largely decided the configuration of the political set-up in the would-be Independent Malaya. UMNO was determined to prove itself to be the credible representative of the Malay electorate and decisively to undermine the IMP. The MCA also had reasons for not trusting the IMP, which tended to define 'Malayan' solely by reference to the Malays. This stance by the IMP was yet another opportunistic *volte face* by Onn. Accordingly, the apparently unlikely alliance between the two communalistic parties, the UMNO and MCA, won nine out of the 12 seats in the elections, while the IMP won only two seats. Essentially, the Kuala Lumpur Municipal Elections were an indication to the colonial government of the political forces in Malaya. The IMP, after the poor showing at the polls, lost its credibility. Soon, with the successful application of this electoral 'Alliance Formula' in the other areas of the country, the arrangement became institutionalized.

During the Emergency, there was reason enough for the Malay rulers in UMNO and the Chinese big businessmen in the MCA to reach a rapprochement in order to defend the status quo and defeat the workers' revolt. At the same time, great strain was placed on the Alliance since, as basically communalist parties, the leaders of the UMNO and MCA constantly had to assuage their respective social bases in the petty bourgeoisie. Within the Alliance, the communalist politics continued on the issues of immigration, educational opportunities, and legislation on the registration and licencing of businesses.[54] Nevertheless, the two parties maintained their common electoral front in all the subsequent polls while keeping the issues at hand as vague and as broad as possible.

But the IMP managed to stir up more communalism before its demise. It still had considerable strength in the Federal Legislative Council, accounting for 30 out of the 75 members. In the last days of its existence, it tried to destroy the UMNO-MCA alliance; it succeeded in having the MCA's 'Social Welfare Lottery' banned in May 1953. When the government introduced the Education Ordinance to control the Chinese-medium schools (which were strong bastions of anti-colonialism), overwhelming pressure from the Chinese community forced the MCA to take an independent stand from the Alliance. Similarly, it had to differ over the licencing and registration of businesses. In 1953, Dato Onn in provocative vein accused the MCA and other Chinese organizations of trying to make Malaya 'the 20th province of China'. In the communalist furore, the colonial government took a backseat. The censure motion in the Legislative Council against Onn for his speech that was 'calculated to stir up interracial discord' was defeated. The government subsequently declared that it had full confidence in Onn.[55]

While the UMNO and MCA still lacked ministerial positions in the government: the IMP was the party preferred by the British. The UMNO and MCA then demanded that elections to the Federal Legislative Council be held by 1954, but the British would not oblige 'while the primary task was the restoration of law and order', and 'self-government could only be contemplated after the Emergency was over.'[56] It is noteworthy that throughout all this, UMNO and MCA never openly conflicted with the colonial authorities.

After the IMP was defeated in the Municipal Elections, it lost interest in further elections and sided with the government's view, maintaining that 'stability of the country would be disrupted if the people and the whole of their elected representatives do not properly understand what they are doing'.[57] The IMP had no base in the Malay masses, which were more responsive to the communalist line of the traditional rulers in UMNO, or were unconcerned. Moreover, the IMP was the party most closely identified with the colonial power.

In March 1953, the IMP attempted to launch a new initiative to gain support by sponsoring a National Conference 'to plan the way to a united, free and independent Malaya'.[58] The British Governor-General gave his whole-hearted support to the Conference;[59] UMNO and MCA boycotted it. At the Conference, the MIC insisted on Federal elections by 1954, and when this motion was not carried they left in protest. At the same time, UMNO and MCA also threatened to resign from the Government Councils if the 1954 deadline was not met. With these various groups vying with each other to lead the so-called nationalist movement, the British had to make some concessions. Consequently, in May 1953 the colonial government announced the formation of a Legislative Committee.

In February 1953, in what was to be its last turn-about, the IMP gave way to the 'Party Negara' and the ideology of this petty bourgeois party once more reverted to that of Malay chauvinism. Dato Onn's political stance had come full circle, back to that of 1946 when he led the Malay revolt over the Malayan Union proposals. In many ways, it reflected the realization that in the prevailing climate, political capital could be gained only through communalism, partly because in 1955, 85 per cent of the electorate was Malay.[60] Party Negara adopted the IMP's programme of the gradual introduction of elections and self-government, and maintenance of the Malay rulers as constitutional monarchs. In addition, to prove that it was even more communalistic than UMNO:[61]

(a) It disallowed membership of the party to non-Malays who had resided in Malaya for more than 10 years but who were not citizens.
(b) It declared Islam as the official religion.
(c) Malay would be the official language along with the English language.
(d) There would be restricted immigration of non-Malays through a quota system.
(e) There would be stringent conditions on application for citizenship by non-Malays.

Party Negara maintained that the immigration restrictions were meant to avoid 'the growing imbalance between the three major races... [since] we are against any attempt at domination by a section of the Chinese community in this country'.[62] Onn even proposed encouraging Indonesian immigration as a way of ensuring the numerical superiority of the Malays. In its campaign to break the UMNO-MCA alliance, Party Negara played upon the theme that by its alliance with MCA UMNO was betraying Malay interests. In 1955, it succeeded in putting pressure on the Alliance by forcing UMNO to take a definite stand on the language issue as well as on citizenship policy. The two parties in the Alliance had kept their programmes as vague as possible while invoking communalist rhetoric to their respective audiences; it was this tenuous bond that held the Alliance together. The IMP motion in the Legislative Council had moved to make Malay the sole official language. The MCA and the Chinese guilds protested, and the Alliance decried the devious nature of the motion, but it was passed. The Chinese interests then petitioned the British Crown demanding a policy of multilingualism.

When the Federal election campaign began in earnest, the

country had a full taste of the communalist politics that was to feature in the years to come. Meanwhile, the 'Alliance' was complete when the MIC joined this 'Communal Formula'. The strain on the Alliance was most severe during the allocation of seats for the elections. In all three member parties, there were protests at what each saw as concessions to the other parties, and the familiar allegations of the leaders having 'sold out their race'. The Alliance leaders had to impose strict internal discipline to keep the electoral front intact, while at the same time they each had to secure the support of the very same communalist base; such was the contradiction of the 'Alliance Formula'. For example, on the one hand the Tungku appealed to the Malays by stressing the 'alien danger' posed by non-Malay immigration, and on the other, he defended the Alliance manifesto compromise of marginally less restrictive citizenship requirements, arguing that the 'loyal' MCA and MIC members did not constitute this alien threat.

The 1955 Federal elections were thus mainly a contest between Party Negara and the Alliance, although neither faction was antagonistic to the interests of imperialism. During the election campaign, Party Negara played on the theme of Chinese domination after Independence and the betrayal of the Malays by UMNO through its compromise citizenship conditions for the non-Malays. Party Negara, however, could not shake off the close identification with the colonial power at a time when Independence and self-government were the main demands of the masses. Its target date for Independence was not until 1960.

The Alliance managed to keep the contentious communal issues as nebulous as possible between themselves, and created an apparent image of opposition to the colonial power to suit the prevailing political climate. It capitalized on all the misgivings relative to the colonial power, but failed to present the electorate with any clearly defined alternatives. It even orchestrated some protests and boycotts, such as the resignation of the three main Alliance leaders from the Legislative Council in May 1955.[63] The question of amnesty for the guerrillas (included in the Alliance manifesto) was intended to appease a war-weary population. Their manifesto, however, made no reference to the eventual union of Malaya and Singapore. Above all, this was owing to fear of Singapore's strong left-wing labour movement, as well as the threat to the Malays, numerical edge should Singapore become part of the Federation.

The 1955 election was a landslide victory for the Alliance, which won 51 out of the 52 seats. The remaining seat was lost to the Pan-Malayan Islamic Party (PMIP) in the Krian rice district of Perak, which was mainly composed of Malay padi farmers. Afterwards Party Negara became a spent force, leaving the Alliance as the only political party worth supporting by the British colonial state; the Tungku became 'Chief Minister'. Subsequently, the

Alliance announced the target date for Independence as four years hence, and also undertook to negotiate amnesty for the guerrillas.

But the British were not prepared to hand over power until they were assured of the Alliance's ability to deal with the CPM and the insurgent masses. Western imperialist interests had to be ensured while the Emergency was still in progress. Only after the Baling talks between the Alliance and CPM leaders had broken down in December 1955 and the former reneged on its amnesty proposals, were the British assured of the Alliance's reliability as the neo-colonial custodians. Soon, negotiations between the British Government, the Alliance, and the Malay Rulers began. The result was a foregone conclusion:

> The Tungku and other Ministers went to London in January 1956 expecting some hard bargaining on this issue. To their surprise and gratification their demand was immediately met and August 1957 fixed as the date of Independence.[64]

The Independence Agreement allowed the British High Commissioner overriding powers 'if in any case he considered it expedient in the interests of public order, public faith and good government of the Federation'.[65] The conduct of the war against the guerrillas remained in British hands, who also retained the right to maintain a military presence, '...not only for the defence of Malaya, but all the Commonwealth'.[66] The Agreement also guaranteed Western imperialist interests against nationalization and any obstacles to free repatriation of capital and profits. The role of foreign capital in the newly Independent Malaya was assured:

> ⅜Foreign capital½ must continue to play an important part in the economic and social development of Malaya... in view of the importance of the Federation's contribution to the strength of the Sterling Area through the direct earnings of dollars from tin and rubber, the Federal Government will continue to consult with the British Government so that it can act in full knowledge of the Sterling Area problems.[67]

MERDEKA: The Communal Formula Enshrined

Merdeka means 'Freedom' in the Malay language. While it was the militant slogan of the Indonesian nationalist movement, it was also adopted by the imperialist-groomed 'Alliance Party' in Malaya as its slogan. Before the Merdeka Mission set off for London, the Malay rulers had obtained a guarantee from the Alliance leaders that their status as Constitutional heads of state would be defended; this was in return for promising to back certain Alliance proposals for self-government. The Merdeka talks in January/February 1956 were remarkable for their lack of contentiousness. Only technical points regarding administration during the transition to Independence had to be resolved; most of these pertained to defence, internal security, public services, finance and economics.

The Constitutional provisions included in their terms of reference: '...the safeguarding of the special position of the Malays'.[68] The Reid Commission that was set up at the Merdeka Conference to prepare a Report on the Independence proposals relied mainly on the recommendations of the Alliance. These comprised the following main proposals:[69]

(a) Special privileges for Malays in the public services, permits and licences in business and trade, government scholarships for education.
(b) English and Malay would be the only official languages.
(c) The principle of *jus soli* citizenship for all born after 1957. All those over the age of 18, born in the country and who had lived for at least five out of the preceding seven years in Malaya, would be granted citizenship, if they had elementary knowledge of Malay. For individuals born outside the country, a residential requirement of eight out of the preceding twelve years would be needed to qualify for citizenship. No dual citizenship would be permissible.

The Commission endorsed almost all the Alliance recommendations, but in order to placate the pressure for democratic rights in the rest of the country, suggested that special privileges for the Malays be reviewed by the Legislature after 15 years.[70] No sooner was this announced than communalist elements within UMNO began to attack this limitation on Malay special privileges; the same provisions created misgivings in the Chinese community. Ultimately, however, the pressures from within UMNO prevailed, for, as Means put it:

> The more extreme communal elements among the Chinese were not in control of the MCA. The Alliance remained more sensitive to Malay criticisms of the Report, particularly since the Malay voters outnumbered all the others.[71]

This ensured the UMNO's decisive political edge over its other two partners in the Alliance during the post-colonial era.

Thus, no time limit was placed on the matter of Malay special privileges; instead it was to be periodically reviewed by the Malay Head of State. Substantial concessions were also made to the Malays regarding the issues of language and religion: Islam was declared as the official state religion on 31 August 1957. Responsibility for the administration of Muslim affairs was to lie with the Keeper of the Ruler's Seal, who was answerable to the Council of Rulers. Within each state, Islamic proscriptions binding on all Malay persons would be enforced by the Sultan's Council of Islamic Religion and Malay Custom (*Majlis Ugama Islam dan Adat Isti'adat Melayu*).[72] The Constitution's designation of Malay as the *official* language laid it open to interpretation by UMNO as being the *only* language in the years that followed.

The 'Razak Report' on Education was enacted in 1957. It recommended, amongst other things that: 'Malay and English would be compulsory subjects in all primary and secondary schools.... A common syllabus and time-table for all schools was to be enforced...'[73] Large sections of the Chinese community saw this as an attempt to curb instruction in Chinese in the Chinese-medium schools. Mohammad Khir Johari, who became Minister of Education in 1957, indicated the scale of the Chinese disaffection in that:

> When I took over the Ministry my office resembled that of a General: wall maps and charts with pins showing the location of school strikes and riots throughout the country hung everywhere...[74]

There were disturbances in many of the Chinese schools in Penang, Ipoh, Kuala Lumpur and Seremban. Chinese eduation became the chief issue in the Ipoh-Menglembu by-election in November 1957, but the MCA adopted the same position as the government.

The Chinese associations and guilds voted in favour of the PPP candidate, D.R. Seenivasagam, who, two years earlier, in the 1955 elections, had lost his deposit against an Alliance candidate. This time however he beat his Alliance rival by a substantial majority, but this was entirely owing to the support of the Chinese community.

The Merdeka Constitution had effectively institutionalized communalism as the state ideology; additionally it reflected the balance of forces within the Alliance. For the newly Independent Federation of Malaya, the basic provisions of bourgeois democracy, of 'juridical equality', had to be compromised simply because the Malay rulers were strongly opposed to it. These feudal elements, preserved by the same colonial strategy, were still a dominant force with political-ideological influence over the Malay masses.

The Alliance, on the other hand, had to accommodate the upper strata of the non-Malay bourgeoisie, who were important linkages in the imperialist domination of the Malayan economy. But not only were there problems of sharing political and economic power between the three communal parties in the Alliance, but the ruling strata within each party had to accede to the demands of their respective social bases, especially among the petty bourgeoisie. The inter-party struggles (still a feature today) have tended to be seen by social scientists crudely as those between the 'English-educated' and the 'vernacular-educated' intellectuals.[75] The comprador elements were, of course, generally the English-educated and these have had to fend off attacks by the other sections excluded from the Alliance deal. Without doubt, the communalist politics has exacerbated these struggles. The various factions involved have never failed to appeal to communalist sentiments in building up their class bases. This has taken the predictable form of charging the respective UMNO, MCA, and MIC leaders with having 'sold out their race'.

The Federation of Malaya adopted a 'Constitutional Monarchy' with a royal Head of State (*Yang di-Pertuan Agong*) elected by and among the nine Sultans. On Independence Day, the ordinances and regulations of the Emergency remained in force. The 'checks and balances' built into most liberal democracies were circumvented by two Articles of the Merdeka Constitution: Article 149, giving Parliament special powers to deal with subversion; and Article 150, giving the Executive special powers to deal with an Emergency. 'Free' elections largely concealed traditional feudal loyalties and duties binding the Malay peasantry to the aristocratic leaders. Apart from the economic bonds familiar to rural institutions, the political-ideological domination by the aristocratic landed interests of the peasantry is further effected by the special charge on the rulers as protectors of Malay religion and custom. This domination was further enhanced by the institutionalization of Islam as the state religion and so incumbent upon each and every Malay person in the country.

Social inequality was not impaired at Independence, and continued to be interpreted in communal terms. The masses in all three main national groups still found themselves segregated in the same communal division of labour. Only in the white-collar occupations (the teaching profession, civil service) was the division slightly minimized. The only free socializing between Malays, Chinese and Indians seemed to exist at the top, between the triumvirate in the Alliance—what has been referred to as 'horizontal solidarity' by pluralists. Intermarriage still is rare, religion and the law being inseparable in Malay jurisprudence: a non-Malay would first have to *masuk Melayu* (become a Malay) before marriage to a Malay person could be considered.

A noteworthy feature of the Alliance is that from its inception, there was never any doubt that UMNO was the dominant partner. This is linked to the special position of the Malay rulers in the colonial set-up, the predominance of the Malays in the electorate, as well as the state's political strategy and ideology of *bumiputraism*. This has been an important factor in subsequent state policies, and it has also facilitated the ascendancy of the state capitalist class from the traditional Malay ruling aristocracy. Consequently, whatever compromise was reached within the coalition, UMNO always had the upperhand regarding 'Malay Special Rights' and the definition of citizenship and education policy.

The issue of education and language again came to the forefront in mid-1960 when the Rahman Talib Education Report was published. There was an instant outcry by the Chinese community over its recommendations:

1. Secondary schools receiving partial assistance from the government which failed to make arrangements to conform fully with the

statutory requirements as from the beginning of 1962 or earlier should be regarded as independent schools ineligible for any assistance from government funds, as from the beginning of 1962.

2. All the official, national, public examinations—the Lower Certificate of Education and the Federation of Malaya Certificate of Education Examinations—should be held only in the nation's two official languages, Malay and English.

3. The Ministry of Education should cease organizing examinations in Chinese, i.e. the Junior Middle III Examination, the Chinese Secondary Schools Promotion Examination, and the Chinese Secondary Schools Leaving Certificate, with effect from 1961.[76]

These recommendations, in effect, meant that languages other than Malay and English was completely useless, even though the 1956 Razak Report had pointed out that:

> We consider that there should be some flexibility in our secondary school system.... For example, we can see no reason for altering the practice in Chinese secondary schools of using 'Guo Yu' as a general medium provided that these Chinese schools fall into line with the conditions mentioned...[77]

Above all, the recommendations in the Rahman Talib Education Report violated Article 152 of the Federal Constitution, which guarantees the use and study of the languages of all communities.

5. Features of the Neo-Colony

At Independence, the imperialist bourgeoisie's domination of the Malayan economy was still very much in evidence. But the new form of imperialist domination, which had to concede political self-determination to the neo-colony, still fell short of bourgeois democracy. This was an indication of the failure of the local ruling class to complete the national democratic stage. In the last chapter, we saw how the mediation of their rule by the local ruling class was achieved. At the same time, the interests of the latter had to be met through reforms. Even the Foreign Office files and records of the pre-Independence period indicate the political and economic reasons for the reforms and 'development' policies. Above all, the threat to imperialist interests in Malaya and the region during the 'Emergency' had warranted reforms, particularly in the peasant sector. In this and the following chapter, the dependent character of the development strategy adopted by the neo-colonial state will be examined. The local ruling class continues to be dominated, because the pursuit of their own interests is circumscribed by the imperialist interest they serve. And while the neo-colonial situation exists, it is still the workers and peasants who are exploited by the local and metropolitan ruling class.

When the peasant sector is examined, the question of how and why the Malay peasantry remain susceptible to the communalist ideology of the neo-colonial state will be foremost in our consideration. In this respect, it is important to note the basically enclave character of imperialist domination of the Malayan economy as well as the forces countervailing the effects of capitalist penetration of the rural sector and of the consequent differentiation of the peasantry. But from a Marxist point of view, it would be erroneous to explain the problem in economistic terms. From the analysis of communalism so far, it can be appreciated that the ideological domination of the Malay masses is effected as much through the various cultural forms and institutions of traditional Malay society and all the other manifestations of the state ideological apparatuses as it is by economic means.

As we trace the period up to the promulgation of the New Economic Policy (NEP) in 1969, the emergence of the Malay state bourgeoisie out of the traditional Malay ruling class can be discerned. The communal explosion on 13 May 1969 can be seen as the inevitable consequence of the contradictions inherent in the Alliance Formula. It revealed the precarious nature of the communalist strategy of the state, even though it has remained the single most important aspect of the neo-colonial state's rule. The reconstituted 'Alliance Formula' into the *Barisan Nasional* (National Front), and the new, prominent role of the Malay state bourgeoisie in the NEP will be considered in the remaining chapters.

The Neo-Colonial Economy

At Independence in 1957, the basic character of the Malayan economy differed little or not at all from what it had been as a colonized nation. Social inequalities persisted since the structure of economic exploitation by imperialism remained unchanged. The property relation was never called into question and the key sectors of the economy remained firmly in the hands of the metropolitan bourgeoisie.

The raw materials crucial to the metropolitan industries, had to be forthcoming, especially tin and rubber, which accounted for over 50 per cent of Malaya's exports. The domination of the rubber industry by foreign interests can be seen in Table 5.1. In the tin industry, three British holding companies—London Tin Corporation, General Tin Investment, British Tin Investment—controlled most of the output. There was the same concentration of management in the tin industry by the Agency Houses as in the rubber industry. For example, the three largest of these—the Anglo-Oriental Group, Neil and Bell Group, Osborne and Chappel Group—contained 47 companies and produced 45 per cent of Malaya's output.[1] Tin smelting was also monopolized by two foreign companies, Eastern Smelting Company and Straits Trading Company. One of the first important studies of the structure of the Malayan economy by J.J. Puthucheary also noted the marked interlocking network of directorships of these various companies and Agency Houses: 'About 25 persons, some of whom are directors of Agency Houses, sit on the boards of directors of nearly 200 rubber companies which own nearly 1 million acres of rubber.'[2]

The British Agency Houses were crucial links for industrial and finance capital in the West. They were consultants and managers to firms in the metropolis and were able to invest their capital profitably, owing to the established positions they held in shipping, insurance, commerce, and other services. To date, the oldest of these Agency Houses (e.g. Guthrie, Boustead, and Harrisons and Crosfield) have ramified their interests throughout the economy, including industrial and specialist activities.

The colonial character of the economy of the newly independent

Table 5.1
Ownership of Malayan Rubber Estates by Nationality, 1960

Size	European		Asian	
	No.	*Acreage*	*No.*	*Acreage*
Below 1,000 acres	110	63,357	1,629	425,470
Over 1,000 acres	382	1,107,474	153	345,871
Total	*492*	*1,170,831*	*1,782*	*771,341*

Source: Ooi Jin Bee, *Land, People, Economy in Malaya*, p.214.

country was further exemplified in that Malaya's sterling reserves were held in London, thus on hand to support Britain's international position and industry.[3] The flight of capital and the repatriation of profits abroad was clearly indicated by Puthucheary: 'Something like 15 per cent of Malaya's national income accrued to foreign capital concerns, and was siphoned out of the country annually during this period.'[4] However, the need to modify this traditional pattern of exploitation, and to reduce reliance on the two main commodities was realized by the colonial authorities as a result of the susceptibility of rubber and tin prices to wild fluctuations on the world market. The need to diversify the economy had been felt especially during the Emergency, as the following note from the Foreign Office files show:

> The improvement of the efficiency of the rubber and tin industries is a vital objective. Of equal and even more importance is the necessity that the price of these commodities should be maintained at a level which will enable them to be produced economically without any reduction in wages and employment. This is particularly relevant to the immediate need to counter the progress of communism in SE Asia.... A danger which arises from the fact that Malaya's economy is based on rubber and tin is that it renders the future prosperity of the country dangerously dependent upon the economic activity in North America, which provides the biggest market for both these materials.... This can only be done by diversifying the economy through encouraging the production of new commodities and through developing secondary industries on an economic basis.[5]

But the US hegemony over the Western imperialist bloc had been established in the immediate post-war period. Point IV of the Atlantic Charter had been implemented with the setting up of the multilateral institutions under US aegis: GATT (General Agreement on Tariff and Trade), with its principle of non-discrimination in world trade; IBRD (The World Bank), to mobilize capital resources for investment throughout the world; the IMF (International Monetary Fund), to supervise the financial aspects of the new imperialist world order which assured the dominance of the US dollar. Again the Foreign Office files show that the 'development' programmes under the auspices of the World Bank were part and parcel of Western imperialist design:

> The British are said to have little expectation that Congress would approve any form of Marshall Plan aid for the Far East at this time. Nevertheless, they think that through the IBRD, the Export-Import Bank, or possibly through money voted under the military aid programme and earmarked for the Far East, large-scale investments could be made as part of President Truman's Point IV Programme...[6]

After the US had been rebuffed by the Communists in China, the Griffin Mission was despatched to SE Asia as part of the revised and updated US policy towards the region. Its task:

> To discuss needs for economic and technical aid and to recommend aid programmes designed to demonstrate the genuine interest of the US in the people of SE Asia and to help governments there strengthen their economies and build popular support.[7]

In 1955, the World Bank was invited by the British 'to make a survey of the Malayan economy and to make recommendations for practical measures to further economic and social development'.[8] It subsequently recommended diversification of the economy into other raw material production besides rubber and tin, and also secondary industrialization.

The international banking system was, and continues to be, an inseparable part of imperialist domination. British overseas banking provided the working capital for the extractive and ancillary industries, and financed international trade. The Agency Houses were the first agents of these western banks: Guthries represented the London Merchant Bankers, Coutts and Co., and Boustead, the Hong Kong and Shanghai Bank. Other Western banks established since the 19th Century included the Rotterdam Bank and the National City Bank of New York. These banks purveyed the credit for merchants to finance purchases during processing and transportation of the raw materials. In the post-war reconstruction, loans from War Compensation were issued through the Chartered, Mercantile, and Hong Kong and Shanghai Banks at low rates of interest to firms operating the mines and estates.

Throughout British colonialism, the industries that had come about were mainly smallscale and served colonial purposes, such as the processing of raw materials and other ancillary activities. In fact, such local industries as existed had been set up during the Second World War, to meet food and consumer needs.[9] Thus, even a decade after 'Merdeka', only about 9 per cent of the labour force in the country was employed in the manufacturing sector which contributed only 11.3 per cent to the GDP.[10] Both Hirschman's and Wheelwright's studies show that even though Chinese small industries were numerically preponderant in this sector, the European firms, nevertheless, dominated the market and employed a disproportionately large section of the manufacturing labour force.[11] Malaya served mainly as a market for British manufactured goods and this was one of the reasons for the constraint on the development of an indigenous industrial base. Besides destroying the local handicraft industry, the presence of British manufactured goods militated against the growth of local industrial capitalists and deepened the dependence on the metropolitan bourgeoisie.

The Malayan Government subsequently acted upon the World Bank recommendations and channelled vast sums of revenue into laying the infrastructure for industrialization; clearing land for industrial estates, etc. To attract private investment, the Pioneer Industry Policy (1958) authorized tax exemptions for companies investing in these industries. This industrialization programme was meant to produce consumer goods for the local market, that is it formed the 'import-substitution' strategy of foreign capital, devised primarily to overcome the problem of import controls that were applied by most independent nations in the post-war period. Foreign industries set up included the production of food, beverages, tobacco, rubber and chemical products, cosmetics, toiletries and paints, which were largely intended to cater for the middle-class home market.

The effect of colonialism was, and is still, reflected in the stark regional disparity—an urbanized west coast, where most of the raw materials are found, and a neglected east coast, where the peasantry are concentrated; consequently, the infrastructure was mainly established on the west coast. An open economy allowed capital to move in and out freely, as Malaya was part of the Commonwealth Agreement. But despite the preponderance of British investments in the extractive industries, in relation to aggregate British investment in other temperate countries, their investment in Malaya was not large. Amounts of nominal capital of British companies in the country varied from £67 million in 1938 to only £69 million in 1957.[12] As well as the strictly colonial pattern of these investments, British capital did not grow substantially because of the Depression in the 1930s, the Second World War, and then the Emergency in the 1950s. Also, much of the foreign investments have relied on domestic savings, centralized by finance capital.

Investments by other foreign capitals were comparatively modest at the time of Independence, although there were sizeable investments in tin by French, US and Australian capital and in iron mining by the Japanese. The oil palm industry from its establishment was a strictly European concern, dominated by such firms as Guthrie and Socfin. But with the eclipse of British imperialism after the war, the US secured a foothold in the SE Asian economies when the triangular pattern of trade was established to aid the recovery of Western Europe after the war:

Beyond commodity availability alone was their (SE Asian economies) importance in the great triangular pattern of international trade involving primarily the US, Western Europe, and SE Asia. At a time when Western Europe was struggling to rehabilitate its industry and agriculture and to close the yawning 'dollar gap' that Marshall Plan aid was temporarily bridging, SE Asia was very important to Europe as a source of raw materials that could be purchased for currencies other than dollars, as a market for its European industrial products, and as a big earner of much needed dollars that tended to flow from Asia to Europe either to purchase these industrial products or as profits, interest, repatriation of capital, or personal remittances.[13]

In addition to Western Europe's recovery, the reconstruction of Japan after the war figured strongly in US strategy:

> The US had an additional, specific interest in the nations of the area as promising trade partners of Japan. Then still occupied by the US, Japan required heavy American aid to rebuild its industry and rehabilitate its economy. If it could sell its services and capital goods in SE Asia, and if it could buy rice, coal, and raw materials cheaply there, its dependence on American aid would be lessened.[14]

Thus, aside from the economic advantage which the raw materials of SE Asia offered the US, the latter had reasons to offer economic 'aid' to bolster the politically fragile countries in the post-war era. The 'development' policies that were being recommended for such countries as Malaya were crucial, not only in terms of political viability, but also to create the demand for Japanese industries since Japan was being nurtured as the junior partner of US imperialism.

The Peasantry

Table 5.2
Production of Rural Commodities in which Malays Predominate, 1958

Smallholding Sector	Production (tons)
Copra	73,303
Rubber	271,457
Rice	787,000
Fishing	109,547

Source: Monthly Statistical Bulletin of the Federation of Malaya, 1958.

In 1957, agriculture took up almost 50 per cent of the GDP and 60 per cent of the labour force of the country. The peasantry, predominantly Malay, easily formed the majority of the Malayan population. The distribution of the Malay peasantry in the various sectors of agriculture can be seen in Table 5.2. Malays are concentrated in the rice sector, but they also represent a sizeable proportion of the rubber smallholders. The variety of crops grown throughout the country has meant a not altogether uniform social structure in the peasant sector. There is a distinct geographical division of the respective occupations. Thus, the main rice-growing areas are in the north western states of Perlis, Kedah, and in Province Wellesley; and in the north eastern states of Kelantan and Trengganu. The Malay peasant fishermen are concentrated along the east coast of the peninsula. In these two sectors, the forces of differentiation operate more strongly than in the rubber smallholding sector, which is scattered all over the west coast states. The poorest sections of the population are also found in the peasantry. Between 1950 and 1958, E.K. Fisk reckoned that the incomes per household in the peasant sector ranged from between R$60 to R$120 per month, the equivalent to a per capita income of US$50-100 per annum.[15]

By the end of the 1940s with the Emergency under way, the colonial state was beginning to realize the consequences of neglecting the peasantry:

> The recent stoppage of US purchases of Malaya's principal products—rubber, tin, cocoa—has severely hurt the territory's economy and has hampered the task of subduing communist insurrection. To counteract this, the British will propose sizeable dollar investments; first, to expand rice production and thereby cut the costly imports from Burma, Thailand and IndoChina; and second, to prevent large numbers of Chinese 'marginal' tin miners from going bankrupt and joining the communists.[16]

As the same Foreign Office files show, the measures to buttress the food producing peasant sector were to be aided by World Bank financing: 'The State Department are interested in projects for development of food production in Malaya and might influence the World Bank to make loans for them'.[17] The desperate need to obtain self-sufficiency in rice was enhanced by the uncertain conditions prevailing in the countries of SE Asia from which Malaya imported most of her rice:

> More than half the food supplies of Malaya are imported from Burma and Siam, and production in this area is therefore particularly sensitive to conditions in these latter countries, or to interruptions in communications therewith...[18]

The political and economic reasons for some positive measures to aid the peasant sector are expressed in the Foreign Office documents:

> The economic case for large-scale capital investment and for commodity agreements to stabilize prices and markets for rubber, jute and tin is being reinforced by the political argument that such policies are essential to resist communism in the Far East.... The plan is designed to restore the old triangular pattern of trade. Under this, European trade deficits with North America were covered, at least in part, by

American imports from Eastern countries, which in turn, were debtors to Europe.[19]

The US's strong interest in this problem is attested to in this despatch from the British Embassy, Washington, to the Foreign Office, and corroborates our observation of US post-war strategy in the previous section:

> The US authorities consider increased food production in the Far East to be so imperative that... they would do their utmost to assist any sound projects put forward by the UK, either by support for loans from the World Bank or by financial assistance under Point IV for projects of a technical character... the region under consideration would have a food deficit for the foreseeable future and that the needed priority for food production projects precluded any appreciable programme toward industrialization in SE Asia for many years... we demurred at [the] tendency to express the problem as largely one of producing more food in SE Asia for Japan.[20]

Table 5.3
Estimated Production and Imports of Rice in Malaya
(in thousands of tons)

	1949	1950	1951	1952	1953
Rice Production	310	330	340	350	360
Rice Imports	470	500	520	540	560
Rice Acreage	907	920	935	950	965

Source: 'Food Production in Malaya', FO Far Eastern Department, F18912 (From the Commissioner-General in SE Asia to Secretary of State for Colonies, 14 October 1949, FO371/1102).

The state of rice production in Malaya in relation to imports can be seen in Table 5.3. Already at the end of the 1940s the continuing and increasing imports of rice were already causing concern to the colonial government:

> Internal disorders have made French IndoChina's postwar rice exports insignificant. If other rice supplies fail, or fall under Communist control, the disruptive political and economic consequences in Asia may be gauged from previous experience; while the secondary effects of a food crisis would hardly be less serious: greater Asiatic pressure upon Sterling Area wheat supplies and a concomitant increase in Commonwealth dependence on dollar grains. Further secondary effects might be... a fall in Malaya's rubber and tin production... the actual Communist conspiracy in Malaya, and the special consideration that in this area UK responsibility is direct, suggest that Malaya should receive equal priority of treatment.[21]

The urgency of aid to forestall peasant disaffection was also necessitated by a potentially serious land problem. Demographic pressure, as well as market forces, was leading to increasing sub-division of land holdings.

Land still remains the most important means of production for the peasantry. Technological innovation, far from counterbalancing the size of land holding, has made it a still more important criterion for identifying classes in the rural sector. The trend has been toward concentration of land ownership on one hand, and proletarianization of the peasantry on the other as class differentiation proceeds. This has developed in contradiction to the state's attempts at preserving the smallholding peasantry both for economic and for ideological reasons.

This attempt has been correspondingly witnessed for the peasantry in the rubber smallholding sector. Lee, G.,and Caldwell, M[22] among others, have pointed out this exigency for the state to aid the rubber smallholders during the critical years of the Emergency. P.T. Bauer's 'Report on a visit to the rubber growing small-holdings' was, besides articulating the interests of the metropolitan industrial capitalists, intended to win over the political allegiance of the Malay smallholders to the state.[23]

The great disparity in landholding in the rural sector has been a direct consequence of colonial policy. The colonial state had endowed generous land concessions to the Malay ruling class, although much of this was then utilized for mining and plantations rather than for peasant agriculture. The ownership of vast tracts of land by the various royal families is a well-known fact. The other strata who are in a position to accumulate land include, those in the government services, and the commercial classes.[24] The 1970 national census revealed that about 342,000 Malay households in the rural sector either had no land or possessed inadequate plots. The minimum farm size for a padi farmer to keep his family above the poverty line is five acres, but the average padi farm size is only 3.1 acres, while 78 per cent of all padi lands comprises less than five acres.[25] The subsistence level for a rubber smallholder to support his family is at least six acres, but the average size of rubber smallholdings in 1976 was only three acres, while 70 per cent of all rubber smallholdings were less than six acres.[26]

The state has consistently prohibited the free appropriation of land by the peasantry even though there is a considerable amount of virgin land available that is suitable for agriculture. At present, 9.4 million acres is cultivated, while roughly 6.2 million acres of cultivable land is still untouched. Consequently the main form of peasant protest and action in recent years has revolved around squatters, such as the Hamid Tuah and Tasek Utara incidents in the 1960s and 1970s.[27] The neo-colonial state has instead opted for the rather expensive land schemes (for example, FELDA, Federal Land Development Authority) which are developed exclusively by urban private contractors. FELDA was formed by the British 'Colonial Development Corporation' (now renamed 'Commonwealth Development Corporation'), '...one of the many shadowy organisations that silently and painlessly made the transition from the colonial to the neo-colonial epoch.'[28] (*The Guardian*, London, 10-2-81: 'Stablilising middle class elites in the Third World'). This political aim was uppermost as revealed by Lord Howick, and is the main method used by the state to buy off the Malay peasantry:

> They had almost a political aim in mind. They thought this would cover the country with reasonably well-off small farmers and was the way to resist penetration of the Chinese Communist ideas after all their trouble in the Malayan Emergency.[29]

Peasant Differentiation and Countervailing Factors

This section examines the process of peasant differentiation as well as the countervailing factors that have tended to mitigate its effects and thereby enable the state to deflect the contradictions within the peasant sector through communalism.

Land ownership patterns are a significant indicator of differentiation. The trend towards concentration of land ownership is reflected in the growing tenancy rate, increasing proletarianization, as well as sub-division and fragmentation of farms. The latter refers to the physical non-contiguity of land owned, whereas sub-divided land may be jointly-owned and in contiguous parcels. Concentration then refers to the diminution of the number of owners on a fixed amount of land. Since the days of British colonialism, the transfer of land ownership has been intense: 'In every decade this century, an average of two-thirds of all padi lots and almost three-quarters of all kampong and rubber lots have changed hands [in Saiong Mukim].'[30] But studies have also shown that concentration has tended to affect a smaller percentage of land than has division.[31] Where sub-division had occurred, the result has usually been joint-ownership rather than physical division of land, because the resurveys and registration involved in the process of sub-division are expensive and time-consuming. This also implies, however, that the sub-division of land is proceeding faster than the records show.[32]

The process of differentiation affects the various agricultural sectors differently, more so for subsistence food crops such as rice than for rubber smallholdings. This is illustrated in Table 5.4 showing the decline of 'Sole' ownership in Ho's study of Saiong Mukim. According to the 1960 Agricultural Census, for all states except Negri Sembilan and Malacca, only a quarter to a third of all padi lands was under sole ownership. On the other hand, some three-quarters of all rubber smallholdings was under sole ownership, the proportion falling to two-thirds in Kelantan and to half or less in Kedah and Perlis.[33] It is clear that in most kampongs throughout the country other than the 'rice bowl' states of Kedah, Perlis, as well as Kelantan, the process of differentiation is much slower either because the peasantry have other side occupations or concentrate wholly on rubber production.

Table 5.4
Percentage of 'Sole' to 'All' Owners by Major Crops and Decades, in Saiong Mukim

Decade	Padi	Rubber	Mixed	Gardens	Averages
1900	48	0	13	100	38
1910	50	100	40	87	50
1920	40	64	33	57	46
1930	33	61	22	52	37
1940	26	56	22	36	30
1950	22	49	18	28	25
1960	15	41	12	27	19

Source: Robert Ho, *The Evolution of Agricultural Land Ownership in Saiong Mukim*, 1968:96.

In T.B. Wilson's study of the North Malayan padi producing states, he further discovered that the share of acreage in co-ownership showed a decline since in 1958:[34] 'Over one-quarter of the shares (26 per cent) now registered for Krian padi lands represent less than 1 acre of land each, and nearly a tenth (9 per cent) of the shares represent less than ¼ of an acre.' Compared to 1900, when in Krian only 2 per cent of the shares were less than two acres and 41 per cent of the shares were more than seven acres; by 1954, 53 per cent of the shares were smaller than two acres and only 4 per cent larger than seven acres.[35]

This trend thus led to land sales and concentration of land ownership, and those in a position to buy up the land (as has been pointed out by Husin Ali, see note 24) were those with means in the *kampong*, as well as government servants and the urban commercial interests who provide the rural credit. The operation of Islamic laws of inheritance also tended to increase the process of co-ownership to absurd proportions: 'Thus we find co-owners with 1/127th shares and still others with 9/64th shares and so forth...'[36] Dissipated joint ownership has led to increasing tenancy and landlordism, and discouraged the peasantry from productive investment in the land. The reasons for this have been indicated by T.B. Wilson among others; namely, the difficulties involved in timing similar planting operations; negligent practices of neighbouring farmers; and so on.[37] Increasing tenancy occurs precisely because farmers are faced with inadequate parcels of land.

The extent of fragmentation in the padi areas can be gauged from the 1960 Census of Agriculture: '56 per cent of padi farmers operated a single parcel, 25 per cent worked on two parcels, 11 per cent on three parcels, 4 per cent on four parcels, and the remaining 4 per cent worked on five to nine parcels.'[38] Elsewhere in Locality II of Muda in Kedah, 60 per cent of farms consisted of more than one parcel, and the mean number of parcels per farm was 3.1.[39] In Saiong Mukim, the proportion of fragmented holdings was 29 per cent.[40]

The actual transfer of land is usually effected through a series of circumstances pertaining to traditional Malay rural society, such as incurring extraordinary expenditure through a wedding, funeral, or illness;[41] indebtedness, especially common in padi growing areas owing to credit needs. The various forms of tenurial arrangements that exist also suggest the survival of pre-capitalist feudal influences in rural Malay society. For example, some form of patronage determines whom the landowner chooses to be his tenant, sharecropper or even wage labourer. Not least, patronage also takes the form of electoral support for the landowners or their representatives. This aspect of the Malay rural social structure has profound significance for the susceptibility of the peasantry to the state's communalist propaganda. Besides the economic constraints, the whole religio-cultural setting of traditional Malay society is the basis for the ideological domination of the peasantry by the Malay ruling class.

At this point it is worth noting that there is no necessary contradiction between the process of concentration, especially amongst the padi-growing peasantry, on the one hand, and the state's propaganda relating to the preservation of the Malay petty commodity producer on the other. As has been pointed out, the strategy of generating a social structure based on a smallholding peasantry worked differently in the different agricultural sectors. In terms of productivity, the survival of the rubber smallholders has been an important factor in the strength of the country's rubber industry, thus ensuring a cheap source of the raw material for the metropolitan manufacturing concerns. At the same time, the attempts to increase productivity in the rice growing sector (with huge investments by the World Bank and the state development agencies) have led mainly to polarization of the rice-producing peasantry. Thus it can be seen that communalism has found a material base in the smallholding peasantry in one sector of the economy, and this has disguised the reality of class differentiation in another.

The various forms of forfeiture of land in Malay rural society owing to non-payment of credit have been noted by scholars.[42] *Jual janji* (promissory sale) is a common form of land transfer when land is held as collateral by the creditor. Indebtedness is certainly the rubber smallholders,[43] who have to pay interest rates as high as the rubber smallholders,[41] who have to pay interest rates as high as 60 to 100 per cent. But the extent of concentration on a national scale has never been assessed owing to the difficulty in relying on cadastral maps. Landowners with holdings made up of smaller lots cannot easily be detected except when they die and their estates have been declared. Wilson, looking at a 10 per cent sample of

Krian landowners who had died between 1945 to 1954, found that the total property of 102 deceased spread over 427 titles and averaged 18 acres each. Half the owners each owned less than six acres, averaging three acres; three-quarters of all the owners together owned only 17 per cent of the total cultivated area; while nine of the largest estates together accounted for two-thirds of the total land area; almost half the total area was owned by two men, one of whom was a member of the Perak royal family; the three largest owners between them owned altogether 180 land titles.[44] In his comparative study of three different areas with different crop specialization, Husin Ali has also shown that while land concentration has affected padi-growing areas most of all, it has also affected other crop areas.[45]

The consequence of these processes have been an increase in tenancy rate in the peasant sector. The 1960 Census of Agriculture in Table 5.5 showed that whereas owner-operated farms predominate in rubber, coconut, fruit and other mixed farms, it was the rule in only a third of rice farms. Almost two-thirds of rice farmers in Malaya were either full or part tenants, and absentee landlordism was most prevalent in this sector. The Census also revealed that padi farms made up 29.4 per cent of all farms, and that 93 per cent of tenant farmers were in the rice sector.[46] This pattern is understandable considering the seasonal nature and production practices connected with rice cultivation, whereas the likelihood of 'slaughter-tapping' by tenants in the rubber sector tends to discourage tenancy.

Table 5.5
Tenure Status by Farm Types (%), 1960

Category	Rice	Rubber	Coconut	Fruit	Mixed
Owner	33.7	80.1	86.8	78.9	59.8
Temporary occupation licence	4.7	1.8	3.8	7.1	1.7
Tenant	31.4	—	—	—	0.8
Other single tenure	5.6	5.1	3.6	8.2	3.0
Owner/tenant	15.0	1.2	0.2	1.0	11.4
Other mixed tenure	9.6	11.8	5.6	4.8	23.3

Source: 1960 Census of Agriculture, R.D. Hill, 1967: Table 2.

The main types of tenurial arrangements found in the peasant areas of Malaya are as follows, defined by the mode of rent payment, ownership and trust arrangement:[47]

fixed rent	— *sewa* (cash or padi rent)
cropsharing	— *pawah*
lease	— *pajak*

loan	— *gadai*
mortgage	— *jual janji* (promissory sale)
sole ownership	— *sendiri*
trust	— *pesaka*

The situation at Independence in North Malaya can be seen in Table 5.6 from T.B. Wilson's study. The pattern of tenurial arrangements of farms growing wet-padi as the main crop in the various states of Malaya according to the 1960 Census of Agriculture is shown in Table 5.7.

Table 5.6
Tenurial Arrangements in Northern Malayan Rice-Growing Area, 1958 (%)

	Owner-farmed	Padi Fixed Rent	Cash Rent	Crop-sharing	Others
Perlis	53	38	—	—	9
Kedah	44	42	8	—	6
Province Wellesley	38	57	—	—	4
Krian, Perak	57	35	—	—	8
Kelantan	50	—	—	47	3

Source: T.B. Wilson, 1958, Tables 4 and 5.

There are several other methods in addition to rents whereby landlords can extract further surplus from their tenants, as Wilson has pointed out. These can, for example, take the form of:

(i) The cash deposit (*pertarohan, duit kopi, 'duit teh'*). This was initially the tenant's guarantee of security of tenure, but the practice increasingly represents the landlord's security for his rent. It is especially common in areas of acute competition for land. In areas of fluctuating tenancy, it has become customary for tenants to have to present gifts of padi (*sagu hati*) to the landlord and for this to be considered as *zakat*, which is the religious tithe incumbent upon all Malay padi growers.
(ii) Labour services (*tenaga*) have to be performed by tenants in certain areas. This can take the form of transporting the harvest to the landlord's house or to the middlemen's collection point, or even construction work for the landlord. Landlords frequently also specify the padi variety (for example, *padi merah* or *padi berat*, which are of higher quality) as the norm for rent payment.[48]

Whatever the form of payment, rent is paid over half the padi land in north Malaya and is the most important cost item facing the peasantry. It is generally held that at least one third of the crop, or its cash equivalent, accrues to the landowner. R.D. Hill encountered cases where the proportion was one half (in Kelantan), and even two thirds of the crop (in Trengganu).[49] To give an idea of

Table 5.7
Tenure of Farms Growing Main Crop Wet Padi, by States, 1960

State	Owner-operated (No./%)	Temporary Occupation Licence (No./%)	Tenant (No./%)	Other Single Tenure (No./%)	Owner Tenant (No./%)	Mixed (No./%)	Total (No./%)
Malaya	115,572/45.4	7,044/ 2.7	42,438/16.6	10,248/4.0	35,774/14.0	44,176/17.3	255,252/100
Johore	1,570/36.5	502/13.4	—	360/9.6	20/ 0.5	1,500/40.0	3,752/100
Kedah	2,076/31.5	704/ 1.0	19,634/28.0	3,664/5.2	9,850/14.1	14,146/20.2	70,074/100
Kelantan	19,882/42.0	102/ 0.3	4,460/ 9.4	1,294/2.7	13,342/28.2	8,230/17.4	47,310/100
Malacca	8,766/80.0	160/1.4	742/ 6.9	160/1.4	528/ 4.8	606/ 5.5	10,962/100
Negri Sembilan	13,804/84.6	120/ 0.7	340/ 2.1	220/1.3	860/ 5.3	982/ 6.0	16,326/100
Pahang	9,898/59.3	284/ 1.7	620/ 3.7	1,046/6.2	1,014/ 6.1	3,850/23.0	16,712/100
Penang/Province	3,932/29.1	260/ 1.9	6,200/45.9	220/1.6	2,092/15.5	815/ 6.0	13,518/100
Perak	18,968/51.2	2,470/ 6.7	6,020/16.3	2,222/6.0	3,236/ 8.7	4,100/11.1	37,016/100
Perlis	3,622/30.9	480/ 4.1	1,622/13.8	622/5.3	1,536/13.1	3,830/32.8	11,712/100
Selangor	4,982/44.7	1,682/15.1	1,060/ 9.5	140/1.3	562/ 5.0	2,718/24.4	11,144/100
Trengganu	8,272/49.5	280/ 1.7	1,740/10.4	300/1.8	2,734/16.3	3,400/20.3	16,726/100

Source: Census of Agriculture, 1960, Vol. 9, Tables 620-31; E. Smith and P. Goethals, *Tenancy among Padi Cultivators in Malaysia*, 1965:18.

the magnitude of the total in rents paid, he summed it up as follows: '...an amount in 1964 that was around $18 million —enough to pay for the installation of an irrigation works as large as the Muda scheme every eight years.'[50]

According to T.B. Wilson and T.G. Lim,[51] with the increasing provision of infrastructure and technical innovation, the trend seems to be for a change from sharecropping arrangements to fixed padi rent, and eventually to cash rent and even payment in advance. The commuting of padi rent to cash rent is tantamount to an increase in the rental rate. The payment of cash rent in advance has also meant the loss of compensatory adjustments in the event of a harvest failure. When rent collection is based on a seasonal basis double cropping in recent years has seen landlords' incomes double without any additional layout on their part. Table 5.8 shows the average rents in north Malaya around the time of Independence. Insecurity of tenure, of course, varies with the different types of tenurial arrangement, but overall, studies have shown that the turnover of tenancy among padi farmers is high.[52]

Table 5.8
Average Rents in Cash and Kind, North Malaya, 1958.

	Padi Rents (Gantang[1]/Acre)	Cash Rents (Cash Equivalent[2])	
		$/acre	$/acre
Perlis	96	48	65
Kedah	127	63	72
Province Wellesley	109	54	70
Kelantan	61	30	56
Krian, Perak	144	108	86

Notes: 1 1 gantang=1 English gallon.
       2 At field price of 50 cents/gantang.

Source: T.B. Wilson, 1958:54.

The process of differentiation is similarly evident in the fishing sector, especially amongst the Malay fishermen on the east coast of the peninsula. To some extent the small fishermen have lost control over the means of production to the big capitalist concerns, both local and foreign (mainly Japanese) interests. The latter have come to monopolize fishing with highly mechanized boats (trawlers) and this has had disastrous effects on the incomes of the small fishing peasantry.[53] The dispossessed fishermen have to either hire themselves out as wage labourers or try to survive on other mixed farm activities, especially coconut cultivation.

Although wage labour throughout the country has increased with greater employment of rural folk in the urban industries, the extension of wage labour relations in the rural agricultural sector has been less rapid. The problem of the dispossessed peasantry migrating to the towns and cities has been the most serious in recent years. Without doubt, the rural economy has been firmly integrated into the world capitalist system. The capital-intensive technological innovations in the rural economy have also accentuated class differentiation. A recent government-commissioned team studying the tenurial patterns in the Muda scheme, which produces half the total rice grown for the local market, discovered that:

> ...there has emerged a clear polarisation in farm size distribution.... At one end is the growing number of large farmers cultivating an increasing proportion of the land; at the other end, also a growing number of small farmers operating a decreasing proportion of land.... ⅜This process of rapid polarisation½ marks the irony of the Green Revolution process in Muda: its very success has placed the more prosperous farmers in a unique position to displace the smaller farmers.[54]

The conclusions from this study also confirm our previous observation that control of the land by the rich landowners is more significant than mere legal ownership.

By the end of the 1950s, the Muda area land ownership pattern had changed from one of wide and even distribution in the early years of the century to one of very uneven distribution. A small class of rural bourgeoisie had emerged, cultivating large tracts of land, employing wage labour and investing in agriculture. At the same time, there was a large and growing class of small and middle peasants faced with land fragmentation and demographic pressure on a shrinking land area. When the Green Revolution was introduced in the late 1960s and mid-1970s, land fragmentation continued but there was no corresponding process of concentration. This was mainly because increased productivity with the HYVs (high-yielding varieties) had mostly benefited the middle peasantry. The large farmers could not take the opportunity to increase production by hiring labour owing to the severe labour shortage, but the middle peasants were able to mobilize their family labour. The position of the small peasantry was also somewhat strengthened because the HYVs had inflated land prices and thus land dispossession was not common. Nevertheless, by the mid-1970s, the population of Muda had grown by 50 per cent above the 1955 figure; the average size of farms had fallen to 1.5 hectares by 1976; and more than 60 per cent of all padi farms were of less than one hectare, the minimum size necessary to keep a family above the poverty line.[55]

More recently, with the increasing use of large-scale mechanization, the big farmers have begun to accumulate land, while the average size of small farms has decreased to only slightly more than half a hectare. Among the small farmers, tenants have fared worst with the repossession of land by the rich landlords, and the increase in owner-operation:

Not much is known about the fate of the 7,000 or so tenant households which were displaced in the last decade. Some have become agricultural labourers; others have migrated to the cities.[54]

The number of combine harvesters used in Muda increased from nine in 1974 to over 160 by the end of the decade. It is believed that this represents about 36,000 displaced workers.[55] These machines are mainly rented from urban-based interests and are contributing to serious unemployment. The principal benefactors of the Green Revolution are thus the rich landlords who number 700 (with land over 9.5 hectares) in the Muda region, made up of 61,000 families. The tenure system of farms in Muda and their various proportions are shown in Table 5.9

Table 5.9
Tenure of Farms in Muda, 1976

Tenure-type	% of Farms		% of Land
Owner-farmers	53.9		44.5
small		(55.0)	
medium		(34.5)	
large		(10.5)	
Tenants	29.8		29.3
Owner-tenants	16.3		26.2

Source: Centre for Policy Research, Penang: Study of Muda's tenurial pattern, 1955-76, quoted in Ho Kwon Ping, 'Victims of the Green Revolution', *FEER*, 13 June 1980: 104.

What then are some of the countervailing factors to peasant differentiation that may have served to minimize the contradictions between the rich and poor peasants? The state has been concerned to preserve the rural Malay social structure based on the smallholding peasantry in the *kampong*. This has been crucial as an *ideology* by which the Malay masses' allegiance is maintained by the Malay ruling class and through which communalism is propagated. Thus a Malayan Government Report in 1957 spoke of:

...the political and social reasons for encouraging the existence of a large smallholding class... a considerable help toward political and social security, and of great value as a basis for sound democratic government.[58]

Besides P.T. Bauer's admonition to the colonial government to preserve the rubber smallholding sector, T.B. Wilson had also justified his call for legislative reforms and rent control by:

the need to improve the farmers' welfare... necessary to secure social stability in rural and national life, and may gain urgency for political reasons, as in Taiwan, in order to prevent communist infiltration of the rural districts.[59]

As an economic policy, this has also succeeded in transforming the social relations of production in conformity with imperialist and local capitalist requirements. The rubber smallholding sector has been an important pillar of the country's rubber industry. Rubber smallholders, after all, constituted 21 per cent of households in Peninsula Malaysia in 1975. Between 1960 and 1975, the output of smallholders grew at an average annual rate three times that of the estates. In 1973, smallholders even surpassed the estates in total production, especially with the shift in estate production from rubber to oil palm cultivation.[60] Thus the smallholding sector is vital as a cheap source of abundant raw materials for the metropolis.

Table 5.10
Acreage Cultivated, Production, and Yields of Rubber on Smallholdings and Estates, Peninsula Malaysia, 1960-75

Year	Mature acreage ('000s)			Production ('000 tons)		
	Total	Estates	Smallholdings	Total	Estates	Smallholdings
1960	2,968	1,405	1,563	696	420	276
1970	3,300	1,346	1,954	1,215	621	594
1975	3,363	1,308	2,055	1,417	599	818

Source: K. Young, W.C.F. Bussink, P.Hasan, *Malaysia: Growth and Equity in a Multiracial Society*, World Bank, 1980, Table 8.7, p.222.

At the same time, the effect of institutional factors (for example, the Malay inheritance system) on differentiation may be applicable while mechanization has not proceeded as far and land is still a significant means of production. Developments in Muda certainly bear this out. Thus while kinship ties may have somewhat mitigated the hardships of the displaced tenants, they did not prevent their dispossession when the rich landowners repossessed their lands:

> If not for the fact that kinship ties were strong, and therefore inhibited landlords from repossessing land operated by relatives, the displacement of tenants would have been even more serious.[61]

The influence of kinship ties on differentiation certainly wanes when commodity relations have become generalized, as Firth noted:

> The economic processes, which have widened the gap between capitalist entrepreneurs and propertyless fishermen, were not cushioned to any apparent degree by the elaborate network of kinship ties in the local social system...[62]

The Malaysian state has managed to sustain its communalist strategy by a number of economic measures such as: the injection of vast public expenditure into the rural sector, rice price subsidies, credit facilities, input subsidies, extension services, etc. These, in part, have contributed to the survival of the small farmers in the padi sector. Double-cropping has enabled some small farms to remain economically viable, and as mechanization has not affected every process of rice cultivation, they can still manage to find off-farm work, in transplanting for example. Even in Muda, not all the harvesting has been mechanized.

But as we have stressed, the economic reasons for the state's strategy of coaxing the Malay peasantry cannot be separated from the political and cultural-ideological domination of the latter by the Malay ruling class. The preservation of the Malay *kampong* social structure has been an important aspect of the reproduction of communalism. Thus, religion (Islam) and the institutions linked to it—the mosque, the *surau* (prayer house where the men congregate at least once a day), the *pondok* school (where all Malay children receive religious instruction after their normal school hours) all provide an important function as part of the state's ideological apparatuses. In the *kampong*, there are also various social institutions centred around the mosque or *surau*, such as the *kenduri* (feast) on the Prophet's birthday, or a wedding; the election of the *penghulu* (headman); or other such village occasions. Social relationship in the *kampong* is necessarily close (*dekat* as opposed to *jauh*, in the local community parlance) also because co-operative work (*gotong royong*) has traditionally been essential in rice production.

Besides aiding the reproduction of the Malay community, the state blamed the problem of rural (Malay) poverty on the Chinese middlemen,[63] instead of it being the effect of the imperialist dominated economy. During the colonial period British officials had used the same charge to mobilize the Malay peasantry against the non-Malay traders.[64] In so far as the non-Malay commercial bourgeoisie form an essential link in the chain of imperialist exploitation of the peasantry, the contradiction that exists between them and the peasantry is real. While this class remains primarily non-Malay (mostly Chinese), the state has continued to play upon communalist appeal and to deflect peasant discontent by pointing to the supposed domination of the economy by the Chinese.[65] As we shall see later, this has served the Malay state bourgeoisie in its efforts to develop an economic base through taking over this commercial role while at the same time inhibiting the unification of the Chinese and Malay masses.

The question of the exploitation of the peasantry has to be examined from the overall view of the marketing and credit structure of the whole country. It then becomes evident that the Chinese commercial class merely serve as the mediators of social relations of exploitation in which they are not the dominant class. The oligopolistic nature of worldwide distribution in the hands of the metropolitan bourgeoisie dictates the terms of trade. From the start, retailers have to accept the base price which is set at the level of the 'international' price. The Agency Houses still control the commercial network of the local market as well as all forms of credit. The basis of their control lies in their domination of a whole range of activities that affect the peasantry, from the export of raw materials to the import of fertilizer, consumer and producer goods, to such services as management, insurance, credit, and shipping.

We can see the anti-Chinese and communalist politics of the Malay ruling class focuses peasant discontent at the point where the peasantry directly experiences its exploitation—the trader who buys from the peasant below the value of the labour power embodied in the product. The trader is, however, simply the intermediary in a relation of exploitation. The Malay ruling class' communalist strategy tries to deflect the opposition of the Malay peasantry to capitalist relations of production by concentrating on the nationality of those who are the agents—and subordinate ones at that—of those relations, i.e. it does not touch on the questions of land ownership and size of landholdings.

State Policy Toward the Peasantry

Although up to the New Economic Policy (NEP) in 1969, the economy was marked by relatively little state intervention, the problem of rural poverty and stagnation had earlier warranted some action. Besides the real possibility of the poor peasants joining the guerrillas during the Emergency, for the ruling class there was the equally important consideration of the enfranchisement of the Malay peasantry in the newly independent Malaya.

It should, however, be noted that even during colonial times reforms in the peasant sector had been considered. The gravity of the tenancy situation among padi farmers had resulted in the 'Padi Cultivation Control of Rents and Security of Tenure Ordinance' of 1955. It legislated a rent ceiling and the prohibition of 'tea money' (*duit teh*— see p.124) and other practices by landlords which discriminated against the tenants. Purportedly to help the tenants, this piece of legislation set a minimum limit on tenancy agreements of not less than one season. However, it also set a maxi-mum limit of not more than one year,[66] which only served to exacerbate insecurity of tenure. T.B. Wilson has pointed out other loopholes for landlords in the Ordinance, while it also specified the various duties required of tenants, including the construction and maintenance of dams, etc., without due remuneration. But perhaps the biggest shortcoming of the reforms was that there was no effective enforcement apparatus, which, considering the class connections between the landowners and the state is hardly surprising. Land reform (proposed by officials like Wilson) was not acceptable for the same political reasons.

When the shortcomings of the 1955 Ordinance were finally faced, a Ford Foundation team suggested comprehensive legislative measures to implement the reforms more effectively. The MalaysianGovernment subsequently passed the Padi Cultivators Control of Rent and Security of Tenure) Act of 1967. Although it was a better piece of legislation than the 1955 Ordinance,[67] it rapidly suffered a similar fate. By handing over responsibility for its implementation to the state governments, where the connections to the rural landed interests are even closer than at federal level, the Act became ineffective. Many studies have pointed to the prevalence of rents that exceed the maximum legal limit; of advance payment of cash rents demanded; of tenancy agreements not put down in writing, and so on.[68]

The First Five-Year Plan (FFYP) of 1956-60 was based on the recommendations of the 1955 IBRD mission. These consisted mainly of more infrastructural facilities for the private sector in industry and for increasing the productivity of the rural sector. The latter was consistent with the need to provide cheap wage goods for the urban working class in the 'import-substituting' industrialization strategy being fostered by Western imperialism for newly independent countries such as Malaya. The FELDA (Federal Land Development Authority) scheme was simultaneouly encouraged to provide cheap commodities (rubber, oil palm) for the metropolitan industries. Thus it has been pointed out that: 'Both the First (1956-60) and the Second (1961-65) Plans, as well as the Interim Report of 1963, were almost exclusively the work of foreign advisers...'[69] But the (FFYP) did represent the first integral national development programme as opposed to the hitherto piecemeal efforts by different government departments. 'Rural development' became an important component of the Government's Plans, as the state became a vehicle for elements within the traditional Malay ruling class to create a social and economic base for themselves. After 1969, they were to emerge as the state bourgeoisie.

The Rural and Industrial Authority (RIDA), a public corporation, had already been formed in 1953, purportedly to look after the interests of 'the Malays'. Hampered by severe financial constraints, it could serve only as a supplementary aid to the state governments, individuals, co-operatives or corporations, but little more than that. When the new Ministry of Rural Development was set up in 1959, RIDA was superseded by MARA (Majlis Amanah Rakyat—Council of the People's Trust), which had wide and complex interests geared toward primarily pursuing 'Malay interests'. The communalist intent also belied the attempt to create a Malay capitalist class. The state justified this by pointing to the 'domination' of the Chinese in the Malayan economy. From the start, MARA tended to be urban and commercial-based, and consequently new state bodies were set up specifically for the rural sector.

Rubber replanting received priority treatment under the FFYP, to increase the productivity of rubber against the growing competition from synthetic fibres. Replanting with HYVs, plus such financial incentives as tax relief and subsidies, were proffered via the Rubber Industry Replanting Board, in addition to technical assistance and extension services through the Rubber Research Institute (RRI). Rubber replanting aid, however, mainly helped the plantation interests and rich producers, because the smallholders could not afford to forgo the interim period required for replanting.

During the Second Five-Year Plan (SFYP) of 1961-65, more funds were pumped into the rural sector. As can be seen in Table 5.11 about $550 million, or double the amount allotted to the First Plan, was earmarked for Agricultural and Rural Development. If infrastructural provisions are also included, the amount is closer to 50 per cent of the total development expenditure. This huge increase in rural sector investment corresponded to the state's economic objective of integrating the rural sector more closely into the world commodity market. It was also an attempt by the ascendant Malay state bourgeoisie to curtail the dependence of the peasantry on the non-Malay commercial bourgeoisie by providing new credit and marketing institutions and co-operatives. The land development schemes were also expanded.

Table 5.11
Federation of Malaya: Public Development Expenditure, 1956-65

	FFYP (1956-60)		SFYP (1961-65)	
	$million	% of total	$million	% of total
Rubber replanting	153.4	15.9	130.9	5.6
Drainage and irrigation	38.3	4.0	108.5	4.6
Land development	16.7	1.7	129.8	5.5
Animal husbandry	1.7	0.2	11.3	0.5
Forestry	2.2	0.2	6.6	0.3
Fisheries	2.4	0.2	2.5	0.1
Others	12.8	1.3	78.3	3.4
Agriculture and rural development	227.5	23.5	467.9	20.0
Commerce and industry	12.1	1.3	59.1	2.5
Infrastructure	520.3	50.7	1,236.7	44.0
Social amenities	138.8	13.8	413.6	15.6
Administration	73.0	7.3	167.1	6.3
Defence and security	35.0	3.4	307.3	11.6
Total	1,007.0	100.0	2,652.0	100.0

Source: FFYP, Table II; SFYP, Tables 2-4; FMP, Table 4-I, pp.28-9.

The reluctance of the Malay landowning class to effect land reform had led the state to opt for the strategy of using land development schemes to absorb the growing mass of rural landless and unemployed. Thus, FELDA was set up in 1956 on the advice of, and with loans from the World Bank and its corollary, the Asian Development Bank. In this scheme private contractors are involved in clearing jungle land and in constructing buildings and infrastructure. The settler family has a house and an average holding of about ten acres each, but these are not fully owned by the settlers until they have paid the debts incurred with FELDA. It was originally estimated that it would take 22 years for each settler's debts to be cleared, but it now appears that it will take much longer, the official reasons being low productivity and low market prices of the commodities which the settlers produce.

During the first 20 years of its existence, FELDA developed 813,000 acres, with a peak development of more than 100,000 acres in 1973.[70] Under the Second Plan, 24,000 families were to be settled under the FELDA scheme and a further 7,000 to 8,000 families under the simpler, less expensive Group Settlement Act. There were to be more rubber replanting programmes, and rice cultivation was to be improved with double-cropping and irrigation schemes. The growing mass of landless peasants was expected to be absorbed into the urban service and industrial sectors. But the gap between target and actual achievements of the SFYP can be seen in

Table 5.12
SFYP (1961-65): Target and Actual Public Expenditure in Agriculture and Rural Development

Sector	Target		Actual	
	$million	*% of total*	*$million*	*% of total*
Rubber replanting	165.0	8.0	130.9	5.6
Drainage and irrigation	100.0	4.9	108.5	4.6
Land development	191.0	9.3	129.8	5.5
Animal husbandry	10.0	0.5	11.3	0.5
Forestry	5.0	0.2	6.6	0.3
Fisheries	7.2	0.4	2.5	0.1
Others	67.1	3.3	78.3	3.4
Agriculture and rural development	*545.3*	*26.5*	*467.9*	*20.0*

Source: SFYP, Tables 2-4; FMP, p.29.

6. Malaysia:
The Pluralist Myth Explodes

At the beginning of the 1960s, British imperialism was still faced with the question of independence for Singapore and the North Bornean states of Sarawak, Brunei and Sabah, all of whose demands for self-determination could no longer be put off. The 'merger' solution in 1963 was a realization of imperialist strategy which completely ignored the democratic demands of the masses in the respective nations. Once again communalism was employed by British imperialism in the application of this neo-colonial solution to incorporate Singapore and the North Bornean states.

The inclusion of Singapore by itself would, in numerical terms, have tilted the communal equation in favour of the Chinese, but this was unacceptable to the Malay rulers. Now, with the new possibilities for gerrymandering by the inclusion of Sarawak and Sabah, the time was ripe for merging Singapore with the Federation. It was the ideal solution to enable British imperialism to maintain its hold on the rich resources of the North Bornean states (oil, timber, pepper, tobacco, gas) and at the same time deal with the left-wing threat in Singapore, since Malaya was secure under the 'Alliance' rule.

But the opposition to this neo-colonialist plan in each of the constituent states was by no means muted. In all of them, this opposition was mercilessly crushed by the repressive machinery at the command of the colonial state.

The larger Federation of Malaysia merely expanded the communal equation, which exerted even greater stress on the Alliance Formula. The contradictions between the local ruling class in the peninsula and that of Singapore inflamed the climate of communalism even more. But even after Singapore's expulsion from the Federation in 1965, the contradictions inherent in the Alliance Formula were not resolved. The Democratic Action Party (DAP) merely took over where the Peoples' Action Party (PAP) had left off, fanning the flames of communalism by opportunistically championing the cause of the non-Malays.

The withdrawal of the PAP and the large Chinese electorate of Singapore altered the political balance of forces within Malaysia in favour of UMNO. From the early 1960s, the emergent Malay state bourgeoisie began to assert their interests. Their ideology was characteristically communalistic and the factional struggle within UMNO between this class and the 'Old Guard' was finally resolved when the bloody riots of 13 May 1969 exploded the myth of Malaya as a 'harmonious plural society'.

Opposition to 'Malaysia'

The opposition to 'Malaysia' in the respective nations involved indicated the scant justification for a union of Malaya with North Kalimantan (northern Borneo), since no significant historical or cultural ties had existed between the peoples of the two nations, except that they had the same colonial master. By contrast, as we saw during the Independence struggle in Malaya, and as almost every political party recognized at the time, was that Singapore should be an inseparable part of Malaya. Singapore's hinterland was peninsula Malaya—the economy, politics and cultures of the two were inextricably linked, as were the kin connections between their peoples.

Singapore

Singapore, with its lucrative entrepot trade, ancillary industries based on Malaya's raw materials, and its strategic position for Western imperialism in the Far East, had a popular left-wing labour movement up to the 1960s. During the post-war period the PAP led militant strikes and was fiercely anti-colonial. At the same time, Lee Kuan Yew (LKY) and his 'moderate' faction were only a small group within it. The strikes and confrontation with the colonial authorities led to the arrest of many workers and PAP leaders, but Lee and his cohorts were not among those arrested. There was never any doubt that the British preferred Lee as their neo-colonial trustee, and eased the passage for his eventual victory. In the words of Clutterbuck, who was himself a serving officer in Singapore and Malaya:

> In the long run these arrests also proved to be of major advantage to LKY and the moderate wing of the PAP, who were able during the next three years to build up the party to a position of political dominance.... If it had not been for the October 1956 riots and these resulting arrests, the story might have been quite different.[1]

While Lee's public posture was to denounce these arrests in order to retain the support of the masses, the absence of the left leaders in the PAP executive owing to their incarceration allowed the Lee faction to push through the Constitutional proposals of March 1957, which involved perpetuating British control through the Internal Security Council (ISC). But the arrests in no way discouraged the left in the PAP, and they managed to win six seats on the Central Executive Committee (CEC) at the annual Conference in August 1957. They took effective control from the Lee faction, who had to resign their posts. Only ten days later, however, their salvation came through the Colonial Government when five out of the six newly-elected left-wing CEC members were arrested in yet another of the Government's 'anti-communist purges':

> Repeated government intervention to ensure LKY's political survival confirmed the feeling that Lee was by now Britain's chosen man for Singapore.... For at least twelve months before the May 1959 elections, Goode (the Colonial Chief Secretary in charge of Special Branch) had maintained close contact with LKY... Lee himself later gave a 'personal tribute' to Goode and implied that Goode's reports when he was in charge of the SB had greatly helped him.[2]

After the 1957 arrests, the Lee faction began to insure themselves against a repetition of left-wing successes in subsequent PAP conferences by changing the Party's democratic structure. They created two classes of Party members: 'ordinary' and 'cadre'. Only a small group of cadres were allowed to elect the CEC, which in turn was responsible for selecting the cadres. At the time, the left membership had not broken from the PAP, because they felt that to form a new independent left party would have invited instant state repression. Thus, while the Lee faction maintained their public posture of defending the PAP's left leadership in prison during the December Municipal Elections, the PAP won 13 out of the 14 seats it contested.

With British connivance and patronage, the Lee faction was assured of victory at the 1959 Legislative Assembly General Elections. Their election campaign was conducted on a radical platform, with the promise not to assume office unless Lim Chin Siong and other trade union leaders had been released. In any case, it would have been impolitic to have leading PAP members in gaol while the PAP was in office:

> In 1961, Lee frankly explained why he did not deal firmly with Lim Chin Siong and other pro-communist stalwarts. It was not because summary arrests were undemocratic or detention without trial repugnant to the rule of law. It was because to detain political opponents when British still held ultimate power in Singapore would be to attract the odium of acting as Britain's stooge. The previous Lim Yew Hock government had done just that and had failed in the eyes of the people.[3]

The PAP contested all 51 seats and 43 were landslide victories, with 54 per cent of the total votes cast. After the 1959 elections, Lee became Prime Minister, narrowly defeating Ong Eng Guan in the Central Executive Committee elections of the PAP. Almost immediately, Lee cut civil servants' and academics' salaries and threatened workers with imprisonment if they disrupted industrial stability. Newspapers either closed, shifted headquarters, or else had to conform to the strict PAP line. The internal security arrangements were tightened, while the new 'Singapore ideology' was constantly emphasized in the media by the PAP stalwarts—Lee,

Goh and Rajaratnam.

Lee managed to survive a challenge for power by Ong Eng Guan, a fellow opportunist, and the vindictive methods used by the former against his political opponent was a foretaste of what to expect in the future. LKY then took advantage of the confusion in the left at the time by floating the idea of a merger with the mainland and the north Bornean states. With the Malayan leaders and the British, he played on the communist bogey and presented his faction in the PAP as the alternative. So while the Lee faction in the PAP was on the brink of defeat by the left in Singapore, the Tungku in Malaya subsequently proposed the 'Malaysian Federation' to comprise the 11 states of Malaya, Singapore, Sabah, Sarawak and Brunei.

The Malayan leaders certainly saw the Lee faction as the lesser of two evils even as they could perceive that contradictions existed between themselves. The Malay rulers in UMNO further feared that their electoral edge would be eroded when the mainly Chinese population of Singapore was included in the Federation. But the 'Malaysian Merger' proposals were a neat compromise, since the Chinese electorate would be manipulated and the communal equation deftly balanced by the electorate of the north Bornean states. For the Lee faction, the end of colonial rule would finally provide them with the opportunity to decisively crush the left without fear of being seen as colonial stooges.

Lee lost not time in taking advantage of the merger issue when the Anson by-election came up in July 1961. Now, while the left had consistently supported the unity of Malaya and Singapore, they were justly suspicious of the merger proposals put forward by Lee and the Tungku. For his part, Lee kept the left within the PAP in the dark regarding his merger talks with the Malayan leaders. He would not discount the idea that in the new Federation, internal security would be in the hands of Kuala Lumpur, and the Malayan leaders would be more repressive than the PAP in Singapore.

Consequently, the left finally decided to split from the PAP just before the Anson by-election. Having had enough of Lee's manoeuvrings, their disenchantment was complete. Among other things, Lee had still not released many opposition members imprisoned since the Lim Yew Hock government; others had had their citizenship revoked under a new bill by the Lee government; the Lee faction was trying to capture the trade union leadership; and finally, the Lee government was also trying to clamp down on Chinese education. But the merger issue was decisive in leading the left break-away from the PAP.

Devoid of left support, the official PAP candidate received barely 37 per cent of the popular vote at the Anson by-election and lost to David Marshall. After the Anson defeat, Lee decided to take the merger issue to the Assembly rather than risk a further fiasco at the Party branch committees, where the left had overwhelming sup-

port. He unleashed every dirty trick at his command: the communist bogey; a purportedly secret document exposing Lim Chin
Siong as a Communist front man; even a British-Communist plot
to overthrow the PAP government! In a further attempt to win
public sentiment, the government announced that the remaining
detainees would soon be released. In the confidence motion at the
Assembly, 27 out of the 51 members voted for the government; the
left abstained.

The left's formal break from the PAP occurred on 26 July
1961, when they founded a new party, the *Barisan Sosialis*, with
Lim Chin Siong as Secretary-General. As much as 70 per cent of
the rank-and-file members of the PAP defected. The control of
almost all PAP branches was lost to Barisan, and 30 out of the 34
staff at the PAP HQ left to join Barisan.

Completely without a mass base, the PAP leaders then resorted
to executive powers to plan their strategy. They announced a
referendum on merger for 1 September 1962, after the Malayan
leaders and the British had decided that Malaysia would be proclaimed in August 1963. The 'importance of merger' was promptly
disseminated throughout the media. But Lee had no intention of
repeating the debacle at Hong Lim (where the PAP had lost to Ong
Eng Guan) and Anson by relying on the ballot box. The referendum on merger was '...not a referendum in the usual democratic
sense of the term; "not quite cricket...", as a PAP leader put it'.[4]
Voters were given three choices, all of which amounted to the same
proposition, viz. a vote for merger:

1) Merger under the terms of a Singapore government white paper
giving Singapore autonomy in education and labour.
2) Merger which would give Singapore the same status and citizenship provisions as the component states of Malaysia.
3) Merger on no less favourable terms than those given to the
Borneo territories.[5]

It can be seen that Singaporeans were not given the choice of
voting *against* merger. At the time, the terms for Borneo had still
not been worked out, and the second choice differed little from the
first. Voting in the referendum was mandatory. Those who protested by recording blank votes were told by the Lee government
that this would be considered as votes for the government. Rumours
were rife that blank votes could be traced to the responsible voters
later on. This possibility could not be ruled out since the ballot
papers were numbered and retained for six months after the poll.
At every ballot since, this possibility of the government checking on
voters' ballot papers has served as an instrument of intimidation to
would-be detractors.

Out of 417,482 marked votes, 397,626 were in favour of the
White Paper.[6] Even then, Lee was not satisfied that 144,077 had
dared to cast blank votes despite his dire warnings. He immediately

jailed 133 political activists, students, journalists and others who had opposed merger. Using the referendum results as a mandate for further executive actions, Lee then moved the date of the General Elections forward to September 1963, just four days after the proclamation of Malaysia. But he still did not dare to gamble on the free play of democracy after the lessons of Hong Lim and Anson. The opposition was allowed only nine days for campaigning and all manner of obstacles were put in their way, for example, limited media coverage and printing facilities. On the other hand, the PAP saturated the media with their propaganda, and their leaflets and pamphlets had been produced months in advance.

Furthermore, the Registrar of trade unions ordered the freezing of the bank accounts (totalling S$420,000) of the three largest Barisan-led unions: the Singapore General Employees Union, the Singapore Business Houses Employees' Union, the Bus Workers Union. Four other unions were threatened with deregistration. A year earlier the government had asked employers to sack about 400 Barisan trade union cadres. The usual rumours were circulating at election time. This time it was that, if Barisan won, Federal troops would be brought in to rule Singapore directly from Kuala Lumpur. Another rumour that played on Chinese chauvinism was that Barisan had connections with the PKI in Indonesia which would 'swallow up' Barisan along with Singapore. Even Lee's old rival, Ong Eng Guan, proved useful to the PAP during the 1963 elections. His 'United People's Party' refused an electoral pact with Barisan.

Finally to ensure that his election plan was foolproof, 'Operation Coldstore' was unleashed. In the early hours of 2 February 1963, the Special Branch arrested and detained more than 100 opposition members belonging variously to Barisan, the unions, journalists, and students. The Barisan's key leaders—Lim Chin Siong, Fong Swee Suan, Sandra Woodhull, James Puthucheary—were all arrested. Lee alleged that they were plotting an uprising to coincide with the Azahari revolt in Brunei. The crackdown itself was directed by the Federal Minister of Internal Security, Dato Dr Ismail, and executed by George Bogaars, the Singapore Chief of Special Branch. The Internal Security Council was overseen by the British High Commissioner for Singapore, Lord Selkirk.

Despite the cold and calculated repression, the PAP managed to obtain only 46.9 per cent of the votes but this gave it 37 out of the 51 seats in the Assembly. Barisan still managed to win 33.3 per cent of the votes in spite of the handicap, but it amounted to only 13 seats. After the 1963 elections, the PAP further ensured that through 'legal fixing' of their election tactics, no challenge by any effective opposition parties would be permitted.

Sarawak, Sabah and Brunei
In Sabah, Sarawak and Brunei, the wishes of the people were

treated with equal disregard. There was not even the farcical referendum that was held in Singapore. Local notables were merely invited to tour the Federation and lavishly feted. The Cobbold Commission that was sent to assess local opinion regarding merger was headed by three British and two Malayans. It based its report on a few memoranda submitted by these local elites.

The local ruling class in Sabah and Sarawak were offered disproportionately more seats in the Malaysian parliament: one seat for every 25,000 people, compared with the allocation of one seat to every 116,000 Singaporeans. This was how the communal equation in the Malaysian society was to be balanced. The conclusion of the Commission after a two week stay was that there was a 'rough consensus' for joining Malaysia.[7]

In Sarawak, the opposition to 'Malaysia' was organized by the Sarawak United Peoples Party (SUPP). Out of a total population of 850,000 in Sarawak, the SUPP managed to hold a demonstration of 10,000 against merger. When some SUPP leaders were subsequently arrested, an even bigger demonstration of 20,000 followed. Altogether, about 1,000 people were detained in Sarawak just before the proclamation of the Federation of Malaysia.[8]

In mid-1963 a UN team also came to Sabah and Sarawak to assess the people's opinions of merger. The head of the team had this to say:

> Because of the short time available, it may not be possible for all those wishing to be heard to be granted oral hearing. Those unable to meet the mission are advised to send written memoranda... as far as possible in English, because of the difficulties in translation.[9]

This 'fact-finding' mission was a farce not only because of the brevity of the visit (two weeks) and the fact that the overwhelming majority of Sarawakians spoke little English, but also because even before the team had concluded its investigation, the Tungku had announced the date for the declaration of the Federation of Malaysia: 16 September 1963.

In Brunei, the Party Rakyat, which had won more than 90 per cent of the elective seats in the 1962 elections, moved a motion in the Legislature opposing the Malaysia Plan. It called instead for a federation of North Bornean states. Knowing that this motion would easily be carried, the British colonial government deliberately postponed the Legislative Council meeting three times and early in December disqualified the motion altogether. Realizing the futility of opposing the merger plan by constitutional means, Party Rakyat went underground and led an armed uprising of nearly 10,000. The revolt led by Azahari was brutally put down by British troops, which remain in Brunei to the present day.

Malaya
There was also opposition to 'Malaysia' in the Malayan mainland.

The opposition parties—Pan Malayan Islamic Party (PMIP), Partai Negara, Socialist Front and the United Democratic Party (UDP) —challenged the government to consult the people first:

> The opposition parties have repeatedly stressed that the present government has not obtained a mandate from the people of Malaya to establish Malaysia, and we therefore urge the government to dissolve Parliament and hold a general election before proceeding with a debate in Parliament on Malaysia.[10]

A number of Labour Party leaders who opposed the merger plan were detained without trial. The anti-colonial forces in Singapore and Malaya also warned of the dangers of the inherent communalist politics involved in the whole neo-colonialist scheme. This stand by the left was to be vindicated just ten months after the formation of Malaysia when there were serious communal clashes in Singapore in 1964.

The Larger Communal Equation

When Malaysia came into being on 1 September 1963, only Brunei stayed out, and it remains a British Protectorate to the present day. Among the Constitutional provisions of the new Federation, Britain retained the right to keep her military bases in Malaysia; the special privileges of the Malays were maintained; and the contentious articles relating to the citizenship of the non-Malays remained. For Britain and the Western powers Malaysia's formation had ensured stability in their South East Asian sphere of influence, which otherwise would have swung in favour of the anti-imperialist forces. Thus Article V of the Malaysia Agreement reads:

> The Agreement on External Defence and Mutual Assistance between the government of the UK and the government of the Federation of Malaya and its annexes shall apply to all territories of Malaysia, and any reference in that Agreement shall be deemed to apply to Malaysia, subject to the proviso that the government of Malaysia will afford to the government of the UK the right to continue to maintain the bases and other facilities at present occupied by their service authorities within the state of Singapore and will permit the government of the UK to make such use of their bases and facilities as that government may consider necessary for the purpose of assisting in the defence and for the preservation of peace in SE Asia.[11]

From the beginning, chauvinistic and communalistic politics had laid great stress on the 'Alliance Formula'. Now, with the inclusion of Singapore, the secondary contradictions between the local ruling class in the peninsula and the industrial capitalists in Singapore again took on a communalistic aspect as Lee pursued the PAP's theme of a 'Malaysian Malaysia'. It was quite evident that the PAP's challenge of 'Malay Special Rights' was basically an appeal to the communalist sentiments of the non-Malays in its attempt to extend its interests in the mainland.

By having gained political sovereignty for Singapore and en-sured the entrenchment of the PAP in the island city, Lee even in-sisted on retaining his designation as Prime Minister. This gave Malaysia the remarkable feature of being the only country in the world with two Prime Ministers! This piqued the Malay ruling class on the mainland even further. Thus within the wider political arena of Malaysia, the communalistic wrangling reached an un-precedented scale.

Within UMNO, the Malay rulers were increasingly alarmed by the PAP's challenge to the ground rules of the 'Alliance'. This un-compromising stand by the PAP was partly the result of having failed to replace the MCA (Malayan Chinese Association) as the representative of the Chinese electorate in the Federation. Conse-quently, throughout 1963-65, Lee and the PAP created a highly-charged atmosphere of communalism within Malaysia.

Thus it was not only the Malay rulers within UMNO but also the Chinese bourgeoisie in MCA who resented this aggressive en-croachment by the PAP. The communalistic mud-slinging reached a climax during the federal elections of April 1964. The PAP fielded 11 candidates in the mainland but lost miserably. Even so, the Alliance leaders who ran the federal government would not tolerate this incursion by the PAP on Alliance territory. There were calls by the Malay 'ultras' in UMNO for the arrest of Lee. Then, on 21 July, communal rioting broke out in Geylang, the Malay district in Singapore, resulting in 20 deaths and several hundred injured, just as the Barisan leaders had predicted.

Throughout 1963-65, Indonesia's *Confrontasi* against Malaysia also contributed toward inflaming communal tensions, especially in Singapore, where the Malays were goaded as the discriminated minority in Indonesian propaganda. George has revealed that after each outbreak of violence, Lee tried unsuc-cessfully to persuade the Tungku to accept the PAP into the Federal government. Tun Razak was quoted as saying:

> When they found they were unsuccessful in persuading UMNO to ac-cept them, the PAP started to criticize and attack UMNO and Malaysia. In this way they hoped to coerce UMNO to accept them.[12]

In May 1965, Lee founded a 'Malaysian Solidarity Convention' of a united opposition whose slogan of 'Malaysian Malaysia' became only a slightly more subtle form of communalism than that bandied around by the Malay ultras. This coalition of the opposi-tion parties in the Malaysian Parliament—13 seats in Singapore, 16 from Sabah, 34 from Sarawak, 15 from the mainland—threatened the status quo itself. There was further fear in Kuala Lumpur that Singapore, Sabah and Sarawak might break away to form their own federation. Finally, on 9 August 1965, the Malaysian Parlia-ment duly passed the Separation Bill, expelling Singapore from the

Federation. When Lee's tears of frustration had dried, the PAP in Singapore proceeded in earnest to build their 'Little Israel'.

13 May 1969: Collapse of the Alliance Formula

The communal riots of 13 May 1969 were the tragic outcome of the contradictions inherent in the Alliance Formula. Social scientists who designate the cause as the breakdown of 'moderate' politics clearly fail to look at the evolving class configuration and at the tight political reins maintained by the Alliance which strained to breaking point. It is noteworthy that, while the state's communalist strategy serves to divide the masses, simultaneously it creates contradictions among the various ruling factions who appeal to their respective social bases in communalist terms.

With Singapore's withdrawal from the Federation, the political balance within Malaysia as a whole was also altered. The ruling class on the mainland could exercise economic and political power virtually unimpeded, thus arousing anxiety in Sabah and Sarawak. Not only were the political leaders in Sabah and Sarawak (let alone their people) not consulted over the Singapore expulsion, but the financial assistance for East Malaysia expected to come from Singapore was now curtailed. The threat of increasing domination from Kuala Lumpur became even more alarming since the 'East Malaysian' states now featured less in the political balance of Malaysia's communal equation.

Indeed the communal politics of the pre-Malaysia period was in no way diminished. The PAP and its opportunistic slogan of 'Malaysian Malaysia' to catch non-Malay votes was superseded by the DAP (Democratic Action Party). Within the dominant Alliance itself, the rival communalist demands between UMNO, MCA, and MIC again surfaced in view of the removal of the PAP challenge. In all this, the Tungku played the role of arbiter, a role that became increasingly eroded as the emergent state bourgeoisie began to assert themselves in the new balance of forces. Within UMNO there were calls for more stringent citizenship laws for non-Malays and a speedier implementation of Malay as the sole official language.[13]

The ascendancy of this Malay state capitalist class can be seen in the contents of the Malaysian Plans. The First Malaysia Plan (1966-70) and the Second Malaysia Plan (1971-75) saw even more agricultural institutions emerge at both federal and state levels. These were aimed at providing further alternative channels for credit, marketing, extension services, and so on, in order to accelerate commercial services in the rural sector. Among these were: the expansion of Bank Pertanian (Agriculture Development Bank); the establishment of Lembaga Padi Nasional (LPN, National Padi Authority); Food Industries of Malaysia (FIMA); MAJUIKAN (Fisheries Development Authority); MAJUTERNAK (Livestock Development Authority); RISDA (Rubber Industry Smallholders Development Authority); FOA (Farmers Organisation Authority), and various State Agricultural Development Corporations, including MARDI (Malaysian Agricultural Research and Development Institute). The vastly enlarged bureaucracy that has been created for the management of all these rural schemes has provided abundant opportunities for corruption and manipulation as well as a Malay petty bourgeois class base for the state bourgeoisie.

The interests of the rich Malay farmers and state bourgeoisie were further boosted in the latter half of the 1960s by the Green Revolution—the World Bank-inspired scheme for increasing agricultural productivity. The 'miracle rice' was accompanied by the construction of water conservancy work since it performed well only under ideal conditions. Thus the Muda (Kedah) and Kemubu (Kelantan) Schemes were built largely with World Bank funds.[14] In addition, the necessary nutrients, fertilizer, and pesticides essential for the HYVs (high-yielding varieties) are all supplied by the multinational agribusinesses. For example, all the fertilizer in the country is supplied by a subsidiary of ICI, 'Chemical Company of Malaysia' at Port Dickson. The association of ICI with the Department of Agriculture and the Rubber Research Institute is longstanding. The nitrogen fertilizer plant is also linked with Esso. The Agency Houses, Harrison and Crosfield, and Guthrie,[15] help to market and distribute their products on the local market.

To a great extent these inputs have been provided to the farmers at subsidized costs, but studies have shown[16] that they have mainly profited the rich farmers. A Guaranteed Minimum Price for padi[17] was introduced by LPN (Lembaga Padi Negara-National Padi Authority) to encourage production and productivity. But all these subsidies have been at the expense of the consumer, and this is another way by which the Malay bourgeoisie buys the loyalty of the Malay peasantry to maintain its communalist policy. In terms of increasing productivity, the Green Revolution has achieved its aim: from 1957 to 1972, the acreage of land under padi production increased by only 28 per cent, while padi production actually increased by 170 per cent (see Table 6.1). By the start of the Second Malaysian Plan in 1971, almost 70 per cent of the local rice consumption had been met by domestic production. But in terms of easing rural poverty, as we saw in the last chapter, the Green Revolution in fact accentuated class differentiation. The Third Malaysia Plan (1976-80) admitted to a serious problem of rural poverty.

From the 1960s, there was clearly a struggle within the Malay ruling class, between the 'Old Guard' conservatives who were content with their economic interests in private capital of the non-Malay and foreign bourgeoisie (even if this only meant sitting on the boards of directorship) and landed interests, and those elements who wanted to expand state capital still further in order to create a strictly Malay state bourgeoisie. The Cabinet crisis which led to the dismissal of Aziz Ishak in 1962 can be seen as a manifestation of that struggle. Ishak was the Minister of Agriculture and Co-

Table 6.1
Production of Principal Agricultural Commodities, 1960-75
('000 metric tons)

Commodity	1960	1965	1970	1975	Annual Rate of Growth
Rubber	770	917	1,269	1,477	4.4
Palm oil kernel	116	185	522	1,514	18.7
Rice	645	813	1,080	1,288	5.0
Coconut oil	n.a.	70	96	79	n.a.
Sawn logs	n.a.	n.a.	12,701	13,725	n.a.
Sawn timber	983	1,230	1,995	2,734	7.1

Source: Ministry of Finance, Economic Report, various years; World Bank, 1980:216.

operatives who favoured measures to establish marketing, credit and processing co-operatives in the rural sector, thereby cutting off the economic hold of the non-Malay commercial bourgeoisie on the Malay peasantry. His dismissal at the time showed that the 'Old Guard', symbolized by the Tungku, still had the upper hand within the Malay ruling class and were reluctant to disturb the status quo. They were satisfied with gradualist measures, such as providing economic and social amenities and utilities as piecemeal electoral rewards to the rural Malays, while allowing the non-Malay bourgeoisie free rein in the private sector. Thus, at the end of the 1960s, Malay capital was negligible: the total amount of credit extended to Malays in 1970 was only 1.4 per cent of all the bank loans and advances.[18]

Contradictions in the rural sector, and peasant discontent had resulted in the electoral victory by the PMIP (Pan Malayan Islamic Party) in the east coast states of Malaya in 1959. The PMIP's leadership was provided by the Malay petty bourgeoisie, both in the urban and rural areas, who were dissatisfied with the performance of UMNO. Their ideology was that of Islamic fundamentalism and to the present day their main criticism of UMNO leaders and followers (who are branded as *kafir* or infidel) is their profligate lifestyle, and compromise with the non-Malays. But the petty bourgeoisie *within* UMNO provide the social base for the ascendant Malay state bourgeoisie since they have gained from the *bumiputra* policies. In 1965, the First Bumiputra Economic Congress was held by those Malay elements who vociferously criticized the government's record in relation to aiding the formation of Malay capital. The ideology they propagated in order to achieve their ends was predictably communalistic. Consequently, MARA (Majlis Amanah Rakyat—Council of the People's Trust) was created out of RIDA (Rural Industrial Development Authority), together with other state enterprises such as Bank Bumiputra and FAMA (Federal Agricultural Marketing Authority), to actively foster Malay business interests.

By the Second Bumiputra Economic Congress in 1968, the clamour by these same elements within UMNO for a vast expansion of state capital to aid Malay interests was overwhelming. It became evident that the section of the traditional Malay ruling class that was satisfied merely with their positions on the boards of the non-Malay companies was rapidly becoming a minority. With increasing state intervention in the economy, the appetite of the Malay state capitalists was whetted accordingly. The growth of this class out of the traditional Malay ruling class had been facilitated by the configuration of political forces since Independence. Above all, it was the state's communalist strategy (Malay Special Rights) that has allowed the Malay ruling class to tip the balance of class forces in its favour. As a result, its incursion into the economy has been presented as a *fait accompli* to the other class forces in the country.

After the Generals' coup in Indonesia in 1965, the demands of the ultra-communalistic Malays within UMNO became even more aggressive. This was partly the response to the cue from General Suharto: 'Our intention is to build a greater Maphilindo, which means we would like to unite with the Malay race and other friendly neighbouring countries.'[19] The expulsion of Singapore also had ensured the Malays' position as the largest ethnic community in the Federation. The predominance of UMNO within the Alliance was thus guaranteed, and the communal bargaining within it had to be on terms acceptable to the top leaders of UMNO. All non-Malays who failed to abide by these rules of co-operation with UMNO by disregarding these 'sensitive issues' of 'Malay Special Rights', language and religion, were barred from access to the political system.

On 31 August 1967, Malay became the *sole* national language, and the enforced use of Malay in the government service and education system was to further ensure the retention of Malay privileges and special rights. Whereas at Merdeka in 1957, there was the assumption that these Malay privileges were a temporary measure only, to be maintained for approximately ten years in order to 'raise the economic and educational level of the Malays to parity with the non-Malays',[20] these special rights were now institutionalized. This provided the setting for the General Elections of 1969.

Communalist wranglings reached an unprecedented pitch. Post-Independence developments were leading to discontent among the workers and peasants, as well as sections of the non-Malay petty bourgeoisie. Income distribution figures showed worsening conditions for the workers and peasants, including an absolute decline in real household income.[21] The non-Malay workers and petty bourgeoisie were even more disgruntled by the state's discriminatory *bumiputra* policies, not only regarding employment, but also in education, scholarships, and licence grants.

These various sections of the population displayed their grievances against the Alliance during the 1969 elections. With the virtual proscription of the left, the main opposition parties in the elections comprised only those which preyed upon communalist sentiments and took advantage of the mass disaffection towards the Alliance. The Labour Party decided to opt out of constitutional politics. *Parti Rakyat* was one of the few political parties that rejected the communalist appeal but concentrated strictly on 'class solidarity'. Its manifesto pointed out that:

> The Malay feudalists and the big Chinese and Indian capitalists who unite within the Alliance Party with the support of the international capitalists, have always and continue to exploit the peasants, workers, fishermen, petty officials and traders, etc. of all races in this country.[22]

The DAP, successor to Singapore's PAP, was a petty bourgeois-led party which championed the interests of the urban non-Malays. The PMIP's basic aim was 'to establish through constitutional means an Islamic state for the benefit of the Malays'.[23] Its ideology of the imposition of a Malay community on the whole nation was fervently propagated by Malay school-teachers and *ulamas* (religious teachers) in the rural areas. Their dedication was in strong contrast to and posed a threat to UMNO's rural organization and power base, and this opposition within the Malay community still exists today. The PPP (People's Progressive Party) was dominated by two lawyer brothers, the Seenivasagams. It attracted non-Malay voters, mainly in Perak state. *Parti Gerakan Rakyat* (Gerakan), was formed only in 1968 by a number of opposition leaders and intellectuals from their Penang stronghold.

These opposition parties made an electoral pact not to split the votes even though they were at opposite ends of their respective communalist propaganda. The results of the 1969 General Elections shook the status quo, for it completely demolished the Alliance edifice that had stood unchallenged since Independence: UMNO lost 17 parliamentary seats mainly to *Parti Islam* (PMIP), winning only 51; MCA (Malayan Chinese Association) won only 13 seats, conceding 20 to the opposition; while MIC (Malayan Indian Congress) won only two out of the three allocated to the party.[24] At the state level, the results were even more surprising: Kelantan was again lost to *Parti Islam*; the Alliance was beaten in Penang and Perak; the seats were evenly distributed in the capital state of Selangor; while the Alliance managed only 13 out of 24 in Trengganu. The worst defeat was suffered by MCA, whose candidates won only in constituencies with a strong Malay representation.

Communal tensions were extremely high, especially in the capital city of Kuala Lumpur, when the results were declared. The victory procession by the opposition and the counter-demonstration by UMNO, each trying to outdo the other in racialist taunting, precipitated the worst communal rioting in the country's history.[25]

The manipulated character of the riots and the interpretation that it was a ruling class offensive against the threat to the status quo cannot be ruled out.[26] Since '13 May', the fascist threat of communal violence, backed by the mainly Malay military, hangs over Malaysian politics to deter any challenge to the ruling class.

But the most significant change during the State of Emergency which followed was the determined quest for power by the Malay state bourgeoisie in UMNO. With the suspension of Parliament under martial law, the National Operations Council was headed by Tun Razak, who replaced the Tungku, since the former was more acceptable to the ascendant state bourgeoisie. The subsequent UMNO leadership began to articulate the interests of this class. The opponents of the Tungku during the 1960s included Mahathir and Musa Hitam, both of whom were expelled during the crisis of '13 May', but who at present are Prime Minister and Deputy Prime Minister respectively.

7. The 'New Economic Policy': Communalism Sustained

The explosion of the Alliance arrangement gave way to a broader coalition which co-opted some of the opposition parties of the pre-1969 period—with the Sarawak United Peoples Party (SUPP) in the 1970 Sarawak elections; with Gerakan in Penang; and with the People's Progressive Party (PPP) in Perak. This new coalition, renamed *Barisan Nasional* (National Front), thus contested the 1974 General Elections. After 1969, the pre-eminence of UMNO within the ruling coalition was further presented as a *fait accompli* to the other member parties.

While the Government's New Economic Policy (NEP), promulgated in 1970, serves as the main vehicle for the interests of the Malay state bourgeoisie, it also represents the latest manifestation of the institutionalization of communalism by the Malaysian state. In its assertion and claim to power, this Malay bourgeoisie has, in no uncertain way, used the same communalist strategy that we have traced so far.

But despite the vastly expanded state sector and the continued trend of capital accumulation, this Malay state bourgeoisie remains a dependent one in relation to metropolitan capital. Above all, the working class in Malaysia has had to bear the brunt of the exploitation inherent in the Government's 'development strategy', based on continued investment by foreign multinational companies. Thus, although the workers' struggles from the 1960s onwards have been less intense than those of the previous three decades, this is largely a reflection of ruthless state repression and its infiltration of the labour movement. Nevertheless, as the data produced below indicates, workers' struggles have not ceased in recent years, despite the state's attempt to present a picture of 'industrial peace' in order to attract foreign investors.

The current situation is marked by increased state repression. While normal democratic processes have never characterized Malayan/Malaysian politics, in recent years, Emergency laws introduced by the state have become more arbitrary as have legal procedures to deal with opposition from the various sections of the masses. Its communalist strategy has involved further denial of the democratic aspirations of the non-Malay nationals. At the same time, the power struggles within the member parties of the *Barisan Nasional* continue to plague the ruling coalition, since the contradictions inherent in the same communal formula have remained intact.

The *Barisan Nasional*: Larger But Same Alliance Formula

The National Operations Council (NOC) that ruled the country by decree, in addition to Tun Razak as Chairman, included eight other members, all senior Malay Alliance leaders, Malay bureaucrats, police and military officers.[1] The MCA and MIC leaders were given only representation on the NOC. This highlighted the new pre-eminence of the Malay state bourgeoisie in the ruling coalition, and the NOC period was intended to demonstrate to the Malay community that political power lay firmly in the hands of 'the Malays', in a leadership avowedly determined to 'improve the economic status of the Malays'.[2]

The state, however, also had to present itself as the cohesive factor of the nation, to return the country to normality. 'Goodwill Committees' were set up throughout the country, including a 'Department of National Unity'. The new 'State Ideology', known as *Rukunegara* ('articles of faith of the state') published in mid-1970, called for 'a united nation, a democratic, just, liberal, and progressive society... belief in God, loyalty to the supreme ruler and to the country, support of the Constitution, good behaviour, and morality'.[3] A National Consultative Council, formed in January 1970, also managed to co-opt some professionals and opposition parties, for example, the Sarawak National Party (SNAP) and Gerakan.

With the suspension of Parliament, the ruling party began to take steps to consolidate its power after the 1969 election debacle. It threatened not to reconvene Parliament as long as the Alliance could not obtain the two-thirds majority needed to allow the Government to amend the Constitution. This blackmail had its desired effect for some of the petty bourgeois-led opposition parties easily capitulated and crossed the floor to join the Alliance, including five SUPP members from Sarawak (elected during the 1970 elections).

The suspended elections in East Malaysia (as a result of the '13 May' riots) were held in June and July 1970. Out of the 40 parliamentary seats at stake, the Alliance needed at least 30 to be certain of its two-thirds majority. The Sabah Alliance, under the mafia of Tun Mustapha,[4] won all 16 seats in that state. In Sarawak, however, the Alliance won only nine seats (including two PESAKA *(Parti Pesaka Anak Sarawak)* seats out of a total of 24. Only after the subsequent decision by the five SUPP members to join the Alliance coalition did the ruling party manage to obtain the two-thirds majority.

With the reconvening of Parliament on 20 February 1971, the Constitutional (Amendment) Act was passed. Under this legislation, certain issues—'which might arouse racial emotions in respect of the National Language ⅜i.e. Malay½, the special position of the Malays and other natives ⅜the *bumiputra*½, citizenship rights and the sovereignty of the Malay rulers'[5]—were declared to be 'sensitive' and it became an offence to raise these questions in public. The amendments also stipulated quotas reserved for *bumiputras* in institutions of higher learning.

From that time, the Alliance began to co-opt more opposition parties into the broader framework. In January 1972, Gerakan agreed to the Alliance becoming a partner in a joint Penang state government. The PPP did likewise and entered into a ruling coalition with the Alliance in Perak, while retaining its independence in the federal parliament. Then, in January 1973, Tun Razak succeeded in co-opting *Parti Islam* (the former PMIP) into the coalition. Dato Asri, *Parti Islam*'s head and Chief Minister of Kelantan, was enticed with a federal Cabinet post as Minister of Land Development and Special Functions.

Thus, although by January 1973, the old Alliance (UMNO, MCA, MIC) had yielded to the now enlarged *Barisan Nasional* (BN) —Alliance plus SUPP, Gerakan, PI, PPP—commanding 122 out of the 144-seat Parliament, the coalition was, if anything, even more tenuous, '...based on the lowest agreeable denominator'.[6]

When the first General Elections after the 13 May riots was announced for August 1974, the DAP (Democratic Action Party) —outside the BN—was the main opposition party voicing communalist demands on behalf of the non-Malays. It led a frail opposition coalition bloc with SNAP and *Persatuan Kebangsaan Melayu Singapura*—Malay National Union of Singapore (PEKEMAS). In the meantime, the Government had redrawn the electoral boundaries to the undoubted advantage of the BN, and added ten more seats to the pre-existing 104 seats in West Malaysia. Within the BN, the undisputed dominance by UMNO was again demonstrated in the way they controlled the electoral bargaining amongst the coalition member parties and ensured that 'government' candidates, and not potential opposition members, were selected. Even the discontent within *Parti Islam* (PI)—easily the more volatile member of the coalition—was contained by the Malay leaders.

It was the dismal showing by MCA at the 1969 General Elections that had prompted UMNO to bring in the other Chinese-dominated communal parties such as Gerakan and SUPP. There had also been mass defections of MCA members and branches to Gerakan in the early 1970s. In the aftermath of 13 May, Tan Siew Sin—the erstwhile leader of the MCA and, since colonial times a member of one of the main comprador families—suffered the same fate as the Tungku.[7] He was unable to inspire the confidence of the MCA social base, but in the power struggle that followed the MCA leadership was assumed by one of his supporters, Lee San Choon. The internal squabbles and factional jostling within the top echelon of the party have continued to the present day.

The results of the 1974 elections were a foregone conclusion. But in the event, DAP still managed to secure around 20 per cent of all the votes cast, while independent Malay candidates in Kelantan (mostly *Parti Islam* dissidents) and *Parti Rakyat* (renamed *Parti Sosialis Rakyat Malaya*) in Trengganu captured around 20 per cent and 30 per cent of the vote respectively.[8] MCA's success was once again attributed to UMNO's ability to turn out *Malay* votes for the former's candidates. The urban constituencies in Kuala Lumpur, Ipoh, Seremban, Malacca, Alor Star, all fell to DAP. The PPP's association with the BN cost it much of its non-Malay urban votes. The results in West Malaysia were as follows:[9]

UMNO	62
PAS	13
MCA	19
Gerakan	5
MIC	4
PPP	1
Total (BN)	104
DAP	9
PEKEMAS	1
Total (W. Malaysia)	*114*

In Sabah, as expected, the Sabah Alliance won all 16 seats. Fifteen of these were uncontested because of Tun Mustapha's maverick style of preventing (through arrest or other means of persuasion) the submission of nomination papers by opposition candidates.[10] Until 1975, Tun Mustapha's corrupt and dictatorial rule was carried out through his United Sabah National Organization (USNO) party and a political apparatus that dominated every department of Sabah.

In the 1974 elections in Sarawak, SNAP in the opposition retained its nine seats in the federal parliament and increased the number of SNAP representatives in the state legislature from 12 to 18.[11] This was in spite of the defeat of its leader, Stephen Kalong Ningkan, and the state government's arrest and detention of its deputy president, Datuk James Wong. But the Sarawak branch of the BN, composed of SUPP, SCA, and PBB (*Partai Pesaka Bumiputra Bersatu*, formed in 1973 through the merger of *Partai Bumiputra* and *PESAKA*), easily absorbed the remaining seats.

The 1974 General Elections thus represented the enlarged BN formula in action. The co-option of the various opposition parties has ensured the Government an overwhelming majority in parliament, which, if the 1969 elections had been left to run its constitutional course, it would have lost. This electoral majority has enabled the Government to carry through its New Economic Policy as well as a gamut of repressive legislation over the ensuing years.

The New Economic Policy

The Government's New Economic Policy (NEP), announced in 1970, was embodied in the Second Malaysia Plan (SMP) (1971-75) and elaborated in the Outline Perspective Plan for the period 1971 to 1990 in the Mid-Term Review of the SMP. The avowed aims of the NEP are:[12]

(i) The restructuring of Malaysian society to correct the economic imbalance between the races.
(ii) The eradication of poverty.

The method by which the government proposed to 'correct the economic imbalance' has been to increase Malay ownership of the share capital of limited companies from about 1.5 per cent in 1970 to 30 per cent by 1990. In this, a large role has been designated for the state—about three-quarters of the target of 30 per cent share ownership is to be held 'in trust' by public *bumiputra* enterprises, and about a quarter left for Malay individuals.[13]

From the main premise of the NEP—couched in terms of restoring the 'racial imbalance'—this can be seen as the latest expression of the ruling class's communalist strategy. With the direct participation by the state in capital accumulation, however, vast resources have been diverted through fiscal and monetarist tools and the channelling of domestic as well as international financing. This has included the direct ownership of private capital:[14]

> The government will participate more directly in the establishment and operation of a wide range of productive enterprises. This will be done through wholly-owned enterprises and joint ventures with the private sector. Direct participation by the government in commercial and industrial undertakings represents a significant departure from past practices. The necessity for such efforts by the government arises particularly from the aims of establishing new industrial activities in selected new growth areas and of creating a Malay commercial and industrial community.

Consequently, public development expenditure during the Second Malaysia Plan was $9,820 million, while public financing of private investments was $3,380 million (see Tables 7.1 and 7.2). The sharp increase in state expenditure since the SMP, especially in commerce and industry, is also revealed in Table 7.1. A Ministry of Land Development was set up in 1973 to co-ordinate the activities of the various land development agencies.[15] Even in terms of 'economic costs', these rather expensive FELDA (Federal Land Development Authority) schemes had been criticized by such economists as Fisk during the 1960s.[16] Between 1956-76, FELDA

Table 7.1
West Malaysia: Public Development Expenditure, 1966-80 ($million)

Sector	FMP, 1966-70 (Actual)	(%)	SMP, 1971-75 (Actual)	(%)	TMP, 1976-80 (Actual)	(%)
Agriculture and rural development	1114.1	26.3	2129.1	21.7	7585.2	23.6
Commerce and industry	141.3	3.3	1618.2	16.5	3205.2	10.0
Infrastructure	1429.4	33.7	3316.5	33.8	10599.1	33.0
Social amenities	752.1	17.7	1347.7	13.7	5561.0	17.4
Administration	138.1	3.3	348.7	3.6	1229.3	3.8
Defence and security	668.8	15.7	1024.2	10.4	3748.0	11.8
Others	—	—	36.5	0.4	111.0	0.4
Total	4242.8	100.0	9820.9	100.0	32074.8	100.0

Source: SMP, Table 5-1; TMP, Table 12.3; Mid-Term Review of the TMP, Table 18-2.

Table 7.2
Financing of Private Investments, 1971-80

Sources of Finance	SMP, 1971-75 ($million)	(%)	TMP, 1976-80 ($million)	(%)
Domestic private investment	6,409	52.2	10,236	37.2
Public sector finance	3,380	27.5	10,616	38.6
Foreign capital	2,496	20.3	6,669	24.2
Total	12,285	100.0	27,521	100.0

Source: Table 6-7; TMP, Table 15-2; Mid-Term Review of the TMP, Table 8-1.

managed to settle only 40,000 families when, as its Director-General admitted in 1974, 10,000 families were being made landless *annually*.[17]

Under the Third Malaysia Plan, public development expenditure in the rural sector increased yet again (Table 7.1). More government agencies were set up to give Malays preference and financial assistance in government contracts, licences, grants, land, and other provisions. In all three Malaysia Plans up to 1980, about a quarter of the total development expenditure by the public sector was in the rural sector alone, not counting infrastructural expenditure.

The Malay state bourgeoisie is thoroughly committed to a policy of co-existence with private capitalism.[18] They are also usually the first to take advantage of the new business opportunities that they themselves have created. In the state propaganda, 'Malays'—from the aristocratic tycoon to the poor peasant in the *kampong*—are encouraged to venture into business in order to 'catch up with the Chinese'. Various incentives are proffered by the state, such as land, licence and financial grants, besides the stipulation of 30 per cent Malay participation in new enterprises.[19] A sizeable section of the Malay petty bourgeoisie no doubt also benefit from these government hand-outs. But besides their corporate interests, the Malay state bourgeoisie also profit from the large salaries and other 'perks' that go with being in command of the state apparatus. The opportunities for gain from bribery and corruption in the hugely enlarged bureaucracy are notoriously widespread.[20]

The increasingly large role played by the state in the peasant sector represents, above all, an attempt by the Malay state bourgeoisie to have an economic base also in the rural sector. In this effort, they have tried to cut into the economic activities of the lower strata of the non-Malay commercial class, who, in official propaganda are usually portrayed as the main exploiters of the Malay peasantry. This is especially evident in the co-operative movement as well as in the other activities of the government agencies such as *Perbadanan Nasional* (National Corporation) (PERNAS) involving credit, marketing, transport, consumer products, the like. The latter has even intruded on the China trade, the traditional preserve of the Chinese commercial bourgeoisie.[21] But as we saw in the last chapter, the poor peasantry have scarcely benefited from the increased government expenditure and activities in the agricultural sector, which, instead, have largely benefited the rich farmers, the main base of the Malay state bourgeoisie. Nevertheless, the survival of the rich commercial non-Malay bourgeoisie shows that they have managed to undercut the government agencies (which suffer gross bureaucratic inefficiencies), or else have come to an accommodation with the state bourgeoisie.

Table 7.3
Ownership and Control of Corporate Sector, 1971-80 (M$ million)

	1971	(%)	1980	(%)
Malaysian residents	2,512.8	38.3	13,817.8	52.5
Malay individuals and				
trust agencies	279.6	4.3	3,273.7	12.4
Malay individuals	168.7	2.6	1,128.9	4.3
Malay trust agencies	110.9	1.7	2,144.8	8.1
Other Malaysians	2,233.2	34.0	10,544.1	40.1
Foreign residents	4,051.3	61.7	12,505.2	47.5
Share in Malaysian				
companies	2,159.3	32.9	7,128.0	27.1
Net assets of local branch	1,892.0	28.8	5,377.2	20.4
Total	*6,564.1*		*26,323.0*	

Source: *FEER*, 10 April 1981, p.77.

Amanah Rakyat—Council of the People's Trust (MARA); Urban Development Authority (UDA); *Lembaga Padi Negara* (National Padi Authority) (LPN); and the State Economic Development Corporations (SEDCs). PERNAS is by far the most dynamic, with investments in almost every aspect of the industrial and commercial sectors, both in the urban and rural sectors. To date, *bumiputra* ownership of the corporate sector is still running short of the 30 per cent target by 1990, but the Fourth Malaysia Plan is aimed at a massive acquisition of shares by the state-funded trust agencies for *bumiputras*. No less than 35 per cent of new capital will be acquired by the state agencies between 1981 and 1985.[23] The expansion of state capital since 1971, represented by the growth of the share of ownership of the corporate sector by the *bumiputra* trust agencies, is illustrated in Table 7.3.

Foreign Capital and the Dependent Bourgeoisie

Throughout the class struggles of the post-Independence period, the state has played a central role in trying to maintain cohesion by espousing 'National Unity'. The ruling class has thus identified what objectively are its own interests (i.e. the New Economic Policy) as the interests of the whole nation. The communalist policies are propagated as being in the interest of national unity and enshrined in the *Rukun Negara* (National Ideology). Additionally, the state has been the indispensable instrument in the pursuit of the interests of the Malay bourgeoisie and the big non-Malay bourgeoisie. We have argued that this Malay capitalist class has emerged out of the reconstituted traditional Malay ruling class (aristocratic landed interests), who, simultaneously, have been in control of the highest echelon of the military-bureaucracy. The pre-1969 'Old Guard' in UMNO are by now all prepared to fall in with the new state power. It is for this reason that the ascendant Malay ruling class has been designated as the 'state bourgeoisie' instead of 'bureaucratic bourgeoisie' opted for by some Malaysian neo-Marxists.[24] The latter have implied that this new Malay bourgeoisie has emerged from the petty bourgeoisie 'in charge' of the state bureaucracy.

But despite the state bourgeoisie's nationalist rhetoric, basically it is a dependent bourgeoisie, for its economic interests are linked to the reproduction of foreign capital. The conditions for economic growth in the national Plans are dependent upon continued private foreign investments. Thus, despite the projected decline in the proportion of foreign shareholding in the Outline Perspective Plan, this does not represent any undue obstacle or antagonism to foreign capital. Significantly, there is to be no overall cut-backs in the ownership of foreign share-capital, as is clear from Table 7.4. This is also a logical progression of the control by finance capital through technological, managerial, and other indirect financial

Table 7.4
Ownership of Share Capital of Limited Companies, Peninsula Malaysia, 1970-90

Ownership	1970 (Actual)		1975 (Estimate)		1980 (Target)		1990 (Target)	
	(M$m)	(%)	(M$m)	(%)	(M$m)	(%)	(M$m)	(%)
Malay individuals	84.4	1.6	227.1	2.3	695.4	3.4	5,914.2	7.4
Malay interests[1]	41.2	0.8	541.0	5.5	2,588.9	12.6	18,095.5	22.6
Malays & Malay interests (Total)	*125.6*	*2.4*	*768.1*	*7.8*	*3,284.3*	*16.0*	*24,009.7*	*30.0*
Other Malaysians[2]	1,826.5	34.3	3,687.3	37.3	8,290.5	40.4	32,012.9	40.0
Foreign	3,377.1	63.3	5,434.7	54.9	8,952.2	43.6	24,009.7	30.0
Total Private Sector[3]	*5,329.2*	*100*	*9,890.1*	*100.0*	*20,527.0*	*100.0*	*80,032.3*	*100.0*

1. Agencies considered to hold shares in trust for Malays, e.g. MARA, PERNAS, Bank Bumiputra, Bank Pembangunan, UDA, and SEDCs.
2. Includes nominee companies, and third-company minority holdings.
3. Excludes government and its agencies, except trust agencies.

Source: *Third Malaysia Plan (1976-80)*; World Bank; K. Young, W.C.F. Bussink, P. Hasan, *Malaysia*, 1980:69.

ties, rather than through the direct ownership of stock to ensure control of the resources and surplus.

Malaysia remains economically dependent on Western imperialism by virtue of capital investments, loans, aid, and financial ties directly controlled by the latter. 'Development' in Malaysia is confined mainly to specialization in raw material supply and ancillary industrial manufacture as part of externally integrated metropolitan industries. This economic domination by Western imperialism is possible only through the political alliance of the metropolitan bourgeoisie and the local ruling class. This is reflected in the foreign policy of the Malaysian State which dovetails with the interests of the Western powers. Malaysia's membership of the regional bloc, ASEAN, a staunch ally of the West, similarly indicates that political alliance. Ultimately, the ruling class in Malaysia can maintain its rule over the masses only with the military assistance of the metropolitan bourgeoisie.

Until the 1960s, Britain was still by far the major foreign investor in the country. Its investments were mainly in plantations and mines, oil, motor assembly plants, printing and publishing, metal and chemical industries, food and beverage production, banking and trade, shipping, insurance and specialist services. Overall British interests in Malaysia and Singapore in the 1960s were valued at £700 million. Out of this, £75 million annually was remitted to Britain as net profit, and a further £35 million as annual profits in invisible earnings from banking, insurance, and other services.[25] British firms controlled 30 per cent of the international trade passing through Malaysia and Singapore, valued at £500 million out of an estimated total trade of £1,600 million. This produced a favourable balance of trade for Britain estimated at £80 million in 1960.[26]

The Lloyds Bank Economic Report of 1971 put the figure for foreign investments in Malaysia at M$5 billion, of which M$3.5 billion were UK-owned. Of the latter, M$1,640 million were in plantations and M$1,095 million in mines.[27] In the plantation sector, the trend has been toward conglomerates of estates as these companies diversify their interests and manage more subsidiaries. These interlinking acquisitions have incorporated elements of the local non-Malay bourgeoisie as well as the Malay state bourgeoisie.

The fundamental point regarding the metropolitan bourgeoisie's hold on the local economy lies in the control of the investments, rather than size of the share-capital itself. This is what lies behind the joint-ventures with foreign capital or putting Malaysians on the boards of companies. The concept of control is, in the last analysis, unquantifiable since decision making by representatives of capital derives from social relations. It has been shown, for example, as little as a 5 per cent stake by a multinational company in a local firm can place it effectively within the former's control.[28]

Another significant feature of foreign ownership and control is the high degree of concentration of the foreign investments. This was noted earlier of the Agency Houses in the plantation sector. In 1973, in mining, London Tin and Charter Consolidated between them owned and controlled over 40 per cent of the tin output in 1973.[29] In this sector especially, noted for its high capital intensity, the reality behind the much trumpeted 'economic nationalism' of the Malaysian state is less radical than it is made out to be.[30] The oil industry (which has financed the Third Malaysia Plan, as well as the current boom) is dominated by the multinational oil companies. That is why the attempt in 1977, the state oil corporation PETRONAS's bid for a bigger share of the profits failed. The indiscriminate exploitation of resources, including timber (especially in East Malaysia), has led not only to despoliation of the environment and pollution but also to lost earnings for the peasantry and fishermen.[31]

In recent years, the manufacturing sector has accounted for an increasing share of the GDP.[32] But characteristic of the industries that have been set up is that they merely complement the worldwide operations of monopoly capital. Malaysia, in common with the other Third World capitalist countries, has been attracting the attention of foreign investors as a source of cheap labour among other advantages for the export-oriented industries. The 1960's strategy of 'import-substituting industrialization' had to be superseded because the local home market had become saturated. Continuing abject poverty of the majority of the masses; population increase; mounting wage costs in the metropolis, all contributed to the new strategy by the metropolitan bourgeoisie. New outlets for employment were sought to absorb the growing mass of landless, a product of the Green Revolution. The World Bank had also emphasized the promotion of export-oriented industrialization as a means of earning foreign exchange.[33]

Private foreign capital thus began to flow into regional manufacture and assembly plants producing consumer or capital goods, in particular textiles, household appliances, vehicles, electronics, watches, and local processing of raw materials. The transfer of deskilled operations to the area was effected. It is more advantageous for Japanese capital, for example, to have export bases in low-wage countries such as Malaysia if its 'cost-competitive' (i.e. labour intensive) industries such as textiles are to survive. This factor is further accentuated by the revaluation of the yen, which makes it more difficult for Japanese manufacturers to sell their goods in foreign markets, and cheaper instead to import the same goods made by their subsidiaries in the Third World. Other factors prompting the 'offshore sourcing' by metropolitan capital include: the high cost of land in the parent country; the prohibitive costs of pollution-curbing measures; as well as the attempt to capture foreign markets by using the Third World base as a subterfuge.[34]

German capital has also been quick to realize the advantages of investing in this part of the world. Siemens in electrical construction and electronics, and Rollei in the photographic industry, are outstanding representatives. In Malaysia, they are exempt from company, and development tax for up to nine years. The hourly wage rate here represents 7 per cent of its equivalent in Germany. Siemen's factory, built in 1974, cost the company only 40-45 per cent of what it would have been if it had been built in Germany.[35]

While British investments remain strong in Malaysia today by virtue of being the old colonial power, in recent years the eclipse of British capital on the world scene has seen the rapid incursion by US, Japanese, and European capital. Thus more than one-third of all capital investments is now American, and Japanese capital is the junior partner to US imperialism, with the former supplying cheap manufactured goods to the area. Correspondingly, the role of military overseer has passed from British to US hands. Since 1966, the latter has been supplying and training the Malaysian military and police forces in repressive operations.

As we saw in Chapter 4, Malaysia is a vital bastion in Western imperialist strategy in the region. The oil boom of the 1970s has brought capital funds into the area at a phenomenal rate. The multinational oil interests were expected to have invested some US$35 billion in the Asia-Pacific region between 1970 to 1980. This is mostly in the Indonesia-Malaysia area, with Singapore as the centre for their financial and transportational dealings.[36] Meanwhile, the 'export-oriented industrialization' strategy has seen the spread of 'Free Trade Zones' (FTZs) throughout the area.[37] Within the perimeter of the zone in the host country, the foreign firms have their own authority. The host country, in turn, has to provide all the necessary infrastructure, services, incentives, as well as local labour power needed to produce the export goods. In addition, such enticements as customs-free privileges, lax capital and income tax, unrestricted repatriation of profits, are provided.

But perhaps the most important condition for foreign capital, that the Malaysian government has guaranteed is the appropriate 'climate for investments'. This includes:[38]

(a) 'healthy and responsible' trade unionism and corresponding labour legislation to ensure this so that wages can be kept attractive to the foreign investor.
(b) fiscal and monetary policies to convince the investor that the government has the correct priorities in his favour.
(c) maintaining currency stability and a large external reserve.
(d) acceptance of obligations of the IMF Agreement, viz. a country may not impose restrictions on payments or transfers on international transactions.

The Government even directly supports foreign investors by offering medium and long-term loans through the government-sponsored

Malaysian Industrial Development Finance Ltd. (MIDF). Easy credit terms are given for factories and sites by the Malaysian Industrial Estates Ltd. as well as the SEDCs. Fiscal incentives to foreign firms include: tariff protection; import duty relief; accelerated depreciation allowances on fixed assets; payroll tax relief; tax holiday up to ten years; and so on.[39]

Since Independence, finance capital has continued its grip on the economy of Malaysia. In 1971, there were 38 commercial banks, 22 of which were foreign, representing British, US, Japanese, German, and other European interests. Their main function has been to service their respective nationals' industries, invest in profitable deposit banking, harness local capital resources, and conduct other international business in the area. In 1969, the share of deposits held by foreign banks amounted to 63.6 per cent.[40] The control of the lucrative international trade finance is also in foreign hands. In 1977, the (British) Chartered Bank was still the largest bank, measured by Malaysian deposits placed with banks.[41] Furthermore, 81 of the 89 insurance companies registered at the end of August 1970 were foreign. Other forms of foreign financial investment include; wholesale trade, shipping, consultancy, audit business, and portfolio investment.

Thus the Malaysia Plans have merely helped to consolidate the hold by the imperialist monopolies over the local production and resources. The Fourth Malaysia Plan is no exception in the dependence on foreign borrowing: 46 per cent of total government borrowing, or M$4.6 billion, came from foreign sources in 1982. The government is also counting on about M$500 million in credits from the World Bank. These loans and investments are to be tied to specific projects and purchases. At the same time, local finance will be forthcoming for use by the monopolies—the government intends to borrow the remaining 54 per cent from domestic sources.[42]

Malaysia is an attractive country for investment by the monopolies. A study by W.B. Reddaway of overseas direct taxes and profitability of British investments in various countries, found that Malaysia ranks third.[43] When post-tax figures are considered, it ranks second only to Germany in terms of profitability. This has been a primary motivating force for such firms as Guinness, British American Tobacco, Dunlop, Bata, Unilever, for example, to continue to invest in Malaysia. The chemical and tyre manufacturing multinational firms have a virtual monopoly over the local and world market. Monopoly rights are frequently granted to foreign companies if a certain product is deemed essential for the country. Thus, for a country that produces the bulk of the world's rubber, an indigenous tyre manufacturing industry has not arisen simply because Michelin and Firestone have already shared out the tyre market among themselves. The local market is too small for a viable tyre industry to develop. The state enterprise, Pernas, may have a stake in Goodyear, but that does not ensure it access to the rest of the world market, because Goodyear's parent company in Luxembourg has different interests from Pernas.[44]

It can be seen that the government's 'development strategy' based on reproduction of metropolitan capital, involves continued exploitation of the Malaysian working class.

Working Class Struggles since Independence

While the number of strikes by workers dropped drastically with the state offensive toward the end of the 1940s, the struggles did not diminish any further since that time. At various times, especially during the 1960s, workers' struggles have been quite intense even though these have not been highlighted in the media. From Table 7.5, it can be seen that the numbers of workers involved reached record proportions.

Table 7.5
Workers' Strikes and Man-days Lost, 1947-77

Year	No. of Strikes	No. of Workers Involved	Man-days Lost
1947	291	69,000	696,000
1950	48	5,000	37,000
1954	78	10,000	51,000
1957	113	14,000	219,000
1958	69	9,500	59,000
1959	39	7,000	38,500
1960	37	4,600	42,000
1961	58	9,045	59,730
1962	95	232,912	458,720
1963	72	17,232	305,168
1964	85	226,427	508,439
1965	46	14,684	152,660
1967	45	9,452	157,980
1968	103[1]	31,062	208,417
1969	49[2]	8,750	76,779
1970	17[3]	1,260	1,867
1971	45[4]	5,311	20,265
1972	66	9,701	33,455
1973	66	14,003	40,866
1974	85	21,830	103,884
1977	40[5]	7,783	73,729

Notes: 1 90 in rubber plantations alone.
2 22 in rubber plantations; 14 in oil palm plantations.
3 12 in planting industry.
4 32 in plantation industry.
5 18 in manufacturing sector.

Source: *Malaysian Yearbook*, various years.

The lull in the number of industrial actions during the 1950s is understandable when one bears in mind the weight of state repression during the Emergency, which included detention, and banishment of militants, in addition to the repressive laws. The Trades Disputes Ordinance (1949), for example, had imposed restrictions on strikes 'likely to affect adversely the public interest'. In 1958, a further 100 trade union officials were detained for 'subversive activities' under the Emergency Regulations.[45] The Emergency gave the colonial Government the opportunity to render (as it had done with the political parties), the erstwhile militant labour movement harmless. The Malayan Trade Union Congress (MTUC) was accordingly set up as the alternative workers' organization in the neo-colony. In the precise words of its Secretary-General:

> The MTUC had, after all, contributed a great deal in countering the communist threat and had brought a large number of unions under its wings, thereby eliminating what could have been a large power base for the communists. Despite a gradual weakening of the communist insurgency there was still a need to counter its subversive activities, and in this respect the Government realized that the MTUC would continue to play a useful role.[46]

But during the economic recessions when labour conditions were at their worst, not even the MTUC, or the government regulations, could stop the workers' actions.

The Trade Union Ordinance of 1959 empowered the Registrar of Trade Unions to register and deregister unions. During the recessions of 1958 and 1959, there was considerable consolidation and reorganization of labour unions. Among these were the formation of a National Union of Telecoms Employees and a National Union of Commercial Workers. During the period of unemployment in 1959, about 50,000 mine and foundry workers were laid off as a result of fragmentation and other causes. In the mining employees unions in particular:

> ...the employers had all along depressed the effectiveness of unions by delaying recognition; refusing to negotiate on certain claims such as wage claims on the pretext that these matters were managerial prerogatives; victimising trade unionists; refusing passage of union vans and vehicles through company property; downgrading active unionists; giving increments to selected workers of the management's choice and dismissing active unionists for the slightest faults.[47]

'Fragmentation' also affected the estates from 1950 onwards. By 1957, more than 52,000 acres had been 'sub-divided' and about 14,000 workers lost their livelihood.

In 1962, while the government proposed amending the Constitution by the introduction of the Trade Union Bill, there were two important strikes for recognition by the Railwaymen's Union and the Cement Workers Union. The police were brutal with the strikers, and union officials were arrested under the Internal

Security Act. Then, in 1965, the government unilaterally pro-mulgated the Essential (Prohibition of Strikes and Certain Pro-scribed Industrial Action) Regulations in the face of Indonesia's 'Confrontation' against the newly-created 'Malaysia'. This piece of legislation also extended to the private sector unions. It was a year in which:

> ...the strike situation was just as bad as in the previous year and the cause of this was the unnecessary delays by employers in dealing with the grievances of workers.[48]

The government's handling of the situation was so bad that at one point a general strike by the government employee unions was im-minent. The Union of Fire Brigade workers gave notice to strike in May 1965. In addition, port and harbour workers, bank employees, teachers, army workers,[49] shoemakers, oil workers, and commer-cial employees, all had grievances against the employers and against the government machinery impeding their progress.

As in the past, because of the stronger labour movement in Singapore double standards were applied by the government as bet-ween that country and the mainland. Thus, while unions could organize on a cross-industry basis in Singapore, they were permitted to organize only along narrow lines within each industry or establishment in the mainland. The government also refused to ac-cept the Postal Arbitration Award or the majority report of its own Commission on the protection of rubber estates against fragmenta-tion. The 1965 Essential Regulations had, furthermore, legislated compulsory arbitration of all industrial disputes.

The Industrial Relations Act of 1967, which replaced the 1965 Regulations, not only consolidated all existing legislation relating to industrial relations, but empowered the Labour Minister to in-tervene in any trade dispute. In the words of the Secretary-General of the MTUC: 'It deprived even the small and ineffective trade unions of whatever virility or strength they might have possessed'.[50] 1968 saw struggles by workers especially in the plantations, due to the large scale retrenchment in the industry as well as in the com-mercial sector: there were 90 strikes in the rubber plantations alone, of which more than 60 per cent involved about 16,500 workers and a loss of 90,000 man-days between April and July, owing to the im-plementation of an award of the industrial court. Two strikes, one in Labis (Johore) lasted 85 days, while the other, in the United Patani Estate (Kedah), lasted nearly 100 days. These alone involved 1,170 workers and a loss of 107,100 man-days.[51]

When the NEP was launched, the labour laws were further tightened in 1969 when the Industrial Relations Act was amended by the Essential (Industrial Relations) Regulations. Whereas hither-to the question of union recognition and dismissals was decided by the Industrial Court, these powers were now transferred to the Labour Minister. Common law rights of management were also delineated on matters affecting promotion, transfer, employment and dismissal of workers, as well as the assignment or allocation of duties. These regulations on rest hours, hours of work, holidays, and other conditions of service were introduced: '...for fuller realisation of the Government's NEP... so as to bring about a manageable and contented labour force which can attract foreign investment.'[52]

Immediately following the draconian labour regulations of 1969 the number of strikes dropped. Once again, however, the recession in 1974 saw industrial action by workers. During the early 1970s, most of the strikes were again in the plantation industry, but unorganized workers also began to account for a growing number of strikes. In 1971, for example, out of a total of 45 strikes involving 5,311 workers and 20,256 lost man-days, 13 were launched by unorganized workers, accounting for 31.4 per cent of the workers involved and 74.5 per cent of lost man-days.[53] This can only reflect on the lack of confidence in the MTUC. But by 1977, the largest number of strikes were occurring in the manufacturing sector. Discontent with the MTUC leadership was becoming quite apparent and vocal by then. The Congress for Industrial Unions (CIU) was inaugurated on 25 September 1977 to cater for the small unions which were 'discontented with the dictatorial manner in which the MTUC was run'.[54]

8. Social Classes and Communalism

The alliance that brought together the local ruling class, including the non-Malay bourgeoisie, is still intact. But even if it were not, any analysis of the Malaysian state that sees the principal contradiction in Malaysian society today as that between 'fractions of the ruling class' (for example, that of the Malaysian neo-Marxists criticized in the Introduction) is seriously mistaken.

This is not to say that the contradictions inherent in the present class rule, through which the various leaders in the *Barisan Nasional* (BN) have to appeal to their respective social bases do not still remain. During the 1970s, the heightened climate of repression which has stifled mass resistance, has tended to amplify the contradictions within each member party of the ruling coalition. Political scientists and neo-Marxists alike have tended to focus on these factional struggles in the UMNO, MCA, and MIC. But it would be turning the Marxist concept of the state on its head if we forget that the starting point of the Marxist analysis of the capitalist state is its relation to the oppressed classes.

In this chapter, we shall examine the Malaysian state vis-à-vis the social classes in the society. Its communalist strategy will be seen to create contradictions within the ruling class even while it is the principal mechanism of class rule, of dividing the masses. In recent years, state repression has increased and more communalist policies have been implemented.

Finally, we shall examine the nature of the Malaysian Government's 'development strategy', the current anti-British stance by the Mahathir regime and the 'Look East' policy, all intended to create the impression of an independent economic nationalism. But the room for manoeuvre by the dependent bourgeoisie in Malaysia is strictly limited by the overall strategy of capital accumulation by the imperialist bourgeoisie in the metropolis, though the interests of the metropolitan bourgeoisie and the local ruling class in Malaysia converge in their joint exploitation of the workers and peasants. Despite the state repression in recent years, the struggles by workers, peasants and their allies (students and intellectuals) in the anti-imperialist, democratic struggle have increased. In this chapter, we shall also acquire some idea of the social conditions of the workers and peasants in the country in the light of the government's plans to 'restructure' Malaysian society.

Contradictions within the Ruling Class

During the 1970s, the state's suppression of the masses' struggles tended to amplify the factional strife within the ruling coalition. In the aftermath of 13 May 1969, the efforts by the main parties in the Alliance (UMNO, MCA and MIC) to reform have been in vain. For most of the period the member parties of the BN were torn by struggles between an older conservative group clinging to the old rules of the power game, and a younger group who wanted to reform those rules to try to regain electoral support amongst each party's social base. But these intra-party struggles were never serious enough to threaten the status quo for, even while the 'Young Turks' have prevailed in each of the parties, the 'Old Guard' have merely retreated to be full-time overseers of their economic empires.

MCA's attempt in the early 1970s to regain their flagging support among the Chinese community included: the 'Chinese Unity Movement' in 1971, which came to an abrupt close when the leadership felt its own position in jeopardy; negotiations for a merger with DAP, was shelved after it was exposed by the press; and in 1973, efforts to merge with SUPP and Gerakan failed when Pekemas was founded.

The resignation by Tan Siew Sin, who represented the old comprador group from the leadership of the MCA, after failing to win the confidence of the party base, led to factional strife between Michael Chen/Lim Keng Yaik and Lee San Choon. The latter, a protégé of the incumbent Tan, won in the end, even though Michael Chen, who represented the reform group of the petty bourgeoisie, was backed by the late Tun Razak. Upon resumption of the leadership, Lee San Choon proceeded to expand and consolidate his party base by embarking on a recruitment drive for new MCA members; the construction of the prestigious MCA headquarters; the setting up of the Multi-Purpose Holdings Bhd, today the second biggest public company; the founding of Tengku Abdul Rahman College to cater for the non-Malay students left out by the *bumiputra* policies; and the formation of the Chinese Cultural Societies to boost the image of the MCA as the 'representative of Chinese interests'.

When the Merdeka University (MU) campaign was revived in 1974,[1] MCA and Gerakan spoke against it in Parliament while in public they had to justify their position to the Chinese community. In an attempt to woo the party base, Michael Chen dissociated himself from Lee San Choon's opposition to MU and set about building his own base through the Youth Unity Movement and his own position as Cabinet Minister for Housing and New Villages.

Through the system of patronage, Chen has managed to accrue support among the sizeable Chinese petty bourgeoisie, workers, and squatters in the New Villages.[2]

The factional squabbles within MCA surfaced again in September 1979 when Chen and his group openly challenged the Lee San Choon leadership by contesting the Party Presidency and other top executive posts. Lee, through some procedural manoeuvres, such as the cancellation of secret balloting, managed to survive the challenge. Another manoeuvre he employed (and a favourite trick among the other parties) was to appoint new executive secretaries for more than 100 MCA divisions throughout the country just ten days before the General Assembly. They provided delegate votes for the Lee bloc, which allowed him to fend off the challenge from Chen.

Throughout the power struggle in 1979, even the Chinese newspapers opined that it had absolutely no relevance to the Chinese people's interest. 1981 saw defections from one party to another between MCA, Gerakan and DAP. Michael Chen led a mass defection from MCA to Gerakan after discovering that his power base in MCA had been eroded. At the same time, there were defections to MCA from Gerakan as well as DAP by MPs who had had enough of the Opposition game. In fact, since the founding of Gerakan in 1968, when it had posed as a multiracial, liberal and reformist party, it has served more as a party of MCA defectors. The founder of the party, Lim Chong Eu, was one-time President of the MCA. Then there was the second wave of defections from MCA led by Lim Keng Yaik in 1972.

To MCA, Gerakan poses a threat to their privileged relationship to UMNO. Gerakan is led by the professional class of the petty bourgeoisie and directs its appeal to the disgruntled non-Malay middle class. The rivalry between the two member parties of the BN even reaches the extent of mutual sabotage at election time. This was seen, for example, in the 1978 General Elections when the Penang MCA put up Independent candidates against Gerakan in the constituencies where the MCA were not allocated seats by the BN to contest. There have been reports, too, of Gerakan and DAP members who have been offered monetary enticements to join MCA.

But the rivalry is not simply between MCA, Gerakan and DAP. The Malay ruling class does not view with pleasure the stronghold of Gerakan's in Penang with its *Chinese* Chief Minister. There are moves by UMNO to erode Gerakan's edge through gerrymandering,[3] and any open conflict between the parties will only fuel the communalist politics. There are already signs of deteriorating relations between the Penang State Government and the Federal Government as the Gerakan State Government tries to implement policies in the Malay constituencies to erode the UMNO power base, as well as move Chinese residents into the Malay areas. A cabinet minister has openly attacked the Penang Development

Corporation for discriminating against Malays and has called for the takeover of the Corporation by the National Housing Board. Now, four months after the April 1982 elections, the squabbles within and among the three main Chinese political parties have erupted again.[4]

The Indian component of the BN, the MIC, has also been wracked by internal dissension. At its general assembly in 1980, riot police stood by amid fears of violence between the two rival factions within the party, one representing the old order, the other for a new deal within the BN. There was trouble again in May 1981 when the MIC called a meeting to discipline one of its vice-presidents, Subramaniam; his supporters turned up to demonstrate against the president Samy Velu. Although each of these altercations has been temporarily patched up, peace in the MIC has become a political joke. Like the MCA, the factional strife has involved constitutional chicanery and procedural methods to prevent the opposing faction from sending its delegates to the assembly. The ruling coalition is concerned for the cohesion of the MIC, for although the Indian population is dispersed among the Malay and Chinese constituencies, MIC votes can decide the fate of UMNO and MCA candidates at election time.

MIC's troubles are mild by comparison with the power struggle in UMNO (the dominant partner of the BN coalition), which has raged ever since the 1969 crisis. The elevation of Hussein Onn to power upon the sudden death of Tun Razak in 1976 did not prevent the emergence of factional interests. In particular, Onn could not prevent the readmission to the party of the former Selangor Chief Minister and UMNO Youth leader, Harun Idris, regarded as the instigator of the 1969 riots, with his base in the Malay petty bourgeoisie and lumpen elements. Then, in June 1976, the UMNO General Assembly elected Syed Jaafar Albar, a supporter of Harun, as UMNO Youth leader over the PM's choice, Mohamed Rahmat. In a dramatic twist to the power struggle in UMNO, the Onn Government brought corruption, forgery and criminal breach of trust charges against Harun in 1976. The latter was convicted in 1978 after a trial that aroused bitterness within the party and alienated the Youth section (Harun's personal power base) from the leadership. It is common knowledge that this move to initiate proceedings against Harun was orchestrated behind the scenes by his political rivals within UMNO intent on preventing the assertion by his faction of Malay 'ultras' in the petty bourgeoisie for swifter and more radical *bumiputra* policies. This would have disturbed the delicate balance of forces within the BN communal formula. But even while Harun was in prison, his supporters continued to nominate him for the party presidency and the UMNO Supreme Council.

The power struggle continued unabated even after the Presidency of the party had been decided upon. Thus, even after Hussein

Onn's 1978 UMNO election victory, the factional strife was persevered over the three Vice-Presidencies since Onn was not expected to stay in office for long owing to ill-health. In 1981, there were party divisions in Penang and Perak; the Chief Minister of Pahang was being forced out; in Sabah, a minister and deputy minister were dismissed by the Chief Minister Harris Salleh for plotting to topple his government; and in Johore, the Chief Minister was charged by several political groups, including the Johore State Sultan, with illegally appropriating state land. These events reflected the class struggle in UMNO within each state.

The first breach in the BN was in 1977, when the riots in Kelantan led to the expulsion of PAS, which controlled the state at the time. The PAS coalition with the BN since 1973 had not been an easy one and the petty bourgeois theocentric party was a perpetual thorn in the side of UMNO because of its uncompromising chauvinistic stand on race and religion. Apart from the ideological aspects, PAS was dissatisfied with the allocation of seats in the federal and state governments. Attempts by PAS to open branches in UMNO areas were blocked. The struggle came to a head in 1977 in Kelantan when PAS state assemblymen demanded the resignation of the Chief Minister, Nasir, a PAS veteran felt to have been compromised by UMNO. After the PAS had dismissed Nasir from the party and pushed through a motion of no confidence in the Chief Minister, riots broke out in the main towns of Kelantan. This led to the imposition of Emergency rule by the Federal Government. PAS subsequently withdrew from the BN and found itself back in the Opposition.

The party still has a firm base in the overwhelmingly Malay states of Kedah, Trengganu, Kelantan and Pahang, and has some support among the Malay peasantry there. In the 1978 elections, the party took 14.9 per cent of the total votes even though it won only five parliamentary seats.

UMNO has had to tread a narrow line between compromising with its non-Malay partners (with whom it has economic and political interests) and simultaneously being as Islamic and chauvinistic as PAS so as not to lose out to that party and the 'ultras' within UMNO itself, which would rend the BN coalition asunder. In the wake of the fervour of Islamic fundamentalism in recent years, the Malay leaders in UMNO have been at pains to warn the Malay masses against the dangers of Muslim extremism[5] while at the same time forced to adopt a 'holier-than-thou' stance by launching a national *dakwah* (missionary) campaign in 1978. A National Council for Islamic Affairs, comprised of representatives from religious affairs departments from all the states, has been created to monitor the activities of the various *dakwah* movements. Kedah and Pahang (both PAS strongholds), however, have consistently refused to co-operate with the Council. The government has also announced that all religious teachers would be thoroughly screened

Table 8.1
State of the Parties in Parliament after the 1978 General Elections in
Peninsula Malaysia

States	Barisan	DAP	PAS	Total
Perlis	2	—	—	2
Kedah	11	—	2	13
Penang	4	4	1	9
Perak	17	4	—	21
Selangor	10	1	—	11
Federal Territory	2	3	—	5
Negri Sembilan	5	1	—	6
Johore	15	1	—	16
Malacca	3	1	—	4
Kelantan	10	—	2	12
Trengganu	7	—	—	7
Pahang	8	—	—	8
Total seats	*94*	*15*	*5*	*114*
Total Votes received	*1,731,939*	*652,700*	*537,251*	*3,141,210*
(%)	*(55.1)*	*(20.8)*	*(17.1)*	*(100)*

Source: Ismail Kassim, 1979:71, Table 5:1.

by the state religious authorities.[6] Among other weapons, the
government can always resort to the Internal Security Act (ISA)
and powers given to the Registrar of Societies to keep Islam within
acceptable bounds.

The State, Social Classes and Communalism

The predominance of the Malay state bourgeoisie should not
distract us from the fact that their alliance with the *non-Malay big
bourgeoisie* is still intact despite the communalist rhetoric. The
upper stratum of the non-Malay bourgeoisie have accommodated
themselves to the new state of affairs, for not even during the 1969
crisis were their interests seriously threatened. The Malay state
bourgeoisie have been their allies since the old Alliance period, except that the former now have new and bigger economic interests in
the capitalist sector. As has been pointed out, the enlarged state
sector has profited the bourgeoisie as a whole, even as the non-
Malay bourgeoisie has had to accept the new balance of forces
dominated by the Malay bourgeoisie in UMNO. In fact now, the
non-Malay bourgeoisie has more opportunities through joint ventures with the state enterprises, as well as foreign capital, in an ever-
widening sphere of economic exploitation.

The state bourgeoisie needs the private investments of the non-
Malay bourgeoisie to fulfil the objectives of the NEP, as the 'investment strike' by private investors over the ICA of 1975 amply

demonstrated. Between 1970 and 1980, private investments, including those in oil, grew at 12 per cent per annum in real terms, from M\$1,490 million to M\$4,635 million, or at current prices, at 21.1 per cent per annum from M\$1,490 million to M\$10,083 million.[7] By 1980, private investments accounted for more than half of total investments. The latest figures on the ownership and control of the corporate sector reveal that the non-Malay share grew from 34 per cent in 1971 to 40 per cent in 1980 (see Table 8.2). The NEP target for the non-Malay share is 40 per cent by 1990. Moreover, the banking capital, in which the non-Malay big bourgeoisie is based, has been indispensable for the expansion of state capital and also for foreign exploitation. The NEP stipulation of 30 per cent *bumiputra* participation in all enterprises further means that the Malay bourgeoisie has a direct stake in the non-Malay investments. The Fourth Malaysia Plan (FMP) has proclaimed that the private sector will now take over the engine of economic growth: private investments will rise by 9 per cent annually while public investment will fall, and will account for 72 per cent of investments during the FMP compared with 63 per cent during the TMP.[8]

Table 8.2
Malaysia: Ownership and Control of the Corporate Sector, 1971-80 (\$ million)

	1971	(%)	1980[1]	(%)	Annual Growth Rate, 1972-80 (%)
Malaysian residents[2]	2,512.8	38.3	13,817.8	52.5	20.9
Bumiputra individuals[3]	168.7	2.6	1,128.9	4.3	23.5
Bumiputra trust agencies[4]	110.9	1.7	2,144.8	8.1	39.0
Non-Malay residents[5]	2,233.2	34.0	10,544.1	40.1	18.8
Foreign residents	4,051.3	61.7	12,505.2	47.5	13.3
Share in local cos.	2,159.3	32.9	7,128.0	27.1	14.2
Net assets of local branches	1,892.0	28.8	5,377.2	20.4	12.3
Total[6]	*6,564.1*	*(100.0)*	*26,323.0*	*(100.0)*	*16.7*

Notes: 1 Estimate.
2 Classified by residential address of shareholders, not by citizenship. Includes foreign citizens residing in Malaysia.
3 Includes institutions channelling funds of individual *bumiputra*, e.g. Lembaga Urusan dan Tabung Haji, Amanah Saham, MARA and co-operatives.
4 E.g. PERNAS, MARA, UDA, SEDCs, Bank Bumiputra, BPMB, FIMA, PNB.
5 Includes shares held by nominee and other companies.

Source: FMP, p.62, Table 3-14.

The MCA's 'investment arm', Multi-Purpose Holdings (MPH), is today Malaysia's second largest public company. It was formed as a response to the 1975 Industrial Co-ordination Act (ICA), which imposed regulations on investments in the manufacturing sector, including equity participation by *bumiputras* and *bumiputra* representation on the payroll. Even enterprises with as few as 25 staff and as little as M$100,000 (US$43,000) capital were to be included in this. As a result of the protest and 'strike' by both local non-Malay and foreign investors, the Act was amended in 1977 and again in 1979. Multi-Purpose was the economic ploy by the Chinese big bourgeoisie in MCA to incorporate the threatened small Chinese businesses under one investment umbrella. This was another method of concentrating and centralizing local funds so that they could expand into new fields of economic activity using modern management techniques. Additionally, the Chinese big bourgeoisie in MCA hoped to draw Chinese support away from the traditional guilds and clan associations, in which the MCA have little support.

Chinese individuals in Malaysia hold the bulk of MPH equity not owned by KSM (Malaysian Multi-Purpose Co-operative Society), an organization linked directly to MCA. Lee San Choon —president of KSM, MCA president and Cabinet Minister of Transport—is MPH's biggest shareholder. The political connections are paralleled by its economic stature. It is the biggest company on the Kuala Lumpur Stock Exchange in terms of paid-up capital, while its main subsidiaries and associates are among Malaysia's biggest companies: Bandar Raya Developments (42 per cent owned by MPH), Dunlop Estates (88 per cent), Magnum Corporation (39 per cent), United Malayan Banking Corporation (UMBC, 41 per cent), Guthrie Bhd (80 per cent).[9] The personal corporate ties of MPH's directors link it to yet another list of the most dynamic companies in the country: Kuala Lumpur-Kepong, Batu Kawan, Highlands and Lowlands, Supreme Corporation, Malayan United Industries, Malayan Banking, to name but a few. In all the corporate acquisitions that Multi-Purpose has been involved in, its connections with the banking capital of the Chinese big bourgeoisie have proved indispensable. The link with *bumiputra* capital is seen in the joint venture with Pegi Malaysia (a publicly traded investment company chaired and mostly owned by Malay politician Ghafar Baba) over the buying of 51 per cent stake in Dunlop Estates Bhd.

The contradictions inherent in the BN noted in the last section constantly threaten to upset the alliance between the Malay state bourgeoisie and the non-Malay big bourgeoisie. For example, in April 1981, the head of the Youth wing of UMNO, Suhaimi Kamaruddin attacked the move by MPH to take a majority stake in UMBC, saying it would 'threaten peace and security' by replacing the *bumiputra* agency, PERNAS (with 30 per cent stake in UMBC) as the major shareholder in the banking corporation. A compromise was eventually reached involving the Prime Minister Mahathir, whereby each would have equal stake (40.68 per cent) and equal representation on the board. Not long after, the UMNO Youth leader again attacked the control of Dunlop Estates Bhd by the Pegi-MPH joint venture. The solution found was to raise the *bumiputra* interest from 37 per cent to 50 per cent.[10]

But in the attempt to establish an economic base for itself, the Malay state bourgeoisie has competed with the *lower strata of the non-Malay commercial bourgeoisie* as well as the *'national' bourgeoisie*, mainly Chinese. This struggle was signalled by the promulgation of the NEP, whose basic premise is communalist, as we have seen. The various aspects of this struggle have focused around the credit and marketing needs of the peasantry. While state subsidies and expenditure in the rural sector are attempts to buy over the Malay peasantry, the state agencies and enterprises simultaneously provide an economic base for the Malay state bourgeoisie.

When the NEP and the ICA were promulgated, these sections of the non-Malay commercial bourgeoisie reacted in various ways, such as economic boycott; bribing government officials, and business manipulation, such as underselling the co-operatives. In this way the well-off sections have survived, but their protests partly contributed to the amendments to the ICA. The poorer sections, who also were active during the anti-colonial struggle, are potential allies of the workers and peasants in the anti-imperialist struggle. They include artisans covering a vast array of trades, retailers, rice merchants, stallholders and hawkers, market gardeners, taxi drivers, workshop maintenance owners, millowners, etc., organized in guilds, trade associations and chambers of commerce. The Chinese Chambers of Commerce have traditionally included the 'national' bourgeoisie as well as professionals, who have been vociferous critics of the status quo in the MCA.[11] The MCA has consistently failed to capture power within the Chambers of Commerce. Throughout the Merdeka University campaign, while the MCA has opposed it, the University's main supporters have been the Chinese commercial bourgeoisie and petty bourgeoisie.

The support for the state bourgeoisie is strongest among the *Malay petty bourgeoisie* in the state bureaucracy. Within the state repressive apparatus, the military and police, there is a preponderance of recruitment of Malays as well as restricted mobility for non-Malay ranks (see Table 8.3). This has served as the ultimate deterrent to any challenge to the status quo, and represents the state's communalist policy at its crudest, as it is intended to demonstrate to the Malay community that political power lies firmly in the hands of 'the Malays'. The highest stratum of the military-bureaucracy is part of the traditional Malay ruling class and they have assumed their position alongside the state bourgeoisie.

The armed forces and police, enlarged during the colonial period, was further expanded during the Emergency in the 1950s. The Chief of Armed Forces Staff, General Tunku Osman Jewa (a relative of the late Premier Tun Razak, and of aristocratic background) was given a seat on the ruling 'National Operations Council' set up after the 1969 riots when Parliament was suspended.

Table 8.3
Ethnic Composition of the Police Service, Division I, West Malaysia (in %)

Year	Malay	Chinese	Indian	Expatriate
1957	26.7	9.0	6.7	67.6
1962	51.1	·29.0	16.7	12.2
1968	45.1	32.0	22.9	—

Source: D.S. Gibbons and Z.H. Ahmad, 'Politics and Selection for the Higher Civil Service in the New States: the Malaysian Example', *Journal of Comparative Administration*, 1971, 3:341.

After 1969, the timetable for expansion of the armed forces was accelerated. Funds were diverted from development projects into defence. The 1980 budget set aside $2.2 billion, or 21 per cent of the operating expenditure for defence.[12] The FMP allocation for defence and internal security is $9.4 billion, or 23.8 per cent of the total.[13] There are also reserve allocations for contingency spending up to $15 billion under the new Plan. The regular army grew from 52,500 in 1978 to 90,000 in 1980. In addition, there are 50,000 reserves in the Territorial Army as well as 58,000 Police Field Force, which were formed during the Emergency as an anti-guerrilla force. The elite Royal Malay Regiment is exclusively Malay; the armed forces senior officers (Division I) corps is 65 per cent Malay, while in the lower ranks, the proportion of Malays is even higher.[14] Above all, the armed forces and police have served the ruling class as a means of absorbing the dispossessed Malay peasantry and urban unemployed Malays, and in this way, buying off these sections of the Malay community as part of the communalist politics at the expense of the other communities.[15]

The Malay petty bourgeoisie have had increasing aspirations, especially since the expanding state sector has provided them not only with opportunities for attractive salaries, corruption, more 'perks', but also scope for private accumulation in the many business opportunities open to *bumiputras*. Through this means, they have constituted the main social base for the Malay state bourgeoisie and they use communalist rhetoric to articulate their demands. At the same time, their increasing aspirations for the quicker implementation of the NEP, and an even greater stake for *bumiputras* in the economy, have to be met or compromised with by the Malay ruling class in order to retain their loyalty. The proportion of Malays in the administrative and managerial occupations has risen from 24 per cent in 1970 to 32 per cent in 1980; while the number of Malays in degree courses at local universities has likewise increased from about 3,084 (40.2 per cent of the total) in 1970 to 19,051 (47.3 per cent) in 1980 (see Tables 8.4 and 8.5).

The Malay state bourgeoisie has, however, come into conflict with a different section of the Malay petty bourgeoisie—mainly school teachers and religious leaders—who tend to originate from rural religious backgrounds. Their increasing numbers are partly the result of the *bumiputra* policies that have increased the educational opportunities for the rural Malays. The opposition to the government by this section of the Malays is to some extent the result of the revulsion at the corruption and profligate lifestyle of the Malay ruling class. They have provided the leadership of the Islamic fundamentalist (*dakwah*) movement, currently a source of concern to the government, as well as of Parti Islam (PAS). In a sense, they are not an altogether new phenomenon since we saw (in chapter three) how the vernacular-educated Malay petty bourgeoisie, who also embodied a religious aspect, had played a crucial role in the rise of Malay nationalism. Since the 1950s, Malay petty bourgeois parties, such as PAS, have enjoyed considerable electoral success in the predominantly Malay peasant areas in the north of the country. The struggle between PAS and UMNO continues in Trengganu, Kelantan, Kedah; the former branding UMNO followers as *kafir* (infidels). There has recently been violence in Trengganu and *imams* with rival political affiliations even lead separate prayer sessions. The government's discriminatory policies in PAS-dominated states are well known. This section of the Malay petty bourgeoisie, who can see through the corrupt practices of the ruling class, may at some stage be won over to the anti-imperialist struggle.

The sections of the *non-Malay petty bourgeoisie* (middle government salariat officers, lower-ranking officers in the armed forces and police, intellectuals and professionals) affected by the discriminatory *bumiputra* policies are disgruntled with the NEP. They have seen their chances of promotion, business opportunities, scholarships and their children's educational facilities curtailed. It has been reported that the implementation of the government policies has been held up, partly because these sections of the civil service have no incentives to work any harder while their prospects for advancement are minimal.[16] It is from among these sections of the non-Malay petty bourgeoisie that the parties such as DAP draw support.

While the NEP has led to the employment of increasingly large numbers of Malays in urban industrial occupations (see Table 8.4), the majority of the *working class* is still non-Malay. While the

Table 8.4
Peninsula Malaysia: Employment by Occupation and Ethnicity, 1970 and 1980

Occupation	Malay		Chinese		Indian		Others		Total	
	1970	1980	1970	1980	1970	1980	1970	1980	1970	1980
Professional & technical	61.2	118.2	48.9	87.1	16.5	26.9	3.1	4.0	129.6	236.2
(%)	(47.2)	(50.0)	(37.7)	(36.9)	(12.7)	(11.4)	(2.4)	(1.7)	(100.0)	(100.0)
Administrative & managerial	5.1	16.2	15.0	29.2	1.7	3.1	1.0	2.7	22.8	51.2
(%)	(22.4)	(31.6)	(65.7)	(57.0)	(7.5)	(6.1)	(4.4)	(5.3)	(100.0)	(100.0)
Clerical	46.8	169.4	71.4	110.8	20.1	21.0	1.8	5.3	140.0	306.5
(%)	(33.4)	(55.3)	(51.0)	(36.2)	(14.3)	(6.9)	(1.3)	(1.7)	(100.0)	(100.0)
Sales	75.4	99.8	204.6	299.0	34.9	32.7	1.2	0.8	316.0	432.3
(%)	(23.9)	(23.1)	(64.7)	(69.2)	(11.0)	(7.6)	(0.4)	(0.2)	(100.0)	(100.0)
Agricultural	938.0	998.9	283.3	289.9	131.5	175.4	11.8	10.6	1,364.5	1,474.8
(%)	(68.7)	(67.7)	(20.8)	(19.7)	(9.6)	(11.9)	(0.9)	(0.7)	(100.0)	(100.0)
Production	112.1	640.6	214.7	601.9	30.8	160.9	0.9	8.7	358.4	1,412.1
(%)	(31.3)	(45.4)	(59.9)	(42.6)	(8.6)	(11.4)	(0.2)	(0.6)	(100.0)	(100.0)
Service	198.2	168.4	196.5	140.1	62.1	40.7	5.5	2.1	462.4	351.3
(%)	(42.9)	(47.9)	(42.5)	(39.9)	(13.4)	(11.6)	(1.2)	(0.6)	(100.0)	(100.0)
Total[1]	*1,436.7*	*2,211.5*	*1,034.3*	*1,558.0*	*297.5*	*460.7*	*25.2*	*34.2*	*2,793.7*	*4,264.4*
(%)	*(51.4)*	*(51.9)*	*(37.0)*	*(36.5)*	*(10.7)*	*(10.8)*	*(0.9)*	*(0.8)*	*(100.0)*	*(100.0)*

Source: *Third Malaysia Plan*, Table 4-15, pp.82-83; *Fourth Malaysia Plan*, Table 9-6, p.175.
Note 1. Totals may not add up due to rounding.

Table 8.5[1]
Malaysia: Enrolment in Tertiary Education by Race and Levels of Education, 1970 and 1980[2]

	1970					1980				
	Bumi-putra	Chinese	Indians	Others	Total	Bumi-putra	Chinese	Indians	Others	Total
Degree courses[3]										
Institiut Teknologi MARA	—	—	—	—	—	719	—	—	—	719
Universiti Malaya	2,843	3,622	525	277	7,267	4,045	3,162	676	162	8,045
Universiti Sains Malaysia	67	126	33	5	231	1,956	1,354	270	17	3,597
Universiti Kebangsaan Malaysia	174	4	1	—	179	4,997	621	180	9	5,807
Universiti Pertanian Malaysia	—	—	—	—	—	1,460	223	88	12	1,783
Universiti Teknologi Malaysia	—	—	—	—	—	680	90	34	9	813
Institutions overseas	—	—	—	—	—	5,194	11,538	2,676	107	19,515
Sub-total	3,084	3,752	559	282	7,677	19,051	16,988	3,924	316	40,279
(%)	40.2	48.9	7.3	3.6	100.0	47.3	42.2	9.7	0.8	100.0
Total	6,106	4,354	600	304	11,364	36,293	34,208	6,771	644	77,916
(%)	53.7	38.3	5.3	2.7	100.0	46.6	43.9	8.7	0.8	100.0

Notes:
1 The breakdown of enrolment of Malaysian students in local and overseas institutions is not available for 1970.
2 This covers students who were attending courses leading to recognised qualifications.
3 Includes enrolment in postgraduate courses.

Source: FMP, p.352, Table 21.3.

workers as a whole have suffered wage-restraining measures and repression, the non-Malay sections of the working class are further, victims of the communalistic state policies embodied in the NEP. The stipulation of 30 per cent quota in *bumiputra* employment in every establishment has seen cases of over-zealous foreign employers, for example, sacking existing non-Malay workers to maintain that quota. Consequently, there have been boycotts by the non-Malays of Malay business premises (hawker stalls, etc.) especially in the capital, which have worsened the communal relations.[17]

These differences among the nationalities within the working class indicate that the state policies are intended to set one section of the working class against another. The NEP *may* have positive consequences for the working-class struggles ahead—exemplified by the MAS airline workers' strike in 1979, in which Malay workers played a prominent role—since it will end the state identification of workers' militancy with 'Chinese Communists'. However, it cannot be assumed that working-class consciousness and solidarity will automatically emerge. The Malaysian state's communalist strategy will undoubtedly (as it already has) evolve new methods of rule, or indeed revert to old methods, to try and buy off the Malay workers.[18]

Identified with the 'economically dominant Chinese', *the poor sections of the non-Malay communities*—workers, petty traders, unemployed, farmers, squatters, fishermen, general labourers—can look to few options to alleviate their abject conditions. They have been left out of the NEP's professed aim of 'restructuring society'. The TMP acknowledged a substantial proportion of the poor, existing in the urban sector. They include the unemployed, hawkers, peddlars, 'New Villagers' (estimated at around one million in the TMP), municipal workers, mine workers, and especially plantation workers. The plight of the Indian estate workers is exacerbated by the diversification into oil palm cultivation and the diminishing acreage of rubber.[19] The incidence of poverty in this sector, according to the TMP, is 40 per cent. Wages and bonuses for rubber and oil palm workers are estimated to average M$10-15 a day respectively, since the NUPW negotiated its last agreement in 1979. General field workers are paid a basic wage plus price bonus of M$4.80 a day, for their bonus is not pegged to the price of the commodities on the world market.[20] The fall in rubber prices since 1981[21] can mean only worse conditions for the plantation workers and smallholders, particularly the non-Malays outside the government-organized schemes who depend on private dealers to buy their output.

All this is in addition to the low wages that the gainfully employed receive in the factories and other establishments, and which form the main attraction for foreign capital investing in the country. It is actually advertised as such in government investment brochures. Wage rates for unskilled industrial workers are advertised at about M$8 per day; semi-skilled workers on the production line at about M$10-12 per day; skilled workers from M$15.20 per day in 1982.[22] The trade union movement, as we saw, has been rendered impotent ever since it was suppressed in the 1940s. Trade union officials today have mostly been co-opted by the state. The current recession and protectionism in the West has hit Malaysia's manufactured exports quite seriously, and this will mean more unemployed workers.[23]

The communalist intent of the NEP is also clear in so far as it cannot benefit the Malay poor peasantry as it claims. At the time of publication of the NEP, government figures on income distribution in the Malay community showed the pattern seen in Table 8.6. Nearly three-quarters of Malay households lived at, or below the poverty line.[24] This indicates the 'enclave development' that has been effected in the neo-colony, despite the rapid growth rate since Independence. It shows that the kind of capitalist industrialization engendered has not been linked to the agricultural base of the country. *The peasantry* still make up the majority in the population, roughly 65 per cent of the total, and according to the Agriculture Census 1977, 89.7 per cent of poor households were in the rural areas; the incidence of rural poverty was 45.7 per cent, while that of the urban 15.4 per cent; Malays still accounted for 75.5 per cent of the total poor households, the majority being employed in agriculture, forestry, hunting and fishing, this sector accounting for 68.8 per cent of the total poor in Peninsula Malaysia.[25]

Table 8.6
Income Distribution of Malay Households, West Malaysia, 1970

Income Range (M$ per month)	Percentage of Malay households
1-199	74.1
200-399	18.3
400-699	5.3
700-1,499	1.9
over 1,500	0.4
Total:	100.0

Source: Mid-Term Review of the SMP.

The 1979 World Bank Research Publication stated that only 39 per cent of rural households and 78 per cent of urban households had electricity, and, notwithstanding the low coverage, rural electrification has received low priority in government planning; only 49 per cent of the rural population (including small urban population) had piped and treated water.[26]

The urban bias in medical health provisions is evident from

Table 8.7
Peninsular Malaysia: Percentage among Poor Households
by Ethnic Origin, 1976

	Total Poor Households ('000)	Percentage of Total Poor (%)	Incidence of Poverty (%)
Malay	519.4	75.5	46.4
Chinese	109.4	15.9	17.4
Indian	53.8	7.8	27.3
Others	5.7	0.8	33.8
Total	*688.3*	*100.0*	*35.1*

Source: FMP, p.46, Table 3-5

the Table 8.8 showing Toddler Mortality Rates (TMR) in various town and country centres. Thus, a child in Kuala Lumpur has an eight-fold better survival expectancy than that of a child in Ulu Kelantan:

Table 8.8
Toddler Mortality Rates by Administrative District, 1969

State	District with Lowest TMR	TMR	District with Highest TMR	TMR
Johore	Batu Pahat	3.25	Kota Tinggi	5.34
Kedah	Kubang Pasu	3.85	Baling (+ Sik)	12.23
Kelantan	Kota Baru	6.29	Ulu Kelantan	17.27
Malacca	Malacca Tengah	3.59	Jasin	4.18
Negri Sembilan	Port Dickson	3.26	Tampin	6.01
Pahang	Kuantan	3.56	K. Lipis (+ Jerantut)	7.23
			P. Pinang	
Penang	Georgetown	2.25	Luar Bandar	5.13
Perak	Kinta (Ipoh)	2.40	Selama	9.32
Perlis		3.43		3.43
Selangor	Kuala Lumpur	2.20	Ulu Selangor	5.63
Trengganu	Marang	6.10	Ulu Trengganu	16.14

Source: *Fijar*, No.2 March 1980, p.11.

In 1973, the neonatal and maternal mortality rates were still relatively high among Malays: 24.5 and 1.61 respectively.[27] The population per physician ratio in 1969 of 4,100, and 43 per cent of the physicians and more than 23 per cent of hospital beds were in the private sector.[28]

The government's development strategy largely accounts for this large proportion of rural poor and the mass exodus from the countryside to the towns. The class structure of rural Malay society and the representation of the landed interests in the state have ensured that technological innovations and subsidies mainly accrue to the rich farmers and landlords. Since colonial days the state has consistently refused to effect land reform, even though inequitable land tenure has been recognized as the crucial inhibiting factor for rural change, and that reform would bring immediate relief to the small farmers.

Thus, instead of focusing on remedying the particular needs of the various poor classes in the country, the state has chosen to blame the plight of the Malay peasantry on 'Chinese dominance of the economy', while foreign capital is presented as the unquestioned necessity for 'development'. At the same time, the state's *bumiputra* policy—involving support and subsidies to the farmers, vast amounts of state expenditure which it can afford while there is ample revenue—is intended to win over the allegiance of the whole Malay community while benefiting the wealthier strata only.

Neo-Colonial Development

The last decade in Malaysia (the 1970s) has been seen as 'boom' years, with annual average GNP growth rate of 7.1 per cent, and manufacturing industry becoming the driving force. The diversification programme has added more commodities to the list of exports, including oil palm, timber and pepper. More recently, what has been billed as a 'power bonanza' has been discovered in Sarawak, Sabah, and off Trengganu.[29] The TMP and the current FMP have been financed with oil revenue, of which Malaysia is a net exporter. However, to note these developments and then hail imperialism as the 'pioneer of capitalism' as some Marxists do,[30] rather than to examine the character of the industrialization engendered in such countries as Malaysia, owes more to Rostow than to Marx.[31] Such Marxists find virtue in the mere fact of capitalist technical progress and the proletarianization process.

Such mechanistic Marxist analyses assume that capitalism would dissolve all the pre-capitalist remnants in Third World countries, such as Malaysia. This is theoretically incorrect and gives support to incorrect political practices. For it is precisely the semi-colonial, semi-feudal characteristics that prevail in many Third World countries which prompted Lenin and Mao to see the necessity for the revolution to pass through a democratic and anti-imperialist stage, especially in the countries where there had been no capitalist agrarian reform.

Our examination of the peasant sector in Malaysia disproves the assumption that capitalism (fostered by imperialism) dissolves all the pre-capitalist forms. For example, the survival of petty commodity production of rubber by the peasantry has proved to be much more profitable than plantation production itself, and monopoly capital would not wish to see the end of this form of exploitation of the Malaysian peasantry.

It is impossible to understand the fundamental changes in the imperialist system—which has seen, for example, the fall in direct foreign investments in Malaysia[32] and the change of emphasis from primary production to manufacturing industry—without seeing the new forms of control through the international financial markets, sub-contracting, technological dependence, managerial and other 'invisible' ties, which siphon off surplus value created by Third World workers. The presence of technology in the Third World country does not itself fundamentally alter this picture as is clear from this candid admission by the Finance Minister of Malaysia:

> Foreign companies are still bogies.... They have not transfered their technology to our people, they have not brought in capital, they are relying on domestic funds and borrowing from banks here, and they have not trained our people. They are still the same.... We need the investments for the markets they provide.... The existing market must be through MNCs because they have tentacles all over the world.[33]

The import of technology, equipment and goods for the Third World capitalist country, as Lipietz has pointed out, signifies no more than 'delivery of commodities' since they cannot serve as fixed capital while they cannot find 'socially formed workers capable of operating them'.[34] The old division of labour thus continues to operate, as Malaysia has to pay with unfinished goods and labour power.

The point has certainly been brought home in the 1980s when Malaysia is facing the recession brought by the Western economies. The 1981 annual report of Bank Negara (the Central Bank) shows rapidly falling revenues in the vital export sector, still dominated by primary commodities; mounting protectionism against manufactured goods in the industrialized countries; a heavy balance-of-payments deficit and shrinking foreign reserves, and growing dependence on commercial loans.[35] Between 1959 and 1975, Malaysia's terms of trade dropped by 49 per cent.[36]

At the time of writing, the Malaysian Government's 'independent stance'—seen in its takeover bids of (mainly primary commodity producing) British companies and its trade embargo of British goods—has captured the international headlines. This has been pointed out as further evidence of the Third World 'national bourgeoisie's' total independence. However, it is the limits placed on the ability of the Third World country's ruling class to pursue its own interests *by* the metropolitan bourgeoisie that is the crucial issue. The hollowness of the populist stance of the Malay state bourgeoisie was witnessed during the 'investment strike' by the foreign and local capitalists against the Government's Industrial Co-ordination Act of 1975, which had attempted to place regulations on investments in order to strengthen the hand of the state bourgeoisie. The latter had to beat a hasty retreat as a result, and the Minister of Trade and Industry (the present 'no-nonsense'

Prime Minister Mahathir) subsequently led a delegation around the Western capitals assuring investors that the Malaysian Government would be 'pragmatic and flexible' in the implementation of the Act.[37] The Act had to be amended in 1977 and again in 1979.

But in pointing out the limits to the independent stance of the local ruling class, we do not opt for the problematic of dependency theory. The inadequacy of the latter in relation to Marxist theory has been amply shown by various writers.[38] Besides their fundamental theoretical (and thus political) inadequacy, their conception of 'underdevelopment' is misconceived. In fact, from an examination of the Foreign Office files in Chapter 5, we saw how British imperialism had recognized the need to initiate 'development' policies in Malaya to meet the exigencies of the time.

Capitalist development in Third World countries has to be seen as part of the overall strategy of capital accumulation in the metropolitan centres. More importantly, the *class* relations between the imperialist ruling class and the local ruling classes in the Third World in this system of accumulation have to be defined. To understand the phenomenon of the 'Newly Industrializing Countries' (NIC) of the Third World today, we need an analysis of the changes in the system of capital accumulation in the post-war decades, its crises and its requirements.[39]

It is in this sense that we say the bourgeoisie in Malaysia is a dependent bourgeoisie. But this is not to say that the local bourgeoisie is reduced to the role of puppets for manipulation by the metropolitan bourgeoisie. In fact, within the framework of the present 'Multilateral Imperialism' under US hegemony, as well as the Malay state bourgeoisie's attempts to create an internal economic base, the latter may (as it has) conflict with a section of the metropolitan bourgeoisie. The weaker section of the Western imperialist bloc in this case is British capital, which also happens to be concentrated in the resources sector, considered to be of 'national interest' and most likely to concern the state capitalist interest. Thus, we have seen the recent takeovers by the Malaysian state agency of British firms, Guthrie Corporation; Barlow Estates; Dunlop Estates; the merging of Malaysian Mining Corporation and Malayan Tin Dredging into the Malaysian Mining Corporation.

But despite the outcry from investors and government circles in Britain over the apparent 'gross acts of economic nationalism', an examination of the recent takeovers will reveal the real nature of the so-called 'backdoor nationalization': the brokers who executed the 'dawn raid' on Guthrie for the Malaysian Government agency, Permodalan Nasional Bhd, were the world-renowned merchant bankers, N.M. Rothschilds and Rowe and Pitman. And, for the benefit of indignant British protectionists, it needs to be pointed out that the latter are none other than the British Queen's own stockbrokers! Also, far from being an instance of backdoor nationalization, the majority holding in Guthrie was obtained at such a high price—901p a share compared with the previous closing price of 662p a share—that London stockbrokers hailed it as a 'fair bid'.[40]

The subsequent reform of the London Stock Exchange Regulations, which has led to the latest trade embargo by the Malaysian Government against British firms investing in Malaysia, further disguises the real nature of the control of resources when it is posed in populist terms of 'Britain Changing the Rules'. The fact is, that the Malaysian government's control over its raw materials still does not alter the rules governing the fixing of the prices of these commodities on the London Commodity Market. Big financial capitalists, like Rothschild, not only control the commodity markets but are the financial managers for the state capitalists in countries such as Malaysia and Singapore today. Posing the question of the control of resources in 'national' terms is merely an obfuscation.

Clearly the interests of the metropolitan bourgeoisie and the local ruling class in Malaysia converge in their joint exploitation of the workers and peasants. Thus, in spite of its apparently antagonistic stance, the Malaysian government is still looking for more foreign investments, even in the mining sector, especially copper and lead in Kelantan, tin in Perak and Selangor. In recent years, the outflow of investible income has continued unabated: the recorded net outflow for 1974 was $600 million and $550 million for 1975.[41] These did not include repatriation of income in the form of royalties, patent fees and other services, for the Deputy Finance Minister revealed that $1,341 million flowed out of the country in 1974 and $1,061 million in 1975 as profits and dividends.[42] This sum of money was equivalent to five times the total education expenditure for 1975.

The repatriation of profits by foreign investors rose to M$1.8 billion in 1980, while net cash outflow in freight and insurance payments rose to nearly M$2 billion in 1981.[43] This outflow of surplus value is likely to retard the 'development' of indigenous capital and its linkages with the local economy. A 1976 study found losses from trade, profit repatriation, shipping and other payments amounted to M$9.4 billion, or 35 per cent of GNP.[44] In recent years, the 'unethical' corporate practices of MNCs in Malaysia have been only too familiar, involving the bribing of corrupt government officials; passing-off second-hand equipment as new; profiting before a project; extortionate charges for capital and technology, and so on.[45] In spite of this, the Malaysian government's investment incentives to foreign capital are among the most attractive (see Appendix).

The recent substantial capital investments by the Malaysian state must be viewed against this background. Above all, even if all the accumulation is made by the state, it is still the bourgeoisie as a whole that profits from its consumption, which is why it is almost impossible to distinguish state capital (or for that matter indigenous 'national capital') from monopoly capital. Ultimately, the 'national bourgeoisie' can best be identified in the context of the (political) national and class struggle against imperialism.

Far from the mechanistic and economistic rendition of Marxist analysis by such as Warren, which sees a progressive role for imperialism's, there is no evidence of dissolution of the natural economy in Malaysia. The marginalized society of *squatters*, the informal sector, the dispossessed peasantry and super-exploited women, these co-exist with the 'progressive' capitalist sector. The TMP estimated some 39,000 squatter families in the Federal Territory alone, or more than a quarter of the total population in the zone. There are also 12-15 per cent of the population living in the New Villages.[46] The government can scarcely cope with the gross housing shortage, nor does it have the will to overcome it while there are economic and political advantages accruing from the existence of this large marginalized sector.

According to the 1977 Treasury Economic Report, even at subsidized rents of M$32 per month, half the squatter families cannot afford to pay the rent; and out of the 31,747 designated low-cost housing that was to be built in the capital in 1977, less than 25 per cent were for squatters. The slums and public low-cost high-rise flats in the city and town centres have reached such a state of dilapidation that even the NST noted:

> The greatest Pekeliling experiment is a low-cost housing flop. Residents cram in sometimes 14 to a small one-room or two-room flat: buildings are potential fire death traps; the old, the sick, the pregnant and even the dead have to take the stairs in the 17-storey blocks.[47]

The 1970 Census noted a total of 2.23 million units of housing needed for the period 1970-90. In the last decade, less than three-quarter million units have been completed, of which only 40,000 were for low-income families. The Malaysian Institute of Architects reckons that housing needs in Malaysia will rise to 1.2 million by 1985.[48] At the same time, in the private sector, housing and property development has been undergoing a boom period with spiralling house prices, as contractors and developers cater for the middle- and higher-income groups where the profits can be made.[49]

Consequently, most of the struggles since the 1960s have centred around squatters, landless and poor peasants 'illegally' opening up state land.[50]

While this informal sector can reproduce labour power at an incomparably lower cost than in the fully developed capitalist conditions in the metropolis, and assure an inexhaustible labour supply, the government's will to cater for the housing needs of the workers, peasants, squatters is absent. At the same time, the influx of rural

Malays into the urban centres is not discouraged while it is a handy means of boosting the Malay electorate in the traditional non-Malay constituencies and so evening up the communal equation. It is well-known, for example, that the Malays on the squatter fringes of the capital city are a vital social base of the former UMNO Youth leader, Harun, and his faction.

It is the labour power, especially of the super-exploited class of *women* that the government advertises in its investment brochures for work in the Free Trade Zones (FTZs) under the auspices of the MNCs. Women are estimated to comprise about one-third of the total labour force in the country, a high percentage of which (56 per cent in 1970) are in the agriculture sector, padi cultivation and rubber production, where the incidence of poverty is highest. Out of this 56 per cent, a third are 'unpaid family workers'. Like women elsewhere, they have to take on the added responsibility as full-time housewives to reproduce the labour power of their husbands and children. In recent years, an increased number of women have been employed in the commercial and industrial sectors, especially in view of rural unemployment and displacement of the peasantry. Women workers are concentrated mainly in the low-wage, labour-intensive industries: food, textiles, and the electronics factories in the FTZs.

This phenomenon of MNC-owned and controlled FTZs in Third World countries began in the 1960s with the crisis in metropolitan capitalism that necessitated a search for cheap wage-zones to increase productivity. Hence the setting up of 'branch circuits' with deskilled labour in many Third World capitalist countries. MNCs found that Malaysian women were the ideal requirement for their Taylorist production units: 'acquiescent and completely involved'. Even the physical requirements for textile and electronic assembly (the two key branches in the externally-integrated circuits of metropolitan capital) were quite similar to women's accustomed domestic work. The frequently-quoted Malaysian investment brochure best sums it up:

> The manual dexterity of the oriental female is famous the world over. Her hands are small and she works fast with extreme care. Who, therefore, could be better qualified by nature and inheritance to contribute to the efficiency of a bench-assembly production line than the oriental girl?[51]

Women make up 90 per cent of the assembly workforce in the electronics factories in Malaysia. Their average daily wage ranges from M$3.00 to M$3.50, or between M$100 to M$200 a month.[52]

Low wages, poor working conditions, overcrowded living quarters, and the problems of adjusting to urban life plus oppressive conditions at the factory, have all added to the frequent outbreaks of 'mass hysteria' which can be seen as a form of workers' struggle—disrupting the work process. The insecurity of factory jobs—the retrenchments in 1974, still loom today[53]—had led to increased prostitution, or similar employment in the mushrooming night clubs, bars and 'massage parlours'.

The 'bloody Taylorism' involved in the MNC-dominated development strategy of the Malaysian government has seen the number of industrial accidents rise by 44 per cent between 1973 and 1977, to 57,911.[54] The *Wall Street Journal* of 9 December 1980 quotes a Health Ministry doctor as saying:

> The government's policy is to attract investors. The first question an investor asks is, 'What regulations do you have, and how well do you enforce them?' If he finds these two areas are weak, he comes in.... You ask [what chemicals the companies use] and they tell you it's a company secret. Although industrial accidents are reported here... occupational diseases aren't. Workers don't connect their illnesses to their jobs, and neither do most doctors. If a man has lead poisoning, the doctor gives him an aspirin.

The remainder of the article contains more such revelations about factory conditions and the admissions by management officials of various companies in the survey by Barry Newman. One company, for example, confirmed that they used asbestos:

> ...but we regret we can't show you round—it's some sort of trade secret. The workers have been offered plastic respirators but have rejected them. The company doesn't provide X-rays to detect asbestos-related disease because X-rays kill tissue. But there is one consolation.... Most of our workers don't stay too long, they move on...[55]

The Mahathir regime's current 'Look East [to Japan and South Korea]' policy merely reflects the predominance of Japanese capital in the Malaysian economy and the obverse of its 'anti-British' stance. Japan has been the country's (as well as the other ASEAN countries') major trading partner for some years now. Mahathir has recently urged the Japanese to shift to Malaysia all their industries found... 'no longer suitable for siting in Japan... so that Japan will continue to reap profits from them instead of having to abandon them altogether'.[56]

Besides helping to ease Japan's own crisis of capital accumulation, environmentalists have bemoaned this open invitation to Japanese capitalists to export their pollution as they have been doing in many Third World countries. Above all, Mahathir's 'Look East' policy goes hand-in-hand with the government's campaign (as in Singapore) to inculcate the so-called 'work ethic of the Japanese'. The British 'irresponsible unions' ('British disease') become the natural negative example to shun. All this merely underlies the state's role in managing labour-power through regulation and repression.

State Repression and Communalism

Even while Malaysia was experiencing a boom during the 1970s, the masses were simultaneously suffering increased state repression. The necessity for dictatorship and Emergency laws under the rule of imperialism and the local ruling class, seems to apply in many Third World countries. As before, the repression by the Malaysian state has included communalist policies to divide the masses.

Since 1969, all manner of repressive laws have been enacted: the Amended Internal Security Act, with powers of arrest and detention without trial; the Printing Press Ordinance (1971), and the Sedition Act effectively muzzles the press, the former requiring every newspaper to obtain an annual licence to publish; an armoury of anti-labour legislation described by the *Times* of London as: 'a bold package of labour legislation that should be a delight to the foreign investor';[57] the Universities and University Colleges Act, which bans any student group from doing anything which can be construed as expressing support, sympathy, or opposition to any political parties or trade unions;[58] the Legal Profession (Amendment) Act, 1977 disqualifies lawyers from membership of the Bar unless he or she has been practising for at least seven years and are not MPs or State Assemblymen or hold office in any organization 'which can be construed as being political in nature, character or effect'. The repressive acts by the Malaysian government over the years have been well documented in the *Report of an Amnesty International Mission to the Federation of Malaysia 18-20 November 1978*, London 1979.

But the most recent additions to the repressive measures are: the Amendments to the 1966 Societies Act and the Amendments to Article 150 of the Malaysian Constitution. The first of the two is intended to be a catch-all to suppress all organizations in the country which have been critical of the government policies. These have included friendship associations, like the Chinese guilds and clan associations, which have been petitioning for the establishment of Merdeka University; dissident Malay religious groups like the *dakway* movement ABIM; and even opposing factions within UMNO. Among its clauses are:

(a) Any society that seeks to influence government policy in any way will be defined as a political society.

(b) The registrar of societies can suspend any non-political society which he deems has become 'political'.

(c) Political societies will not be permitted to have connections with foreign bodies, nor receive funds from abroad.

(d) The registrar is empowered to freeze the assets of any society pending investigation of its affairs, as well as instruct a non-political society to remove any committee member or adviser.

(e) Appeal against the registrar's order can only be made to the Minister of Home Affairs, and not to the courts.

(f) Convicted criminals cannot hold office in any society.[59]

This piece of legislation is intended to define 'political' activity and to single it out for repression. While the Bill was rushed through Parliament, opposition to it, on a scale unprecedented since Independence, was mounted by diverse organizations from the various communities, and spearheaded by the Malay religious organization, ABIM. The Amendments to Article 150 empowers the Cabinet to act through the King in proclaiming a State of Emergency without first seeking Parliament's approval. In this case, even the rule of law has been brazenly contravened, for under Article 150, Clause 8(A), the King's decision cannot be called into question in any court on any grounds.[60]

In addition to the curbs on the labour movement, the government has recently imposed further restrictions on the country's 500,000 unionists. With the Amendments to the Trade Union Ordinance 1959 and the Industrial Relations Act 1967, sweeping powers have been granted to the Minister of Labour and the Registrar of Trade Unions. Among other things, the Amendments seek to:

(a) Reduce the ground on which unions can take strike action; for example, sackings will no longer be a valid reason.
(b) Increase the voting margin for strike action from simple majority to two-thirds majority.
(c) Grant the Minister power to declare trade unions unlawful, and to amend their objectives.
(d) Empower the Registrar to prevent the use of secret ballot. He will also have the power to declare the ballot invalid.
(e) Extend the 3-year restriction on workers in pioneer status industries to organize trade unions.
(f) Bar unionists from holding any political party positions, and prohibit the use of union fund for any 'political purposes'.[61]

In the advent of the FTZs, there is no official minimum wage level in Malaysia, and although there is no specific prohibition, it has proved to be impossible to form unions in pioneer industries. For example, the government has decided that the Electrical Industries Workers' Union is not entitled to organize electronics workers. According to the International Metal Federation:

The government insists that 'there is no similarity between the electrical and the electronics sector' which cannot be explained by the industrial classification adopted by all other nations. This kind of government policy, states the EIWU, is to 'divide and rule' and 'proliferate the trade union scenery with peanut unions'. The government does openly advertise during all trade missions for investment that employees in FTZs are not permitted to join unions.[62]

Perhaps the most repressive of the state's armoury of legislation and the ultimate recourse it has to deal with opposition is the ISA 1960, and the special trial procedures enacted by the Essential (Security Cases)(Amendment) Regulations, 1975 (ESCAR). Since March 1980, the government has sentenced 64 persons to death, of whom 31 have been hanged, for offences under the ISA 1960 and tried under ESCAR. The special procedures under ESCAR contravene the accepted boundaries of what is internationally accepted as the rule of law, and is repugnant to the principles of fundamental liberty:

> 1) A lone judge sits without a jury and is compelled by the Regulations to impose, upon conviction, the maximum sentence, which is death.
> 2) The Public Prosecutor may alter, amend or prefer additional charges before judgement, and is effectively allowed to choose the judge.
> 3) The rules governing the admissibility of evidence are drastically reduced, while those challenging the credibility of Prosecution witnesses by the Defence are more stringent. For example, evidence by witnesses can be heard 'in camera', with their identities hidden; hearsay and second-hand evidence is also admissible.[63]

Lawyers have commented that under the Regulations, 'the accused goes into court with his hands and feet tied while his counsel has his hands tied behind his back'. The International Commission of Jurists has also observed that these Regulations appear 'to go beyond what is strictly required for protecting the "life of the nation" as opposed to the life of the government in power'.[64] For all ESCAR cases, the traditional right of appeal to the Privy Council in London has been abolished. Furthermore, ESCAR 1975 has retroactive effect to Merdeka Day on 31 August 1957. Consequently, all political detainees held before 1975 are liable to be tried under the Regulations. Amnesty International has pointed out that this 'legalises any past abuses of constitutional rights and freedoms'. The full horror of the Regulations was highlighted both domestically and internationally when the mandatory death sentence under the Regulations did not spare even the life of the 14-year old schoolboy in 1977. An international campaign eventually got the boy's sentence commuted to life imprisonment.

Not least, the state repression has included communalist policies aimed at national oppression. In this book, we have traced this strategy back to the colonial days. While non-Malay vernacular education and culture have scarcely received much government assistance, the state seems intent on curbing these even further. A new Cabinet Committee Report has proposed to bring the Chinese Independent Schools under greater control and to give the Registrar of Schools disproportionate powers regarding curriculum and staffing. In early 1982, the government attempted also to encroach upon the Chinese primary school system by introducing teaching aids in Malay to implement its '3Rs' (reading, writing and arithmetic) policy on primary education. However, strong opposition from within the Chinese community seems to have persuaded the government not to overstep the bounds of the 'communal formula'.

We have seen how, over the years, education policy has been

an inseparable part of the state's communalist strategy. While Malay has been recognized by all groups as the national language and main medium of instruction, as embodied in the 1957 Constitution, Article 152 of the Constitution also guarantees the right of education in the respective mother-tongue languages of the peoples of the country. The government has taken to interpret Malay as the *sole* language of the Federation. Likewise, it has consistently rejected the proposal by the Chinese community for the setting up of the 'Merdeka University'. These are instances of national oppression which, as we have tried to show, are ultimately an instrument of class oppression.

Conclusion

The main thesis of this book is that continued repression through communalism is the cardinal mechanism by which the Malaysian ruling class can maintain the loyalty of the Malay masses. Resolving the National Question in Malaysia is the urgent task of the National Democratic Revolution, for the democratic struggle is today the principal component of the anti-imperialist struggle.

Up to the present, this struggle against national oppression has been left mainly to the minority nationalities to demand their just democratic rights. The government's communalist policies in recent years have consisted of the continued curbs on Chinese-medium education (see Chapters 4, 6 and 8) including the suppression of 'Merdeka University' (MU).

As far as MU is concerned, sections of the 'Left' in Malaysia[65] —tending to be the non-Chinese-vernacular-educated—have for various reasons, also argued for its suppression. These reveal both the economism of the Malaysian 'radicals' criticized in the Introduction, and the crass opportunism in conceding the government's position. The common strand in their argument basically accepts the same premises as the government's; namely, that MU will not help 'National Unity'. From the point of view of these 'Leftists', it will not help 'class mixing'.

This, as we have stressed, merely endorses the state's ideological view of national unity, which is intended to fuel Malay chauvinism. The *real basis* of national unity rests fundamentally upon the recognition of the equality of all nationalities. It is a better and firmer basis for mutual understanding between the masses in Malaysia, for anything short of this principle will give succour to the state's ideology of communalism. Since Independence, the lessons of communal relations show that the imposition of one language and one culture on all the nationalities produces only a hollow unity.

The democratic demand for the cultural aspirations of the nationalities is *not* a defence of segregation, for in the process of the struggle for greater (genuine) democracy, the masses will, without doubt, come into contact with those from the other cultures. It is the state, ever since British colonialism, that has consistently placed obstacles in the way of the democratic organization of the Malaysian masses. But it is *not* contradictory to recognize Malay as the lingua franca and at the same time demand the right of education and culture in the vernacular of the various nationalities.

The basic foundations of national unity have to embody a commitment to democracy and policies that will improve the living standards of the workers and peasants and at the same time unite them. These components are inextricably bound and involve the lifting of restrictions on legitimate political organization and activity, as well as the encouragement of social and political institutions that ensure genuine popular control.

Those radicals who see the demand for the democratic right to the pursuit of the nationals' cultures only betray their economism. Their adherence to an abstract 'Left Unity' ('...in order not to alienate the Malay progressives') is usually mixed with the illusion that the socialist revolution is the unchanging stage of the class struggle.[66] However, socialism will not be victorious until it introduces complete democracy. The defence and struggle for democracy is so vital for the struggle for socialism because it provides the best conditions for the self-organisation of the oppressed: 'The proletariat cannot perform the socialist revolution unless it prepares for it by the struggle for democracy.'[67]

The National Question and the defence of the democratic rights of the nationalities is one that has to be taken up by ALL progressives, whether non-Malay or Malay. Defending the democratic rights of the non-Malay masses will, in the long run, benefit the Malay masses as well, as the struggle for greater democracy goes on. The struggle for the unity of the masses on a basis of equality involves the Malay masses' rejection of the neo-colonial state. It strikes at the very basis of that state—the division of the masses through communalism.

Notes

Introduction

1. For example, J.S. Furnivall, 'Colonial policy and practice', NY 1948; C.H. Enloe, 'Issues and integration in Malaya', *Pacific Affairs*, XLI No. 3 1968; K.J. Ratnam, 1963; R.K. Vasil, 1971; Von Vorys, 1975.
2. K.J. Ratnam, 1963:1.
3. After the 1969 riots, a Department of Race Relations was in fact set up in Universiti Sains, Penang.
4. Von Vorys, 1975:14.
5. *Ibid*. p.162.
6. See M.R. Stenson, 1970; M. Morgan, 1977.
7. B.N. Cham, 1975, 1977; M.R. Stenson, 1976; J.K. Sundaram, (Thesis) 1977; M.H. Lim, 1981.
8. B.N. Cham, 1977:195.
9. M.H. Lim, 1981:211.
10. *Ibid*.
11. *Ibid*.
12. *Ibid*. p.210.
13. *Ibid*. p.225.
14. This is borrowed from I. Shivji, 1976. In this respect, it must be remembered that Shivji was talking about the Tanzanian bureaucratic bourgeoisie's 'progressiveness' mainly owing to the fact that its ideology was such that it put socialism on the agenda in Tanzania. The Malaysian state bourgeoisie makes no pretence to pursue even vaguely socialist policies.
15. V.I. Lenin, 'Critical remarks on the national question', Moscow 1951:17.

Chapter 1

1. Sakai ancestresses were said to have intermarried with Malays in Minangkabau legend. See J.M. Gullick, 1965:74-80.
2. R.O. Winstedt, 'Malaya and its history', *Journal of the Malayan Branch of the Royal Asiatic Society (JMBRAS)*, xiii, 1935.
3. F. Swettenham, 'Annual Report Perak' 1890, quoted in Gullick, *op. cit.* p.30.
4. *Ibid*. p.29.
5. J.M. Gullick, 'Indigenous Political Systems of Western Malaya', London, 1965.
6. See Moshe Yegar, *Islam and Islamic Institutions in British Malaya*, Jerusalem, 1979, p.269.
7. In comparison, the Minangkabau settlements in Negri Sembilan were comparatively recent and some form of centralized government arose only about 1780. By then the district chiefs had come to terms with the Minangkabau immigrants and their distinct class structure and matrilineal arrangement, known as *adat perpateh*.

8. See Gullick, *op. cit.* pp.65-80.
9. H.G.Q. Wales, *JMBRAS* xviii, 1940; R.O. Winstedt, *op. cit.*
10. P. Chandrasekaram, 'Some dominant concepts and dissenting ideas in Malay rule and Malay society from the Malacca Sultanate to the colonial and Merdeka periods', Ph.D. thesis, Singapore University, 1977.
11. V. Purcell, 1967, pp.31-9.
12. Holland lost all her outposts in India and the west coast of Sumatra, in the war with Britain (1780-84).

Chapter 2

1. Something like £4 million worth of tea was sold by the Company each year at prices roughly double those paid in Canton. A.L. Morton, *A People's History of England*, Lawrence and Wishart, 1938:462. By 1740, the East India Company had capital worth £3 million, paying out dividend of 7 per cent. *Ibid.* p.306.
2. V.Purcell, 1948:40.
3. 'The manufacturers had nothing to fear from the import of foreign industrial products since their establishments were technically and economically far superior. On the other hand, however, the price of grain constituted the most important element in the 'price of labour', and this factor was all the more important in determining industrial costs, because the organic composition of capital was still low and the share of living labour in the value of the total product correspondingly high. The openly avowed motive of the English tariff campaign was the cheapening on the one side of raw materials, on the other side, of the price of labour power.' R. Hilferding, 1923:377-8.
4. R.N. Jackson, 1961:21.
5. Guthrie started business in 1821; Syme and Company in 1823; Boustead and Company in 1830.
6. V. Purcell, *op. cit.* p.43.
7. K.G. Tregonning, 1964:81.
8. W.L. Blythe, *Historical sketch of Chinese labour in Malaya*, Singapore, 1953:2.
9. V.I. Lenin, Moscow, 1970:58.
10. See debates in R. Owen and B. Sutcliffe, 1972.
11. In 1872, there were petitions from the Chambers of Commerce of Malacca and Singapore. In 1873, 248 big Chinese merchants in the Straits Settlements did the same. Every capitalist and merchant interest who had risked capital wanted state protection.
12. See glossary of local terms. J.C. Jackson, 1967:17.
13. Yip Yat Hoong, 1969:59.
14. C.N. Parkinson, 1964:99.
15. See M. Amin, 'British intervention and Malay resistance' in M. Caldwell and M. Amin, 1977.
16. C.N. Parkinson, *op. cit.* p.228.
17. See 'The anti-colonial struggle led by Datuk Bahaman' in *Communist Party of Malaya*, 1979.
18. K.G. Tregonning, *op. cit.* p.134.
19. Pattani is currently fighting a secessionist war against the Thai authorities.
20. Clive Kessler, 1978:45-50.
21. *Malaysia, Journal of the British Association of Malaysia*, April 1968:14, quoted in M. Caldwell and M. Amin, *op. cit.* p.66.
22. The most recent being A. Burgess, 'The Pinball Peninsula', *The Guardian* (London), 10 January 1981; 'A kind of failure', BBC2, 15 January 1981.
23. See J. de V. Allen, 'The Kelantan Rising of 1915', *Journal of SE Asian History*, IX, 2, 1968.
24. W. Linehan, 'A history of Pahang', *JMBRAS*, XIV, 1936:167.
25. M. Amin in Caldwell and Amin, *op. cit.* p.67.
26. W.R. Roff, 1974:21.

27. *Ibid*. p.14.
28. Moshe Yegar, 1979:263.
29. *Ibid*. p.264. This was especially so in Johore and Trengganu.
30. Annual Report, Perak, 1900:24.
31. Despatch from High Commissioner to Colonial Office, CO 273/197, 9 December 1898. The FMS, with a population of less than a fifth of Ceylon's had twice as many European officers. Quoted in W.R. Roff, *op. cit*. p.22.
32. *Ibid*. p.23.
33. *Ibid*. p.24.
34. Birch, 'The FMS', quoted in *ibid*. p.25.
35. Annual Report, Perak, 1904, p.11.
36. W.R. Roff, *op. cit*. p.27.
37. Report on the census of the FMS, 1901, London, 1902:28.
38. Federal Council Proceedings, 1936:18.
39. 1931 Census of British Malaya, pp.50, 69.
40. W.R. Roff, *op. cit*. p.111.
41. Annual address of the High Commissioner, Federal Council Proceedings, 1920:65.
42. This process has been accompanied by the state's employment of the most brutal means, whether it was the earlier days of the European peasantry or the later colonial plunder of Africa, Latin America, India and elsewhere.
43. E.g. '...the declared aim of British policy since the beginning of protectorate rule... the protection of Malay lands and the preservation of Malay peasant life.' W.R. Roff, *op. cit*. p.122.
44. See T.G. Lim, 1976.
45. Death rates were high, especially from malaria: in one year alone, 9,000 out of 143,000 labourers died from malaria; the Highlands Para Rubber Ltd lost 20 per cent of its labour force annually in its first years of operation. Ooi Jin Bee, 1963:219.
46. W.R. Roff, *op. cit*. p.25
47. Report of the Commission of Inquiry into the state of labour in the Straits Settlements and Protected Malay States, 1890, Singapore, para. 452.
48. R.H. Goldman, 1975:251.
49. T.G. Lim, 1976:129.
50. *Ibid*. p.134.
51. *Ibid*. p.55.
52. A.O. Vonles, 'The laws of the FMS, 1877-1920', London 1921.
53. T.G. Lim, 1971:154.
54. *Ibid*. p.206.
55. In Kelantan, Clive Kessler found that village land was being amassed by four main categories of Malays: the aristocracy, salaried government servants, merchants and rich peasants. C. Kessler, *op. cit*. p.69. Here is a virtual absence of non-Malay commercial interests. Raymond Firth also noted that by 1940, landlordism in the form of a rentier class in the countryside had increased considerably as a result of colonial land policy. R. Firth, 1966:296.
56. See for example, T.B. Wilson, 1958.
57. T.G. Lim, 1971:209.
58. *Ibid*. pp.59-60.
59. R.H. Goldman, 1974:27.
60. *Ibid*. p.29.
61. *Ibid*. p.23.
62. C. Kessler, 1978:65.
63. C.Y. Lim, 1967:146.
64. F.C. Benham, 'The Rubber Industry', in T.H. Silcock, 1961:284.
65. T.G. Lim, 1971:114.
66. L.A. Mills, *The British in Eastern Asia*, 1942:192. The plantations had expensive overheads, not least, their profits had to be distributed not only among shareholders but also managers, directors, secretaries, etc.
67. C.Y. Lim, 1967:144.

68. E.N. Pickett, 'The rubber age and synthetics', enclosed in Despatch to the Secretary of State, Foreign Office (Public Records Office, FO 371/1280, 1948. The *Financial Times* article compared British methods with those of the Dutch in their Indonesian colonies; the latter were viewed as more competent. Pickett pointed out that the Dutch method was to impose enormous taxes on the native producers who out of 1/- (one shilling) got 2d, while 10d went into the coffers of the Dutch colonial government and was transmitted to Holland.
69. Pickett, *op. cit.*
70. P.T. Bauer, 1948:148.
71. P.K. Voon, 1976:4.
72. J.J. Puthucheary, 1960:8.
73. J.H. Drabble, 1973:36.
74. *Ibid*. p.70.
75. 'Report of the Royal Commission on Labour', Vol. II, British Sessional Papers, 1892, Vol.36, Pt.5, Paper C.6795-XI, p.157, quoted in World Council of Churches (WCC), 1972:5.
76. D.W. Figart, 'The plantation rubber industry in the Middle East', US Department of Commerce, Washington DC 1925, p.174; WCC, 1972, p.6.
77. Weld to Holland, 24 September 1887, CO 273/146; quoted in T.G. Lim, 1977:101.
78. J.N. Parmer, 1957:141.
79. Kernial Singh Sandhu, 'Some preliminary observations of the origins and characteristics of the Indian migration to Malaya', in WCC, *op. cit.* p.7.
80. T.H. Silcock, 1954:14. Between 1932-3, 100 small owners went bankrupt. Caldwell and Amin, 1977:48.
81. Caldwell and Amin, 1977:45.
82. K.S. Sandhu, 'Indians in Malaya, immigration and settlement', quoted in WCC, *op. cit.* p.8.
83. See Shirley Gordon in WCC, *ibid*.
84. K.S. Sandhu, in WCC, *ibid*. p.10.
85. C. Kondapi, 'Indians overseas, 1838-1949', 1951:7; quoted in WCC, *ibid*. p.4.
86. M.R. Stenson, 1970:46.
87. K.S. Sandhu, in WCC, *op. cit.* p.16.
88. C.H. Enloe, 1973:22.
89. C.A. Vlieland, 'The population of the Malay peninsula', quoted in B.N.Cham, 1977:2.
90. *Journal of the Royal Anthropological Society* (JRAS), June 1897:1-18; quoted in P.P. Lee, 1978:89. When the secret societies became an obstacle to the colonial authorities (for example, they controlled labour—e.g. domestic servants), their activities were then limited by the creation of the 'Chinese Protectorate' in 1877. There was a general strike in 1857 organized by the secret societies, because of Police and Municipal Acts to move hawkers and vendors off the street.
91. This explains the radical stances adopted by the Chinese Associations and other organizations, even though these were founded and patronized by the rich community leaders. It must be noted, however, that Chinese from all walks of life—even hawkers and trishaw drivers—quite often donated toward various causes of the community; the most well-known instance of this was the contributions to found Nanyang University.
92. K.G. Tregonning, *op. cit.* p.143.
93. *Monthly Review of Chinese Affairs*, 48, 1934:35; quoted in M.R. Stenson, *op. cit.*p.50.
94. W.R. Roff, *op. cit.* p.54.
95. *Selangor Journal*, Vol.IV, 1895:438; quoted in Caldwell and Amin, 1977:97.
96. S.Husin Ali, 1975:25.
97. For example, the supposed 'secret society riots' in Singapore in 1851, 1854, 1857, 1876. See P.P. Lee, 1978.
98. See M. Mamdani, 1976; Shivji, 1976. This is often compared to the 'Protestant Ethic'.

99. P.P. Lee, *op. cit.* p.25.
100. In 1848, the combined value of gambier and pepper produced in Singapore amounted to about $190,000, while the value of imports and exports was $12 million and $11 million respectively. C.B. Buckley, 'An anecdotal history of Singapore in old times', 1965; quoted in P.P.Lee, *op. cit.*p.81.
101. The Chinese in Thailand up until today are mainly Teochews.
102. See Tan Ee Leong, 'The OCBC', 1953:467-8.
103. H.G. Callis, *Foreign capital in SE Asia*, NY 1942; quoted in V. Purcell, 1948:235.
104. *Ibid.* p.237.
105. FMS, 'Proceedings of the Federal Council', 1923:31.
106. *Ibid.* 1931, B, pp.17-18.
107. S. Arasaratnam, 1970:94.
108. The concession was that 75 per cent of the interest should be paid as a condition of postponement of sale; *ibid.* p.94.
109. Malayan Yearbook 1930; quoted in *ibid.* p.96.
110. By the early 1920s, more than half the junior officers in the government services were Tamils from Ceylon, while as late as 1957, almost all the station-masters and booking clerks in the railways were also Tamils; WCC, *op. cit.* p.12.
111. The first Indian member of the Legislative Council was B.K. Nambyar, a Penang barrister, in 1923. This process was slower in the FMS because of Malay sensitivities to 'the encroachment of non-Malays'. An Indian was appointed to the Federal Council of the FMS in 1928. In 1929, Mr L. Thivy, a planter, got into the Perak State Council. In 1932, Dr S.R. Krishnan was appointed to the Negri Sembilan State Council. See Arasaratnam, *op. cit.* pp.85-6.
112. *Ibid.* p.88. They were more concerned with matters affecting the Indian middle class, such as those concerning retrenchment during the Depression.
113. R.H. Kenion, Federal Council Proceedings 1915:B67; quoted in W.R. Roff *op.cit.* p.136.
114. V. Purcell, *op. cit.* p.222.
115. FMS Resident-General's Report for 1901, 1902:20; quoted in WCC, *op. cit.* p.21.
116. S.M. Ponniah, 'Multi-lingual education: The disinheritance of the Tamil workers' child'; quoted in *ibid.* p.21.
117. *Ibid.* p.22.
118. Discussed in D. Latiff, 'Contradictions in pre-war colonialism, 1930-41', in Caldwell and Amin, *op. cit.*
119. CO 273/188, quoted in Simandjuntak, 1969:9.
120. In 1930, domestic rice production made up only 21 per cent of total consumption. Malayan Statistics, FMS, 1934.
121. D. Latiff in Caldwell and Amin, *op. cit.* p.74.
122. J. de V. Allen, 1967:3.
123. Arasaratnam, *op. cit.* p.89.
124. Report of Brig.-General Sir Samuel Wilson, 1932, Cmd 4276, p.90, and *ibid.* p.96.
125. FMS Proceedings of the Federal Council, 1934:B104.
126. Arasaratnam, *op. cit.* p.86.

Chapter 3

1. M.R. Stenson, 1970:7.
2. 'Night-soil' carriers empty the human excreta from the bucket latrines in the towns. This job is usually done at dusk.
3. S. Arasaratnam, 1970:55.
4. FMS, Proceedings of the Federal Council, 1923, pp.107-10; and *ibid.* 56.
5. Between 1925 to 1940, Chinese tappers were generally paid on average 50-100 per cent more per day than the Indian tappers. See J.N. Parmer, 1957:277.

6. *Monthly Review of Chinese Affairs*, 48, 1934, pp.35-6; quoted in M.R. Stenson, *op. cit.* p.45.
7. S. Arasaratnam, *op. cit.* p.78.
8. Rubber prices rose 250 per cent between 1933 and 1936.
9. G.Z. Hanrahan, 1954:22.
10. K.A.N. Neelakandha Aiyer, *Indian problems in Malaysia*, quoted Arasaratnam, *op. cit.* p.46.
11. R.K. Jain, 'Migrants, proletarians, or Malayans?' p.38.
12. C. Gamba, 1962:14.
13. M.R. Stenson, *op. cit.* p.89.
14. Islam as practised by the Malay masses has always been an admixture of the orthodox faith and Malay *adat* (customs), which includes various superstitious practices.
15. Census of British Malaya, 1921, pp.18, 66.
16. Zainal Abidin Ahmad, 'The poverty of the Malays', *Malay Mail*, 1 December 1923; quoted in W.R. Roff, 1974:151.
17. Ibrahim Yaacob, *Nusa dan bangsa Melayu* (Malay Country and People) Jakarta, 1951, pp.60; quoted in Roff, *op. cit.* p.222.
18. Ibrahim Yaacob, *Sekitar Melayu Merdeka* (Concerning Free Malaya), Jakarta, 1957:24.
19. *Majlis*, 7 August 1939; quoted in Roff, *op. cit.* p.218.
20. Roff, *op. cit.* p.218. Among those known, Roff names a civil servant, a cooperative official, a police special branch official, all Malay.
21. E.S.V. Donnison, 1956:281.
22. V. Purcell, 1948:249 reckons the figure as closer to 10,000 and 40,000 during the first week of the Occupation.
23. See also Chin Kee Onn, 1976.
24. The Malay rulers' collaboration with the Japanese was a sore point in the early post-war relations with the returned British. See pp.76-85.
25. See W.R. Roff, *op. cit.* p.231n.
26. R.K. Jain, 1970:303-4.
27. E.L. Wheelwright, 1965:2.
28. Spencer Chapman, 1949:216.
29. K.O. Chin, *op. cit.* p.15.
30. A.Short, 1975:103.
31. *Ibid.* p.24.
32. Force 136 was sent by the British Military Command to liaise with the resistance.
33. There is speculation that they were betrayed by Lai Teck, the CPM Secretary General at the time, who was later unmasked as a double agent.
34. V. Purcell, *op. cit.* p.264.
35. *The Times* (London), 25 June 1945.
36. Clementi, 'Note on a CO Conference', 10 March 1931, Clementi Papers, File: Malaya 9; quoted in J. de V. Allen, 1970.
37. G. and J. Kolko, *The limits of power*, p.61.
38. Annual Report of the Federation of Malaya, 1948, Introduction.
39. A comparison with the Malayan post-war situation that is perhaps worth studying, is the Greek resistance movement.
40. See Cheah Boon Kheng, 1979; M.R. Stenson, *op. cit.*
41. M.R. Stenson, *op. cit.* p.94.
42. Raymond Firth, quoted in Cheah Boon Kheng, *op. cit.* p.147.
43. The BMA began to be ridiculed by Malayans as the 'Black Market Administration'.
44. Cheah Boon Kheng, *op. cit.* p.147.
45. M.R. Stenson, *op. cit.* p.119.
46. The Pan-Malayan Council of Government Workers, 1947; quoted in M. Morgan, 1977:55.
47. Morgan, *op. cit.*
48. *The Times* (London), 30 January 1946. Soong Kwang was charged with killing

a collaborator during the immediate post-war period. He was twice acquitted until a third court of all-European assessors eventually found him guilty. About 200,000 workers in Malaya and 150,000 in Singapore were on strike. See V. Purcell, *op. cit.* p.272.

49. *Straits Times*, 16 February 1946.
50. M.R. Stenson, *op. cit.* p.104.
51. *British Malaya*, September 1946, p.69; quoted in M. Morgan, in Caldwell and Amin, 1977:170.
52. C. Gamba, *op. cit.* p.38.
53. M.R. Stenson, *op. cit.* p.96.
54. *Ibid.* pp.83-4.
55. Examples were *Shih Tai Jit Pao* and *Pai Ma Tao Pao* in October 1945, charged with having used the phrase 'economic exploitation'. See G.Z. Hanrahan, *op.cit.* pp. 54-5.
56. See V. Woddis, 'The Mask is off' in W. Bowan, *Colonial Trade Unions*. British trade unionists, rabidly anti-working class, were sent over to neutralize the threat to British imperialism. One of the most notorious was John Brazier.
57. Most of the planters and European commercial interests only started returning to Malaya in 1947 owing to internment or departure during the war.
58. Bearing in mind the patronizing attitude of the British for the Malay rulers, it cannot be ruled out that just after the war (but certainly before the strong protest by the rulers), the British intended to teach them a lesson. This is the view also of J. de V. Allen, *op. cit.*
59. There was a meeting in Taiping on 12 August 1945 between Ibrahim Yaacob, Burhanuddin, and Sukarno and Hatta.
60. Memo of the Malay Students Society in Great Britain, 25 April 1944; quoted in J. de V. Allen, *op. cit.*
61. *Ibid.* p.7.
62. K.H. Khong, quoting N. Sopiee, 1974:19. (Thesis, 1975).
63. Private letters of J.M. Gullick, 5 September 1964; quoted in J. de V. Allen, *op.cit.* p.12.
64. See 'Malayan Union and Singapore: Statement of policy on the future Constitution', 24 January 1946, Vol.7, p.3.
65. The Malay rulers made representations in the British courts, press and Parliament. They had allies among the old colonialists, such as Frank Swettenham (*The Times*, London, 29 October 1945.)
66. *Utusan Melayu*, 12 October 1945.
67. J. de V. Allen, *op. cit.* p.34. The Sultan of Johore was a staunch Anglophile and these other Malay leaders tried to revoke his signature from the treaty by securing his abdication in favour of his son.
68. Ishak Tadin, 1960:59.
69. *Utusan Melayu*, 22 December 1945.
70. See letter from Trengganu Malay Union to MacMichael, MU Secretariat File 344/46/S; quoted in K.H. Khong, *op. cit.* p.179.
71. *Ibid.* p.180.
72. These 'Advisory Councils' had been set up by the British to represent the various communities. In fact they were made up of Malay aristocrats, top business representatives of the non-Malay groups, as well as the European interests.
73. BMA Monthly Report, February 1946, Part I, p.3; quoted in K.H. Khong, *op. cit.* p.186.
74. J. de V. Allen, *op. cit.* p.19.
75. *Malayan Tribune*, 30 April 1946.
76. HQ Malaya Command, Intelligence Summary No.7, MU Secretariat File 335/46/S; quoted in K.H. Khong, *op. cit.* p.201.
77. *Malaya Tribune*, 18 April 1946.
78. Ahmad Boestaman was released soon afterwards but detained again from 1948 to 1955. He founded the *Parti Rakyat* in 1955 and became its President. He was elected to the House of Representatives in 1959 as a Socialist Front

member but was detained again by the government in 1963.

79. See K.H. Khong, *op. cit.* pp.191-2.
80. Section 86(2) in MU Sec. File 325/46; and *ibid*. p.195.
81. *The Democrat*, 12 May 1946.
82. J. de V. Allen, *op. cit.* p.42.
83. *Ibid*. p.38.
84. *Straits Times*, 29 March 1946.
85. *Malaya Tribune*, 5 March 1946.
86. Federation of Malaya: Summary of Revised Constitutional Proposals, 1947:3.
87. In the Federal Legislative Council, there was to be 22 Malays, 14 Chinese, five Indians, seven Europeans, one Ceylonese and one Eurasian appointees.
88. *Straits Times*, 8 August 1946.
89. Cheah Boon Kheng, *op cit*. p.80.
90. The Straits Chinese British Association had up to then been very loyal to the British.
91. *Malay Mail*, 23 December 1946.
92. *Malaya Tribune*, 10 February 1947. The Chinese press, *Utusan Melayu*, and *Malaya Tribune* were all sympathetic to the PMCJA.
93. *Warta Negara*, 11 December 1946; *Majlis,* 10 December 1946; quoted in K.H. Khong, *op. cit.* p.244.
94. *Straits Times*, 9 July 1947.
95. *Indian Daily Mail*; quoted in K.H. Khong, *op. cit.* p.238.
96. *Straits Times*, 21 October 1947.
97. *Ibid*.
98. *Ibid*. 23 September 1947.
99. *Ibid*. 17 March 1947.
100. M. Morgan, *op. cit.* p.178.
101. MIC, 'The findings of the board of inquiry into the Kedah incidents', in *Dalley Papers*, Ta Chung Press, KL, 1947.
102. *Financial Times* (London), 25 March 1947; in M.Morgan, *op. cit.* p.179.
103. G. Netto, *Indians in Malaya*, Singapore 1962:78; quoted in M. Morgan, *op. cit.*
104. *Straits Times*, 24 October 1947; and *ibid*. p.181.
105. *Straits Times*, 25 February 1948; and *ibid*. p.182.
106. The CPM leadership had been indecisive over the entire strategy for taking over after the war. The Batu Cave ambush during the war had also created suspicion about agents within the Central Committee itself.
107. *Straits Times*, 17 May 1948.
108. *Ibid*. 2 June 1948.

Chapter 4

1. L.C. Gardner, *Economic aspects of the New Deal Diplomacy*, 1964, Madison, pp.272-91; quoted in D.W. Nabudere, 1980:172.
2. *Ibid*. pp.172-3.
3. A.Creech Jones, 5 April 1948, FO 371/55178/10/48.
4. Minister of State, UK Delegation to the UN, SECRET; 2 April 1949, FO 371/76049/5704.
5. Top Secret: Malcolm MacDonald, Commissioner-General in SE Asia to Rt. Hon. Ernest Bevin, FO Despatch No.16, 23 March 1949, FO 371/1073.
6. *Ibid*.
7. Letter from British Embassy, Washington to SE Asian Department, FO, FO 371/13658, 16 September 1949.
8. Telegram from Sir G.Thompson, Bangkok to FO, FO 371/1017/1949.
9. Benjamin Welles, 'British want US to invest in Asia: Proposal for Point IV Program, specifically in Malaya, may be made at Policy Review', NYT, 1 September 1949, FO 371/1017/1949.
10. From R.H. Scott, SE Asia Department to W. Dening, FO, FO 371/1016/1949.
11. Dr W.J. Jonge, 'SE Asia, Indonesia, and the Entrepreneurs', Amsterdam, 25

January 1949; FO 371/1016/1949.

12. 'Anti-Communist Front in SE Asia', British Embassy Washington, 21 February 1949; SECRET, No.3215; FO 371/1017.

13. Singapore Conference of H.M.Representatives on SE Asian and Far Eastern Affairs, FO 371/1280/1948.

14. Philip Noel Baker, Commonwealth Relations Office to Dr Evatt (Australian Government), FO 371/1280, 1948.

15. J.J. Paskim, CO to W. Dening, FO, FO 371/10140/1949.

16. Telegram, Sir H. Gurney to Secretary of State for Colonies, 6 October 1949, No.1132, FO 371/10140.

17. R.A. Hibbert, FO to O.H. Morris, CO: FO 371/1017/1949.

18. SECRET, Note by CO and FO: 'Attitude toward communism in Malaya and China', FO 371/17639, 24 November 1949.

19. Telegram, Sir H. Gurney to Secretary of State for Colonies, 6 October 1949, *op.cit.*

20. Malcolm MacDonald, Commissioner-General to FO, Despatch No.57, 18 May 1948, FO 371/7558.

21. T.S. Tull, FO, 25 May 1948, *ibid.*

22. P.F. Grey to M. MacDonald, 7 June 1948, FO 371/7558.

23. J.D. Higham, CO to R.H. Scott, FO, 17 October 1949, FO 371/1017.

24. 'On Emergency Regulations directed against Chinese squatters', From Secretary of State, CO to Foreign Secretary, 17 January 1949, FO 371/1011.

25. *Ibid.*

26. See 'Letters to the Editor', in the *Guardian* and the *Times* (London), during the 'My Lai' revelations, by former British servicemen who admitted committing the same atrocities in Malaya during the Emergency. See photograph of British soldier posing with severed head of Malayan on page 13 of *A People's History of Malaya: The New Emergency*, by Asoka Guikon, Bersatu Press, Oldham, 1980. Similar atrocities at Tanjong Malim are mentioned in Caldwell and Amin, 1977:222, 239. Chemical warfare was first perpetrated by the British in Malaya (See *Le Monde Diplomatique*, 1978).

27. Commonwealth Relations Office to Australian Government, FO 371/1280/1948.

28. W.J. Pomeroy, *Guerrilla Warfare and Marxism*, p.75.

29. See J.W. Gould, *The US and Malaysia*, Harvard U.P. Cambridge, Mass, 1969:82.

30. See S.P. Hayes, 1971:140. The Griffin Mission also suggested recruiting US missionaries who had just been kicked out of China to teach in the Malayan Chinese schools so as to subvert the orientation of their curriculum.

31. War Office Report, 'Far East Land Forces, Situation Report No. 65', 8-14 October 1949, Malaya, FO 371/9862/1013/61.

32. Situation in Malaya: Telegram from Chief of Intelligence Staff, Far East to Admiralty, DNI, 11 January 1949. FO 371/1013.

33. A. Short, 1975:208-9.

34. Quoted in B.K. Cheah, 1979:63.

35. The *Times* (London), 20 March 1950.

36. *Straits Times*, 6 May 1950.

37. *Malayan Monitor*, III, 12 December 1950.

38. From Sir H. Gurney to Secretary of State for Colonies, 19 December 1948, FO 371/1583.

39. A. Short, *op. cit.* p.265.

40. *Malayan Monitor*, 12 June 1952.

41. 'Rules of the MCA' (mimeo), Rules 4-7; p.42.

42. See Ishak Tadin, 1960.

43. *Indian Daily Mail*, 20 September 1949; quoted in K.H. Khong, 1975:87.

44. G. Means, 1970:124.

45. M.Osborne, *Region of Revolt: Focus on SE Asia*, Pelican, 1970:97.

46. *Straits Times*, 12 June 1950.

47. *Ibid.* 9 October 1950.

48. Federation of Malaya, Annual Report 1950, p.24.
49. M.V. de Tufo, 'A Report of the 1947 Census of Population'.
50. Federation of Malaya Agreement (Amendment) Ordinance, 1952.
51. V. Purcell, 1954:196.
52. K.J. Ratnam, 1963:92.
53. K.H. Khong, 1975:146.
54. Federal Legislative Council debates, November 1952; cited in K.H. Khong, *op.cit.*
55. Debates 6 and 7, May 1953; and Khong, 1975:146.
56. *Straits Times*, 11 February 1952.
57. *Malayan Monitor*, Vol.6, August 1953; quoted in K.H. Khong, *op. cit.* p.176.
58. *Malay Mail*, 20 March 1953.
59. R.K. Vasil, 1971:76.
60. K.J. Ratnam, *op. cit.* p.186.
61. *Straits Times*, 3 January 1955.
62. *Singapore Standard*, 23 January 1955, cited in G. Means, 1970:159.
63. *Ibid.* p.161.
64. J.M. Gullick, 1969:135.
65. *Malayan Monitor*, 1 January, 1956, quoted in K.H. Khong, *op. cit.* p.186.
66. *Ibid.*
67. *Ibid.*
68. Federation of Malaya Information Services, Bulletin No.6072/56, pp.1-2.
69. Report of the Federation of Malaya, Constitutional Commission, KL, 1957, p.183.
70. *Ibid.*
71. G. Means, *op cit.* p.174.
72. Moshe Yegar, 1979:276.
73. Federation of Malaya Report of the Education Committee, 1956, K.L. Government Press, 1956.
74. R.K. Vasil, *op. cit.* p.232.
75. See for example, G.W. Wang, 1970.
76. Federation of Malaya Report of the Education Review Committee, 1960:29-33.

Chapter 5

1. G.C. Allen and A.G. Donnithorne, 1957:145.
2. J.J. Puthucheary, 1960:160.
3. W.M. Corden, 'The Malayan balance of payments problem', in T.H. Silcock, and F.K. Fisk, (ed.), 1963:126.
4. J.J. Puthucheary, *op. cit.* p.159.
5. 'Draft outline of Note on the Federation of Malaya & Singapore': FO 371/F10510/1103/6131949.
6. Benjamin Welles, 'British want US to invest in Asia: Proposal for Point IV Program, specifically in Malaya may be made at Policy Review', *New York Times*, 1 September 1949 (FO 371/1017/1949).
7. S.P. Hayes, 1971:xi.
8. IBRD (World Bank), 1955:2.
9. E.L. Wheelwright, 1965:2.
10. C. Hirschman, 1971:21.
11. In Singapore, European firms made up only 3 per cent of firms in the late 1950s, but employed 31 per cent of the labour force in manufacturing. See C. Hirschman, *ibid.* p.22; E.L. Wheelwright, *op. cit.* p.6. The pattern was much the same in Malaya.
12. 'Britain's international investment position', Central Office of Information, Pamphlet 98, HMSO 1970.
13. S.P. Hayes, 1971:21.
14. *Ibid.* p.22.
15. Fisk, in E.K. Fisk, and T.H. Silcock, 1963:98.

16. Memo by Mr Ford, enclosing extract from NYT article of 1 September 1949, entitled: 'British want US to invest in Asia', to Mr Dening, FO 371/1017/1949.
17. *Ibid.*
18. 'Economic war potential of British and foreign territories in SE Asia', Far East Defence Secretary, Singapore, 23 December 1948 FO 371/1102/1949.
19. *Ibid.*
20. British Embassy, Washington, to R.H. Scott, FO, 26 October 1949 FO 371/1102/49.
21. 'The first meeting of the Far Eastern (Official) Committee Working Party', F7438/1103/61, FO 371/1103/1949.
22. M. Caldwell and M. Amin, 1977:238; George Lee, 1973:448-9.
23. P.T. Bauer, 1948:38.
24. S. Husin Ali, 1975:78.
25. S. Selvadurai, 1972:46.
26. Ministry of Finance, Economic Report 1974-75, p.97.
27. See Husin Ali, *op. cit.* pp.144-60.
28. The *Guardian*, 10 February 1981: 'Stabilizing middle-class elites in the Third World'.
29. *Ibid.*
30. Robert Ho, 1970:2.
31. Robert Ho, 1968:25; T.B. Wilson, 1955:54.
32. T.B. Wilson, *ibid.*
33. R.D. Hill, 1967:99-116.
34. T.B. Wilson, 1958:83.
35. *Ibid.*
36. Aziz, UA, 1958:23.
37. T.B. Wilson, 1958:97.
38. S. Selvadurai, 1972:28.
39. T.G. Lim *et al*, 1974:45.
40. Robert Ho, 1968:Table 2.
41. Noted by, for example, M.G. Swift in M. Freedman, 1967:251.
42. Example, Husin Ali, 1975; T.B. Wilson, 1958.
43. Husin Ali, 1975:81, Table V.
44. T.B.Wilson, 1958:64-7.
45. Husin Ali, 1972:102.
46. C.Y. Lim, 1967:168.
47. T.B. Wilson, *op. cit.* p.75.
48. *Ibid.*
49. R.D. Hill, 1967:108.
50. *Ibid.* p.109.
51. T.B. Wilson, 1958:32; T.G. Lim, 1974:54.
52. The Rice Production Committee, KL, 1952:46, in T.B. Wilson, 1958:Tables 58-61.
53. R. Firth, 1966:325.
54. Centre for Policy Research Report, quoted in Ho Kwon Ping, 'Victims of the Green Revolution', *Far Eastern Economic Review* (*FEER*), 13 June 1980, p.103.
55. *Ibid.* p.104. There are at present 61,000 families living in the area.
56. *Ibid.* p.105.
57. *Ibid.* p.106.
58. Quoted in U.A. Aziz, 1958:27.
59. T.B. Wilson, 1958:93.
60. IBRD (World Bank), 1980:220-1.
61. Ho Kwon Ping, *FEER*, 13 June 1980, p.104.
62. R. Firth, *op. cit.* p.348.
63. This has been propagated by government sources as much as by social scientists such as U.A. Aziz, 1958:25.
64. T.G. Lim, 1971:238-9.

65. This is the main assumption in M.Mahathir, *The Malay Dilemma* too.
66. T.B. Wilson, 1958:94.
67. S. Selvadurai, 1972:29-30.
68. K. Horii, 1972:59.
69. Just Faarland, 'The Malaysian economy', Development Advisory Service (World Bank) Paper, 1970:ii.
70. IBRD (World Bank), 1980:217.

Chapter 6.

1. R. Clutterbuck, *Riot and Revolution in Singapore and Malaya*, pp.135-6.
2. T.J.S. George, 1973:43.
3. *Ibid*. p.65.
4. *Ibid*. p.64.
5. *Ibid*. p.66.
6. *Ibid*.
7. Caldwell, 1979, (Fuemsso), p.35.
8. *Ibid*.
9. *Ibid*. p.37.
10. *Ibid*.
11. The Malaysia Agreement, London, HMSO, 1963.
12. T.J.S. George, *op. cit*. p.81.
13. *Singapore Times*, 18 August 1965, p.7; 16 September 1965, p.10.
14. Muda I Scheme cost M$228m (US$105m). The Muda region produces about one-half of all the local-grown rice.
15. Guthrie has been since taken over by the Malaysian state enterprise corporation.
16. See K.P. Ho, *FEER*, 13 June 1980, p.104; K. Griffin, 1974.
17. The rice subsidy was M$2 per pikul in 1980, costing M$64m annually; *FEER*, 13 June 1980, p.106.
18. Abdul Rahim Said (thesis), 1974:68. Thus although the period between 1957 to 1969 was characterized by steady economic growth, with GDP increasing from $4,500m in 1957 to $10,708m in 1970, a Malay capitalist class had not emerged. By 1969, the total number of Malay capitalists employing more than ten workers was about 155 only in the whole of West Malaysia. See O. Popenoe, 1970 (thesis). He found that about half of these were former politicians or civil servants. Others were mainly in batik manufacture.
19. *Newsweek*, 5 September 1966, p.43.
20. R.K. Vasil, 1971, p.134.
21. The Treasury Economic Report, 1974.
22. Parti Rakyat Manifesto, R.K. Vasil, *op. cit*. p.179.
23. *Malay Mail*, Kuala Lumpur, 13 April 1969.
24. I. Kassim, 1979:9.
25. For documentary of the 13 May riots, refer to issues of the *FEER* during the time; A.R. Tungku, *May 13: Before and After*, Von Voorys, 1975.
26. See Document 5 in *CPM*, 1979, 'On Racialism'. This fascist threat of communal violence has hung over Malaysian politics much like the 'Orange Order' threat in Northern Ireland.

Chapter 7

1. It included Chief of Armed Forces Staff, General Tunku Osman Jewa, a relative of Tun Razak.
2. Avowed aim of the NEP, SMP, pp.42-5.
3. 'Rukunnegara', Federal Department of Information, Ministry of Information and Culture, Malaysia.
4. Tun Mustapha's cavalierly and dictatorial rule embarrassed the Federal government and he was eventually charged for corruption.
5. *Singapore Herald*, 24 February 1971.
6. A Parti Islam official quoted in M.G.G. Pillai, 'Consensus Time', *FEER*, 15

January 1973.

7. Tan Siew Sin is today one of the main figures in the Malaysian corporate scene, heading such companies as SIME DARBY and a long list of others.

8. J. Funston, 1980:234. Parti Rakyat further improved its showing at a by-election for the Kedah state assembly in April 1975 when its candidate lost by only 136 votes.

9. See I. Kassim, 1979:91.

10. See *FEER*, 15 October 1973.

11. SNAP failed to form a united opposition bloc in 1970 with SUPP and PESAKA. The Malaysian PM had threatened SUPP leaders that should the proposed coalition gain power, the Emergency would not be lifted in Sarawak and there would be no return to Parliamentary democracy there. The BN also bought over a SUPP leader with a Cabinet post in Kuala Lumpur. *FEER*, 16 July 1970.

12. SMP, pp.42-5.

13. There has since been some alterations: the government intends to spread the ownership of corporate wealth to private Malay individuals. All the shares in the profitable corporations—PERNAS, Bank Bumiputra, Malaysia Mining Corporation, etc.—now go into a national unit trust for *bumiputras*. This 'Permodalan Nasional Berhad' (PNB) will be responsible for managing the national unit trust, *Amanah Saham Nasional* (ASN). There will be roughly 50,000 $1 units in ASN, and dividend will be paid at least once a year with a guaranteed minimum payout of 10 per cent per annum plus bonus issue. See *FEER*, 22 August 1980.

14. Second Malaysia Plan, p.7.

15. Besides FELDA, there are Youth Land Schemes; Fringe Alienation and Rehabilitation Schemes; Group Replanting Schemes; Public, Joint Venture and Private estates; etc.

16. See Fisk, in E.K. Fisk and T.H. Silcock, 1963:178.

17. *New Straits Times*, 22 June 1974.

18. This may be contrasted with the ideology of 'socialism' that is espoused by the state bourgeoisie in, for example, Tanzania.

19. This has often been interpreted to cover *all* existing enterprises by over-zealous employers. See Chapter 8, note 17.

20. Even while the Bank Rakyat scandal was still fresh in the news, a bigger scandal was uncovered in 1979, involving RISDA (*FEER*, 24 August 1979). Recently Malaysia was discovered to rank high on an international 'corruption scale' as devised by *Time* magazine (*FEER*, 10 April 1981, p.71). Corruption in high places is common knowledge in Malaysia even though only once in a while a 'big fish' like Harun is brought to light as part of a factional struggle. Last year, there were allegations of corruption in the lands and mines department in Penang, Perak, Selangor, Johore and Sabah involving senior civil servants and top politicians (*FEER*, 26 June 1981).

21. The Malaysian government came to an agreement with the Peoples' Republic of China in 1979, whereby the imports of Chinese produce would be directly handled by PERNAS.

22. F. Halim, 1982:38.

23. *FEER*, 10 April 1981.

24. M.H. Lim, 1980; Sundaram, 1977.

25. I. Buchanan, 1972:93.

26. *Sunday Times* (London), 14 January 1968.

27. *Malaysian Digest*, 17 April 1971.

28. See M.H. Lim, 1977 (thesis).

29. *Ibid.* Table 4.1.

30. Lim has shown how in recent years, London Tin shares have been bought up by Charter Consolidated and Pernas, with considerable amounts being taken up by the latter. However, Pernas does not have the technical nor managerial expertize to run the company, so that it is ultimately controlled by Charter. So in fact, Charter has managed to extend its control over the tin supply without

having to lay out a cent in the takeover bid. Charter is of course the dominant force in the tin mining world.

31. See Consumer Association of Penang, *Kuala Juru*. Also Kor Kok Wah, 'Progress and Pollution', *New Internationalist* No.114, August 1982.
32. The share of manufacturing output in the GDP at factor cost increased from less than 10 per cent in 1960 to 17 per cent in 1970; IBRD, 1980:33.
33. For years, Malaysia has had a consistently strong foreign reserves position, which is attributed to its extremely rich resource endowments. However, this is rapidly changing in the 1980s. See Chapter 8, note 35.
34. The Japanese, for example, use Malaysia and Singapore as export bases for entry into Britain by taking advantage of the latter's preferential treatment for developing countries under the General Preference System of Tariffs.
35. M. Freyssenet, *La Division Capitalist du Travail*, 1977.
36. Singapore International Chamber of Commerce Economic Bulletin March 1970:24.
37. See *AMPO*, 1977; *FEER*, 18 May 1979.
38. FIDA, *Malaysia: Your Profit Centre in Asia*, 1975.
39. Treasury Economic Report, 1979/80, pp.201-10.
40. V. Kanapathy, *Foreign Investments in Malaysia*, 1971:6.
41. *The Times* (London), 15 April 1977, p.5.
42. *FEER*, 20 November 1981. Bank Bumiputra has recently extended a US$700 million loan to the government, the largest ever floated in Asia.
43. W.B. Reddaway, 1968.
44. See *FEER*, 22 August 1980.
45. S.J.H. Zaidi, 1975:95.
46. *Ibid*. p.86.
47. *Ibid*. p.142.
48. *Ibid*. p.195.
49. With the creation of Malaysia in 1963, the British Forces discharged over 3,000 employees and relegated them as personal servants of their soldiers, thus depriving them of their union membership status.
50. Zaidi, 1975:239.
51. 1968 Malaysia Yearbook, p.354.
52. 1969 Malaysia Yearbook, p.383.
53. 1971 Malaysia Yearbook, p.335.
54. 1977 Malaysia Yearbook, p.324.

Chapter 8

1. The MU was first mooted in 1967 after the education minister, Khir Johari had announced that in future only students with the overseas Cambridge School Certificate or its equivalent could go abroad for university education. This in effect barred those in the Chinese-medium schools.
2. The TMP estimated the population of the, mainly Chinese, New Villages at one million. These were the creation of the 'Briggs Plan' of containment of the population which the state had deemed were supporting the guerrillas during the Emergency.
3. At the moment, there are 24 state seats in Penang, 10 of which are in Malay constituencies. If MCA were to bargain for five other seats, MCA-UMNO would be able to capture the Penang state government.
4. See *FEER*, 3 September 1982.
5. In recent years, there have been violent actions by the *dakwahs*, e.g. their attack on a police station in Batu Pahat; the desecration of Hindu temples. See *FEER*, 28 November 1980.
6. *FEER*, 28 November 1980.
7. FMP, p.133.
8. *Ibid*. p.252.
9. See *FEER*, 3 September 1982, pp.93-4.
10. *Ibid*. p.95.

11. See below (p.) for qualification of the class category 'national bourgeoisie'.
12. *Singapore Times*, 3 December 1979.
13. FMP, Table 13-1, p.243.
14. *FEER*, 6 March 1981.
15. The DAP and MCA have called for national service for the entire population regardless of ethnicity, but the government has refused to oblige.
16. See *FEER*, 13 January 1978.
17. For example, in 1978, when there were allegations that Chinese workers had been sacked from the 'Anchor' brewery.
18. The Irish case shows that the solidarity of a working class (in this case) of diverse religious affiliations can be impeded by the state.
19. The TMP estimates the incidence of poverty in the New Villages at 58 per cent.
20. *FEER*, 23 October 1981, p.86.
21. The rubber price for benchmark RSSI grade fell from M$3.12 (US$1.32) per kg. in 1980 to M$2.04 in February 1982 (*FEER*, 5 March 1982, p.58).
22. *FEER*, 13 August 1982, p.80.
23. The sales of Malaysian manufactured exports have slumped by 17.3 per cent in 1982. *FEER*, 6 August 1982.
24. Note that the figures in the Table are for 'households', not individuals. The gravity of poverty is, of course, liable to be statistically adjusted. For example, while we are told that the percentage of poor households declined during the SMP, absolute numbers actually increased. See Ishak Shari, 1977.
25. FMP, pp.43,45.
26. J. Meerman, 1979:pp.181, 197.
27. *Ibid*. p.171.
28. *Ibid*. p.139.
29. The world's largest LNG supply will come on stream at Bintulu in Sarawak in 1983. Mainly financed by foreign capital, most of this power supply will go toward powering Japanese industries and homes. Again in Sarawak, a 5,000 megawatt HEP project is to be harnessed on the Pelangus river. Much of this power bonanza will find its way across the South China Sea to West Malaysia (*FEER*, 22 August 1980). The exploitation of the resources of the peoples of North Kalimantan ('East Malaysia') will also ruin the traditional homes of the Ibans, Kayans, Kenyahs, etc. and will no doubt meet with increasing resistance. Gas, oil, and HEP projects are also about to start in Trengganu.
30. Bill Warren, *Imperialism, Pioneer of Capitalism*.
31. See critique of Warren by Alain Lipietz, 'Towards Global Fordism?' *New Left Review*, 1982.
32. While the proportion of foreign corporate assets has fallen, the value of those assets has risen by more than 200 per cent.
33. *FEER*, 22 August 1980, p.49.
34. A. Lipietz, 1982:38.
35. Total merchandize exports fell by almost one-tenth to M$25.6 billion (US$11 billion) compared to a rise of 17 per cent in 1980. For the first time, unit valuesof all Malaysia's main commodity exports dropped simultaneously, including oil, the nation's top revenue earner for the second year running. Manufacturing exports, after nine years of solid growth sales, have slumped by 17.3 per cent to M$5.05 billion. Import volumes remained almost unchanged from 1980, but prices last year rose by 14 per cent. This resulted in Malaysia's first-ever deficit on merchandize account of M$735 million, and current-account deficit of over M$5.7 billion—equal to 10.2 per cent of GDP—more than 10 times the 1980 deficit. The pressure of having to prop up flagging domestic demand and of meeting the FMP targets has meant major increases in government spending; and, with the short-fall in revenue, the public debt expanded 30.2 per cent to M$30.1 billion by the end of the year; total domestic debt was up 22.4 per cent to M$22.4 billion. Foreign debt has swelled even more dramatically: net borrowings from overseas have grown from M$310 million in 1980 to M$2.9 billion. Two new Eurodollar loans were raised in 1981—US$450 million from a Bank Bumiputra-led syndicate in April and

US$700 million from a 54-bank group in November. Malaysia also drew a no-strings M$510 million on the IMF. Bank Negara's international reserves shrank by M$510 million to M$9.8 billion. (*FEER*, 9 April 1982, pp.59-62). The prospects for the future are expected to be worse. Malaysia is currently raising another $1 billion credit in the Euromarkets, the largest loan yet. (*Financial Times* (London), 10 June 1968.) The government is expected to make an unprecedented review of the FMP to slash public spending.

36. Keith Addison, 'Malaysia has yet to find a suitable economic model', *Asian Business*, May 1982.
37. *New Straits Times*, 24 March 1979.
38. See J. Petras, 1978; G. Kay, 1975.
39. A competent example is the work by A. Lipietz, 1982. Although it is necessarily economistic in terms of what he was trying to achieve, there are pointers to the political tasks facing Third World peoples.
40. *Financial Times* (London), 13 October 1981.
41. Treasury Economic Report 1976/77.
42. See Ishak Shari 1977.
43. Keith Addison, *op. cit.*
44. *Ibid.*
45. For example, the Northrop scandal involving high-ranking personnel in the armed forces in 1977. (*The Times*, London, 15 April 1977).
46. TMP, p.166.
47. *New Straits Times*, 23 November 1980.
48. *Fijar* No.15, November 1981, p.3.
49. Property prices and rent increases increased by 15-50 per cent in 1981. It cost M$150-160,000 to buy a two-storey terrace house in Kuala Lumpur at the beginning of 1981 and M$170-180,000 at the end of that year, and it was expected to rise to M$190,000 in 1982. Monthly rents for the same (unfurnished) terrace house rose to a range of M$400-450 by the end of 1981 (*FEER*, 19 February 1982).
50. For example, Hamid Tuah, the Tasek Utara squatters from the 1960s to 1970s. The actions by squatters continued to make the local news at the turn of the 1980s.
51. Linda Lim, 'Malaysia: The solid state for electronics', in *Women workers in MNCs: The case of the electronics industry in Malaysia and Singapore*; Michigan Occasional Papers, No.IX, Fall 1978:7.
52. *New Straits Times*, 7 July 1981; *S.E. Asia Chronicle*, 'Changing role of S.E. Asian Women', p.10.
53. Thousands were laid off during the recession of 1974. Ordinarily workers are sometimes sacked for the least reason so that the firm does not have to pay increments. Microscope work in the electronics factories also means that the eyes fail after only four to five years. See *S.E. Asia Chronicle, ibid.*
54. *Wall Street Journal*, 9 December 1980.
55. *Ibid.*
56. Quoted by Keith Addison, *op. cit.*
57. *The Times*, 5 August 1968.
58. The UUCA was passed after the strong support by the student movement and academics in Malaysia for the Baling peasants protesting in 1974.
59. See *FEER*, 17 April 1981; 29 May 1981.
60. *Ibid.*
61. *The Star* (Penang), 30 January 1980.
62. The Third IMF Asian Electrical Seminar, June 15-16, 1981, KL: 'Social and Economic conditions in the Asian Electrical Engineering Industry', p.67.
63. *Fijar*, No.17/18, Jan/Feb 1982, p.13.
64. *Ibid.*
65. Among them, Aliran (the reformist movement) has come out openly with their publication, 'MU: The Real Issues', 1979. PSRM is also against the setting up of MU for almost the same reasons. The latter had split from the 'Socialist Front' during the turn of the 1960s because they had disagreements with the 'Labour Party' over opposition to the Government's Education Reports.

Others in the 'Left' who oppose MU include those 'radicals' from mainly English-educated backgrounds criticized above.

66. Likewise, the Ethiopian regime's so-called 'Socialism' is used to justify the suppression of the Eritrean people's right to self-determination.

67. V.I. Lenin, *Collected Works* 23, Progress Publishers, 1964:74.

Bibliography

Official Records: Unpublished

Great Britain (Public Record Office, London):
FO 371/1280: Original correspondence from the Colonial Office (CO) to the Foreign Office (FO), 1948-49.
FO 371/7558: Original correspondence from Governor-General of Malaya to Secretary of State for Colonies, 1948-49.
FO 371/9554: Original correspondence from Commissioner-General, SE Asia to Secretary of State for Colonies, 1948-49.
FO 371/76049: Economic Intelligence Department, FO, 1949.
FO 371/1583: Original correspondence from High-Commissioner, Malaya to Secretary of State for Colonies, 1948-49.
FO 371/F1011: Original correspondence from Secretary of State, CO to Foreign Secretary, 1949.
FO 371/1073: Original correspondence from Commissioner-General in SE Asia to FO, 1949.
FO 371/F13658: Original correspondence from British Embassy, Washington to SE Asia Dept., FO, 1949 (SECRET).
FO 371/1017: Telegrams from British Embassy, Bangkok to FO, 1949.
FO 371/10110: Singapore Conference of HM Representatives on SE Asian and Far Eastern Affairs, 1949.
FO 371/1280: Original correspondence from British Rubber Industry, Malaya to Secretary of State, FO, 1948.
Note by the War Office on Military Situation in Malaya, 1948 (TOP SECRET).
FO 371/1016: Report on the Franco-British conversation on the situation in SE Asia in the Quai d'Orsay, 1948.
FO 371/1102: Economic War Potential of British and Foreign Territories in SE Asia—Original correspondence from Far East Defence Secretary, Singapore to FO, 1948.
FO 371/1013: War Office Reports, F9862, 1948-49.
Telegrams from Chief of Intelligence Staff, Far East to Admiralty, 1949.
FO 371/1103: Report by the Working Party on economic and social development in the Far East and SE Asia, F8882, 1949.
Draft Outline of Note on Federation of Malaya and Singapore, F10510/61, 1949.
FO 371/10345: US Policy toward SE Asia and the Far East, 1949, FO.

Malaysia (National Archives of Malaysia, Petaling Jaya):
Federation of Malaya, Secretariat Files, 1948-57.
British Military Administration Files, 1945-46.

Official Records: Published

Great Britain
House of Commons:
Parliamentary Debates, Selected Volumes, 1946-57.
HMSO (London):
Federation of Malaya, Summary of Revised Constitutional Proposals, Cmd. 7171,1947.
Malayan Union and Singapore, Statement of Policy on Future Constitution, Cmd.6724, 1946.
Labour and Trade Union Organisation in the Federation and Singapore, Colonial No.224, 1948.
Overseas Economic Survey, 1952.
Britain's International Investment Position, 1971.
Income Taxes Outside UK, 1972, 1974.

Malaysia
British Military Administration:
Report on the military government of the Malay Peninsula for the period 12-9-45 to 30-9-45.
Monthly Reports.
Advisory Council Proceedings.
Statement of Policy for the future Constitution of the Malayan Union and Singapore.
Report on a mission to Malaya by Sir Harold MacMichael, October 1945 to January 1946.

Malayan Union:
Report of the Consultative Committee on the Constitutional Proposals, 21 March 1947.
Proceedings of the Advisory Council, 1946-48.
Secretariat Files, 1946-48.
Labour Department Files, 1946-8.
Trade Union Advisers Files, 1946-7.
Annual Reports, 1946, 1947.

Federation of Malaya (KL Govt Press):
Annual Reports, 1948-57.
Report on Employment, Unemployment, and Underemployment, 1962.
Report of the Rice Production Committee, 1953.
Final Report of the Rice Committee, 1956.
Annual Report of the Labour Dept, 1948-60.
Annual Report on Education, 1949-61.
Report of the Education Committee, 1956.
Report of the Education Review Committee, 1960.
Census of 1957. Report no.14 by H. Fell, 1960.
Report on the Subdivision and fragmentation of estates, 1957.
Labour Dept. Files.
Federal Legislative Council Proceedings, 1948-57.
Trade Union Registry, Annual Reports, 1948-57.
Detention and Deportation during the Emergency, No.14, 1953.
Federation of Malaya Constitutional Proposals, 1957.
Dept. of Information: Communist Terrorism in Malaya, 1952.
A general survey of New Villages, by W.C.S. Corry, 1954.
The Squatter problem in the Federation of Malaya. Council Paper no.14, 1950.
Resettlement and the development of New Villages in the Federation of Malaya, 1952. Council Paper no.33, 1952.
1950 Draft Development Plan.
1956 First Five-Year Plan, 1956-60.
1961 Second-Five Year Plan, 1961-65.

Government of Malaysia (KL Govt Press):
  First Malaysia Plan, 1966-70, 1966.
  Second Malaysia Plan, 1971-75, 1971.
  Third Malaysia Plan, 1976-80, 1976.
  Mid-Term Review of the TMP, 1979.
  Mid-Term Review of the SMP, 1973.
  The Path of Violence to Absolute Power.
  The resurgence of armed communism in West Malaysia, 1971.
  Ministry of Finance, Economic Report, selected years.
  FELDA, Annual Report, Selected years.
  FELDA, The Jengka Triangle Report, 1967.
  Ministry of Labour and Manpower, Annual Report, selected years.
  KL Municipality, Report on surveys of squatters on State land and private land, 1970.

Statistical Publications:
  FMS Census of Population 1901, compiled G.T. Hare, KL 1902.
  Census of the FMS 1911, compiled A.M. Pountney, KL 1912.
  Census of British Malaya 1921, compiled J.E. Nathan, London, 1922.
  British Malaya: A Report on the 1931 Census, compiled C.A. Vlieland, London, 1932.
  Malaya: A Report on the 1947 Census of population, by M.V. del Tufo, HMSO, London, 1949.
  1957 Population Census of the Federation of Malaya, Report no.14, KL 1960, by H. Fell.
  Socio-economic sample survey of households, 1967/68, KL 1970, by N.S. Choudry.
  Field count summary, 1970 Population and Housing Census of Malaysia, KL 1970, by R. Chander.
  Farm economic survey of the Muda River Project 1966, Ministry of Agriculture and Cooperatives, 1967.
  Rice statistics for West Malaysia, 1966, Ministry of Agriculture and Cooperatives, 1967.
  1960 Census of Agriculture, Reports 1-18, Ministry of Agriculture.
  Handbook of Labour Statistics, Ministry of Labour and Manpower.
  Handbook of Rubber Statistics.
  Malayan Agricultural Statistics, 1931-39, KL 1940: D.H. Grist.
  Nationality of ownership and nature of constitution of rubber estates in Malaya, KL 1933, by D.H. Grist.

Theses and Academic Exercises: Unpublished

Abdul Rahim Said, Developing indigenous entrepreneurship in West Malaysia, MA Cornell, 1974.
Abraham, C.E.R. Race relations in West Malaysia, with reference to modern political and economic development, D.Phil, 1977, Oxford.
Bamadhaj, H. The impact of the Japanese occupation of Malaya on Malay society and politics, 1941-45, MA University of Auckland, 1975.
Barnard, R. Organisation of production in a Kedah rice growing village, PhD Australian National University, 1970.
Chan Heng Chee, The Malayan Chinese Association, MA Singapore University, 1971.
Chee Peng Lim, Role of small industries in the Malaysian economy, PhD University of Malaya, 1975.
Clark, M.F. The Malayan Alliance and its accommodation of communal pressures, 1952-62, MA University of Malaya, 1964.
Doering, Otto, Malaysian rice policy and Muda Irrigation Project, PhD, Cornell, 1976.

Edwards, C.B. Protection, profits and policy: an analysis of industrialisation in Malaysia, PhD East Anglia, 1975.

Edwards, R.H. Public agricultural finance and technological change, PhD, 1975.

Enloe, C.H. Multi-ethnic politics: The case of Malaysia, PhD University of California, Berkeley, 1967.

Goh Kim Huat, Sino-Malay relations 1945, BA University of Malaya, 1960.

Haron, Ishak Bin, Social class and educational achievement in a plural society: Peninsula Malaysia, PhD Chicago, 1977.

Khong, Kim Hoong, British rule and the struggle for Independence in Malaya, 1945-57, PhD Pittsburgh, 1975.

Lee, E.L.H. Income distribution in a developing economy: Case study of West Malaysia, D.Phil Oxford, 1975.

Leong, Stephen, Sources, agencies, and manifestations of overseas Chinese nationalism in Malaya, 1937-41, PhD University of California, 1976.

Lim Mah Hui, Ownership and control in a dependent economy, PhD Pittsburgh, 1977.

Lindenberg, M. Foreign and domestic investment in the pioneer industry, PhD, University of South Columbia, 1973.

Mamajiwala, R.K. Ownership and control of public limited rubber planting companies incorporated in the Federation of Malaya, 1948-58, MA University of Malaya.

Mayerchak, P.M. An analysis of the distribution of rewards in the Malaysian Alliance coalition, 1959-73, PhD, The American University, 1975.

Milner, A.C. The Malay Raja: A study of Malay political culture in East Sumatra and the Malay peninsula in the early 19th century, PhD Cornell, 1978.

Moore, D.E. The UMNO and the 1959 Elections, PhD, University College, London, 1960.

Munro, A. Race relations in Malaya with reference to the 1969 riots, BA Dissertation, University of Sussex, 1978.

Ng Gek Boo, Growth and Unemployment in West Malaysia in the 1960s, PhD Sheffield, 1976.

Othman, M.A. Ethnic identity in a Malay community in Malaysia, PhD Illinois, 1977.

Popenoe, O. A study of Malay entrepreneurs, PhD London School of Economics, 1970.

Pryor, R.J. Malaysians on the move: A study of internal migration in West Malaysia, PhD University of Malaya, 1972.

Ridzuan, A. Growth, structural change and employment creation in Malayan manufacturing industries, PhD Hull.

Saham, J.B.A. The role of British industrial investment in the development of the Malaysian economy, PhD Hull, 1975.

Shockley, H.A. The reluctant Raj: Britain's security role in Malaysia, 1940-70, PhD The American University, 1973.

Sieh Mei Ling, Structure of ownership and control of manufacturing companies in Malaysia, PhD Sheffield, 1978.

Sim Ah Ba, Decentralisation and performance: A comparative study of Malaysian subsidiaries of different national origins, PhD University of California, 1975.

Sundaram, J.K. Class formation in Malaya: Capital, the state and uneven development, PhD Harvard, 1977.

Tan Tat Wai, Income distribution and determination in West Malaysia, PhD Harvard, 1977.

Teh K.P. Protection, fiscal incentives and industrialisation in Malaysia since 1957, D.Phil Oxford, 1975.

Thillainathan, R. An analysis of the effects of policies for the redistribution of income and wealth in West Malaysia, 1957-75, PhD London School of Economics, 1976.

Ting Chew Peh, The Chinese in Peninsula Malaysia: A study of race relations in a plural society, PhD Warwick, 1977.

Wafa, S.H. Land development strategies in West Malaysia: an empirical study, PhD Stanford, 1972.

Yap Chan Ling, The capitalization of the Fishing industry in the Dindings district of West Malaysia, PhD Hull, 1973.

Yeo Kim Wah, British policy toward the Malays in the FMS, 1920-40, PhD Australian National University, 1972.

Books and Articles

Abu Sharaf, H.K.S. (ed.), *Public Enterprise in Asia: Studies in Coordination and Control,* KL Asian Centre for Development Administration, 1976.

Afifuddin, H.J.O. The social, political and economic framework of Muda rice farmers: A historical perspective, MADA, Alor Setar, 1973.

Agarwal, M.C. Rural cooperative credit: A Malaysian case study, *Kajian Ekonomi Malaya,* 2(2),December 1965.

Alavi, H. The state in post-colonial society, *NLR* no.74, 1972.

Alias Muhammad, The PMIP, *SE Asian Affairs,* 1978.

Allen, G.C. and Donnithorne, A.G. Western enterprise in Indonesia and Malaya, NY 1957, Allen and Unwin.

Allen, J de V, The Malayan Union, Yale 1970.

——The Kelantan Rising of 1915, *Journal of SE Asian History, IX, No.2, 1968.*

Amin, S. Accumulation on a world scale, NY 1974.

AMPO, Free Trade Zones and industrialisation in Asia, Tokyo 1977.

Anand, S. Size distribution of income in Malaysia, WB, 1973.

Apter, D. The politics of modernisation, Chicago 1967.

Arasaratnam, S. Indians in Malaysia and Singapore, KL OUP 1970.

Areas, Imperialist domination of Malaysia, London 1974.

Arles, J.F. Ethnic and socio-economic patterns in Malaysia, *International Labour Review,* Vol.104 No.6 1971.

Asian Development Bank, SE Asia's economy in the Seventies, Hla Myint, 1971.

——Asian agricultural survey 1976: Rural Asia, challenge and opportunity, Manila 1977.

Associated Chinese Chambers of Commerce and Industry, Malaysia's Chinese Business Community's views on the Industrial Co-ordination Act, *Asian Business Quarterly,* Volume 3, No.2, 1979.

Awberry,S.S. and Dalley,F.W. Labour and trade union organisation in the Federation of Malaya and Singapore, KL 1948.

Ayre, P.C.I. (ed.), Finance in developing countries, Frank Cass 1977.

Aziz, U.A. Poverty and rural development in Malaysia, *Kajian Ekonomi Malaysia,* Vol.1, No.1, June 1964.

Aziz, U.A. Land disintegration and land policy, *Malayan Economic Journal,*1958.

——Subdivision of estates in Malaya, 1951-60, 3 Vols.1963, University of Malaya.

——Economic survey of 5 villages in Nyalas, Malacca, Dept. of Economics, UM, KL 1957.

Balibar, E. On the dictatorship of the proletariat. Translated by Grahame Lock, NLB 1976.

Banaji, J. Kautsky's The Agrarian Question, *Economy and Society,* 5(1), 1976.

——Modes of production in a materialist conception of History, CSE, *Capital and Class,* Autumn 1977.

Baran, P. The political economy of growth, MR 1957, NY.

—— & Sweezy, P. Monopoly Capital, 1968, Harmondsworth.

Barber, N. The war of the running dogs, London 1971.

Barlow, C. 'The Natural Rubber Industry', 1978, OUP.

Barnard, R. Role of credit and capital in a Malay rice producing village, *Pacific Viewpoint,* 1973.

Barratt-Brown, M. Economics of Imperialism, Harmondsworth, 1974.

Bauer, P.T. The rubber industry, competition and monopoly, 1948, London.
——Report on a visit to the rubber smallholdings of Malaya, 1946, London 1948.
——The Malayan rubber slump, in T.H.Silcock (1961).
——Malayan rubber policy, in T.H.Silcock (1961).
Beaglehole, J.H. Malay participation in commerce and industry: the role of RIDA and MARA, *Journal of Commonwealth Political Studies,* 1969.
Berstein, H. Underdevelopment and Development, 1973, Penguin, London.
Bettelheim, C. 'Theoretical Comments' in A. Emmanuel, 1972.
——The transition to socialist economy, Harvester Press 1975.
——Economic calculation and forms of property, Routledge 1976.
Bhati, U.N. Some social and economic aspects of the introduction of new varieties of paddy in Malaysia, 1976.
Blythe, W. The impact of Chinese secret societies in Malaya, a historical study, London OUP 1969.
Boestaman, A. Merintis Jalan Ke-Puncak, KL 1972.
Brimmel, J.H. Communism in SE Asia, London 1959.
——A short history of the MCP, Singapore 1956.
Brown, C. Rice price stabilization and support in Malaysia, *The Developing Economies*, June 1973.
Buchanan, I. Singapore in SE Asia, 1972 London.
Buraway, M. Race, Class, Colonialism, *Social and Economic Studies*, Vol.23, No.4, 1974.
Burridge, K.O.L. Race relations in Johore, *Australian Journal of Politics and History,* Vol.II, No.2, 1957.
——The Malay composition of a village in Johore, JMBRAS, Vol.XXIX 1956.
Caldwell, M. *Oil and Imperialism in East Asia*, Spokesman Pamphlet No.20, 1971.
——and Amin, M. *Malaya: The Making of a Neo-colony*, Spokesman 1977.
Cham, B.N. Class and communal conflict in Malaysia, JCA Vol.5, No.4, 1975.
Colonialism and communalism in Malaysia, JCA, 7:2, 1977.
Chang, Y.S. The transfer of Technology economics of Off-shore assembly: The case of semi-conductor industry, UNITAR Research Reports, 1971.
Chapman, S. *The jungle is neutral*, London 1949.
Cheah, B.K. *The masked comrades: a study of the communist United Front in Malaya, 1945-48*, 1979 Singapore.
Chee, S. and Khoo S.M. (ed.) *Malaysia and the MNCs*, 1974.
——*Local institutions and rural development in Malaysia*, Cornell 1974.
Chin KO *Malaya Upside Down*, 1976 Singapore.
Claudin, F. *The Communist Movement: From Comintern to Cominform*, Peregrine, 1975.
Clutterbuck, R. *Riot and Revolution in Singapore and Malaya, 1945-63*, London, 1967.
——*The Long Long War*, London 1966.
Communist Party of Malaya, *Selected Documents, 1979*, SE Asia Documentation Group.
——*Declaration regarding the present situation*, 1945.
Consumer Association of Penang, *Kuala Juru.*
Cowan, C.D. *19th Century Malaya: Origins of British political control*, London, 1962.
——*Economic development of SE Asia*, London 1964.
Cross, M. On conflict, race relations, and the theory of Plural society, *Race*, Vol.XII, No.4, 1971.
Das, S.A. and Suppiah, K.B. *Chalo Delhi: The Indian Independence Movement*, Kuala Lumpur, 1946.
Das, S.K. *The Torrens System in Malaya,* London, 1963.
Derek, D. The racial balance sheet, *FEER*, 10 July 1969.
Donnison, F.S.V. British Military Administration in the Far East, 1943-1946, HMSO London 1956.

Drabble, J.D. *Rubber in Malaya, 1876-1922: The genesis of the industry,* London, 1973

Elsbree, W. *Japan's role in SE Asia's Nationalist movements,* 1959, Harvard, Cambridge.

Emerson, R. *Malaya: a study in direct and indirect rule,* London, 1964.

Emmanuel, A. *Unequal exchange,* London 1972.

Enloe, C.H. Issue saliency of the military-ethnic connection: some insights on Malaysia, *Comparative Politics,* Jan. 1978.

——Issues and integration in Malaya, *Pacific Affairs,* Vol.XLI, No.3, 1968.

FAO, *The state of food and agriculture,* 1971 (Rome 1971).

FIDA, International seminar on investment opportunities in Malaysia, 1975.

Financial Times, *Survey on Malaysia,* 25-2-74, London.

Firth, R. *Malay Fishermen,* R & K Paul, London, 1966.

——*Themes in economic anthropology,* London, 1967.

Fisk, E.K. Rural development problems in Malaya, *Australian Outlook,* Vol.16 No.3, 1962.

——Productivity and income from rubber in an established Malay reservation, *Malay Economic Journal* (MEJ), 1961.

——Features of the rural economy, in Silcock & Fisk, 1963.

Frank, A.G. *On capitalist underdevelopment,* OUP 1976.

——*Capitalism and underdevelopment in Latin America,* MR 1971.

Federicks, L.J. (with R.J.G. Wells & B.W. Dissanayake), *Patterns of labour utilization and income distribution in rice double cropping system: Policy implications,* KL 1977.

Freedman, M. *Social Organisation*: Essays presented to Raymond Firth, London, 1967.

——The growth of plural society in Malaya, *Pacific Affairs* 33, No.2, June 1960.

Frobel, J.H. & Kreye, O. *Export-oriented industrialisation of underdeveloped countries,* MR 1978.

——*The new international division of labour,*1980 Cambridge UP.

Funston,J, *Malay Politics in Malaysia,* Heineman, Kuala Lumpur, 1980.

Furnivall, J.S. *Colonial Policy and practice,* NY 1948.

——*Netherlands India: A study of plural economy,* Cambridge UP 1967.

——Political education in the Far East, *Political Quarterly,* Vol.XVII, 1946.

Gamba, C. *Origins of trade unionism in Malaya,* Singapore 1962.

George, T.J.S. *Lee Kuan Yew's Singapore,* 1973 Singapore.

Goh, C.T. *The May 13 Incident and Democracy in Malaysia,* OUP, KL 1971.

Goldman, R.H. The evolution of Malaysia's rice policy in the context of economic and political development, 1974 (mimeo).

——Staple food self-sufficiency and the distributive impact of Malaysian rice policy, *Food Research Institute Studies,* XIV, 3 1975.

Gordon, S. The condition of our plantation workers, in WCC, 1972.

Gould, J.W. *The US and Malaysia,* Harvard 1969.

Griffin, K. *The political economy of agrarian change,* London 1974.

Gullick, J.M. *Indigenous political systems of West Malaysia,* London 1965. Malaysia, London, 1969.

Hanrahan, G.Z. *The communist struggle in Malaya,* NY 1954.

Hayes, S.P. (ed.), *The beginnings of American aid to SE Asia: The Griffin Mission of 1950,* Mass. 1971.

Hilferding, R. *Finance Capital,* Vienna 1923.

Hill, R.D. *Agricultural land tenure in West Malaysia,* MEJ 1967.

Hirschman, C. Ownership and control in the manufacturing sector of West Malaysia, *UMBC Economic Review,* Vol.7(1), 1971.

——Ethnic Stratification in West Malaysia, PhD Thesis, Wisconsin, 1972.

Ho, Robert, Economic prospects of Malayan peasantry, *Modern Asian Studies,*1970.

——The evolution of agriculture and land ownership in Saiong Mukim, *MER,* Vol.13, No.2, 1968.

——Land settlement projects in Malaya: FELDA, *Journal of Tropical*

Geography, Singapore, June 1965.

Hoalim, P. *The Malayan Democratic Union*, Singapore 1972.

Hobsbawm, E. *Industry and Empire*, 1969, London.

Hobson, J.A. *Imperialism, A study*, 1938, London.

Horii, K. The land tenure system of Malay padi farmers: Case study of Kampong Sungei Bujor in Kedah, *The Developing Economies*, 10(I) 1972.

Huang, Y.K. Some reflections on padi double-cropping in West Malaysia, in D. Lim, *Readings in Malaysian Economic Development*.

——Tenancy patterns, productivity, rentals in Malaysia, *Economic Development and cultural change*, 1974/75, V.23.

Husin Ali, S. Malay peasant society and leadership, 1975.

——Land concentration and poverty among rural Malays, *Nusantara*, Vol.1, 1972.

——Social stratification in Kampong Bagan, 1964.

Hussein, M. *Class conflict in Egypt*, 1945-70, MR 1973.

IBRD, *The economic development of Malaya*, 1955.

——Report on the economic aspects of Malaysia, 1963.

——Problems of rural poverty in Malaysia, Rome 1975.

——(World Bank) *Malaysia: Growth and Equity in a multiracial society* by Young, K., Bussink, W.C.F., Hasan P. 1980.

ILO, *The trade union situation in the Federation of Malaya*, Geneva 1967.

Jackson, J. Smallholding cultivation of cash crops, in G.W. Wang, 1964.

——Rice cultivation in West Malaysia, *JMBRAS*, 1972.

——*Planters and speculators: Chinese and European enterprise in Malaya, 1786-1921*, 1967.

Jackson, R.N. *Immigrant labour and the development of Malaya*, KL 1961.

Jain, R.K. *South Indians on the Plantation frontier in Malaya*, Yale, 1970.

Jalee, P. *The Third World in the World Economy*, MR 1969.

Jegathesan, S. *The Green Revolution and the MUDA Irrigation scheme*, 1977.

Jomo, K.S (mimeo), 'The NEP Revisited: 1980.

Kanapathy, V. Industrialisation of Malaysia, *UMBC Economic Review*, Vol.1, No.2, 1965.

Kasim, I. *Race, Politics and Moderation*, 1979 Singapore.

Kay, G. *Development and Underdevelopment*, 1975, Macmillan.

Kessler, C.S. *Islam and Politics in a Malay state: Kelantan, 1838-1969*, Cornell, 1978.

Khoo, K.K. *The Western States, 1850-1873*, KL OUP 1972.

Kidron, M. *Western capitalism since the war*, 1969 London.

Kondapi, C. *Indian overseas, 1839-1947*, New Delhi 1951.

Kuper, L. & Smith, M.G. *Pluralism in Africa*, Berkeley 1969.

Labour Research Dept., *British Imperialism in Malaya*, London 1926.

Lee, George, Commodity production and reproduction amongst the Malayan peasantry, *JCA* Vol.3, No.4, 1973.

Lee K.H. The 1960 Agricultural Census, *KEM* 4(2) 1967.

Lee S.Y. *The Monetary and banking development of Malaysia and Singapore*, 1978.

Lee S.A. *Economic growth and the public sector in Malaya and Singapore, 1948-60*, KL OUP 1974.

Lenin, V. *Imperialism, the highest stage of capitalism*, Moscow 1970.

——*The development of capitalism in Russia*, Moscow 1974.

——*The agrarian program of the Social Democrats in the First Russian Revolution*, CW No.13.

——*On the National and Colonial Questions*, 1975 Peking.

Lent, J.A. (ed.) *Cultural pluralism in Malaysia*, New York, 1977.

Leys, C. *Underdevelopment in Kenya*, Heinemann, 1975.

Li, D.J. *British Malaya: an economic analysis*, NY, 1955.

Lim, C.Y. *Economic development in modern Malaya*, KL 1970.

Lim, D. (ed.) *Readings in Malaysian economics*, KL, 1975.

——*Economic growth and development in West Malaysia*, KL, 1974.

Lim, F. Ha, 'The state in West Malaysia', *Race & Class*, 1982. XXIV.

Lim. L.L. Some aspects of income differentials in West Malaysia, KL, 1971.
Lim, Linda Y.C. Women workers in MNC's, Michigan occasional Papers, IX, Fall 1978.
Lim, M.H. Ethnic and class relations in Malaysia, *JCA* 1980.
——& Canak, W. Political economy of the State policies in Malaysia, *JCA*, 1981, Vol.II:2.
Lim, S.C. Analysis of smallholders' rubber marketing in West Malaysia, Natural Rubber Conference.
Lim, T.G. *Land tenure survey: Farm Locality II*, Muda Irrigation Scheme, KL, 1974.
——*Peasant agriculture in colonial Malaya*, PhD ANU, 1971.
——*Origins of a colonial economy*, London, 1976.
——*Peasants and their agricultural economy in colonial Malaya, 1874-1941*, London, 1977.
Loh, F.S. *Seeds of discord: British politics and education policy in the FMS, 1874-1940*, London, 1976.
Luxemburg, R. The accumulation of capital, 1951 London.
McCormick, J. and Halliday, J. *Japanese imperialism*, 1973 London, Penguin.
McVey, R.T. *The Calcutta Conference and the SE Asia Uprisings*, 1958.
Magdoff, H. *The age of imperialism*, 1969, MR, NY.
Mahathir, M. The Malay Dilemma, Singapore 1970.
Malayan Indian Congress, Memorandum on the Indian education in the Fed. of Malaya by the Indian Education Com. 31-8-47, 1951.
Malayan Monitor, 1950-56.
Mamdani, M. Politics and class formation in Uganda, 1976, MR.
Mao Tse-Tung, Selected Works, Peking 1975.
Marx, K. *Capital* Vols.I, II, III, Lawrence and Wishart, London.
——Pre-capitalist economic formations, 1964, Introduction by E. Hobsbawm.
Means, G. *Malaysian Politics*, NY 1970.
Mills, L.A. *British Malaya, 1826-67*, KL OUP 1966.
Milne, R.S. The politics of Malaysia's NEP, *Pacific Affairs*, Vol.49, No.2, 1976.
Morgan, M. Britain's imperial policy and the Malayan labour movement, *Race & Class*, Vol.XIX, No.1, 1977.
Munro, G.R. & Chee, S. The economics of fishing and the developing world: the Malaysian case, 1978.
Nabudere, D.W. *Imperialism and revolution in Uganda*, 1980, Dar-es-Salaam.
Narkswadi, U. & Selvadurai, S. Economic survey of padi production in West Malaysia, Ministry of Agriculture, 1967, Selangor.
Ness, G. Bureaucracy and rural development, 1967.
O'Ballance, E. Malaya: The Communist insurgent War, 1948-60, 1966, Conn.
Ooi, J.B. *Land, People, Economy in Malaya*, London, 1963.
Owen, R. & Sutcliffe, B. Studies in the Theory of Imperialism, 1972 London.
Panker, G. New American Perspectives on SE Asia, 1975, Rand Corporation.
Parkinson, C.N. British Intervention in Malaya, 1867-77, UM Press 1964.
Parmer, J.N. Colonial labour policy and administration, PhD Cornell 1957.
Peiris, D. The emerging rural revolution, *FEER* 10-1-75.
Petras, J. Critical perspectives on Imperialism and social class in the Third World, MR 1978.
Pirie, P. Squatter settlements in KL, Third Conference of Malaysian Economic Society 1976.
Poulantzas, N. Political power and social classes, NLB 1968 London.
——Classes in contemporary capitalism, NLB.
Purcell, V. The Chinese in Malaya, 1948 London.
——Malaya: Communist or Free? 1955, Stanford.
Puthucheary, J.J. Ownership and control in the Malayan economy, 1960, Singapore.
Ratnam, K.J. Communalism and political process in Malaysia, KL 1963.
Reddaway, W.B. Effects of UK direct investments overseas, Cambridge 1968.
Reid, A. Pre-colonial state systems in SE Asia, Monographs of the MBRAS,

No.6, 1975 KL.

Roff, W.R. The Origins of Malay Nationalism, KL 1974.

——(ed.), Kelantan, KL 1974.

Rudner, M. Nationalism, Planning and Economic Modernisation in Malaysia, California, Sage, 1975.

Sandhu, K.S. Indians in Malaya: Immigration and Settlements, 1786-1959, London, 1969.

Sastri, V.S.S. *Report on the conditions of Indian labour in Malaya*, 6-2-37, KL, 1937.

Selangor Chinese Chambers of Commerce, *Malaysian Chinese Economic problems*, KL 1973.

Selvadurai, S. *Padi farming in Malaysia,* KL, 1972.

——*Socio-economic survey of rubber smallholdings in West Johore*, 1972.

——*Krian padi survey, 1972.*

Selvaratnam, V. *Some aspects of Race and Class*, IDS Discussion Paper 75, Sussex.

Shari, I. Some comments on the eradication of poverty under the TMP, *SE Asian Affairs*, 1977.

Shivji, I. *Class struggles in Tanzania*, MR 1976.

Short, A. *The communist insurrection in Malaya,1948-60*, London 1975.

——Communism, Race and Politics in Malaysia, *Asian Survey*, Vol.10 No.12 1970.

Silcock, T.H. & Fisk, *The political economy of Independent Malaya*, London, 1963.

——(ed.), *Readings in Malayan economics*, London, 1961.

Simandjuntak, B. *Malayan Federalism, 1945-63*, KL 1969.

Smith, E. & Goethals, P. *Tenancy among padi cultivators in Malaysia*, KL, 1965.

Smith, M.G. *The plural society in the British West Indies,* London 1965.

——Pluralism in Africa, in Bowker and Carrier (ed.), *Race & Ethnic relations*, London 1976.

Snodgrass D. R. Trends and patterns in Malaysian income distribution, 1957-70, 1974 (mimeo).

Soenarno, R. Malay nationalism, 1896-1945, *Journal of SE Asian History*, Vol.1, No.I, 1960.

Sopiee, N. From the Malayan Union to Singapore Separation, KL 1974.

Stahl, K.M. The metropolitan organisation of British colonial trade, London 1951.

Stenson, M.R. Industrial conflict in Malaya, London 1970.

——Class and Race in West Malaysia, *Bulletin of Concerned Asian Scholars*, April 1976.

Straits Times, Information Malaysia, Annual.

Swift, M.G. Malay peasant society in Jelebu, London, 1965.

——Economic concentration and Malay peasant society in Freedman, M., 1967.

Tadin, I. Dato Onn, 1946-51, *Journal of SE Asian History*,Vol.1, No.1, 1960.

Tan, C.L. *Malayan problems from a Chinese point of view*, Singapore 1946.

——*One country, one people, one government*, KL, 1966.

Tham, S.C. *Malays and modernisation*, Singapore, 1977.

Thio, E. *British policy in the Malay peninsula*, London, 1974.

Thoburn, J.T. Ownership of shares in UK-incorporated public rubber planting and ——tin dredging companies in Malaysia, *KEM* Vol.VII 1970.

Tregonning, K.G. *A History of Modern Malaysia and Singapore,* KL, 1964

Tunku, A.R. May 13 *Before and After*, KL, 1969.

UNCTAD/GATT, *Malaysia: The market for selected manufactured products from developing countries*, Geneva, 1969.

UNIDO, *Industrial Free Zones as incentives to promote export-oriented industries*, Geneva, 1971.

UNRISD, *Social and economic implications of large-scale introduction of new varieties of paddy: a village case study in West Malaysia*, KL, 1975.

US, Report to the President by the Commission on International Trade and Investment Policy (*Williams Report*), 1971.

Utusan Konsumer, *South China Sea Fishermen Protest*, No.48, July 1978.

Vasil, R.K. *Politics in a Plural Society*, KL 1971.

Von Vorys, K, *Democracy without consensus: Communalism and political stability in Malaysia,* 1975, Princeton.

Voon, P.K. Malay reservations and Malay land ownership in Semenyih and Ulu Semenyih Mukims, Selangor, *Modern Asian Studies*, October 1976.

Wang, G.W. *Malaysia: A Survey*, London 1964.

——Malaysia: Contending Elites, *Current Affairs Bulletin*, 28-12-70.

Warren, B. 'Imperialism, Pioneer of Capitalism', Imperialism and capitalist industrialisation, *NLR* 81, 1973.

Wharton, C. Marketing, merchandising, and moneylending: a note on middlemen monopsony in Malaya, *MER*, 1962.

——*Subsistence agriculture and economic development*, Chicago 1969.

Wheelwright, E.L. *Industrialisation in Malaya,*1965, Melbourne.

Wikkramatileke, R. FELDA in West Malaysia, 1957-71, *Pacific Viewpoint*, May 1972.

Wilson, T.B. *The economics of padi cultivation in North Malaya*, KL, 1958.

——The inheritance and fragmentation of Malay padi lands in Krian, Perak, *Malayan Agricultural Journal*, 1955.

Witton, R. Malaysia: Changing masters, *JCA*, 1972.

Wong, D.S. *Tenure and Land Dealings in the Malay States*, KL, 1975.

Wong, I.F.T. *Present land use of West Malaysia*, KL, 1974.

World Council of Churches (WCC), *Plantation workers of Indian Origin*, KL, 1972.

Yamashita, H., Jegathesan, S. & Yong C.Y. *Agro-economic studies in the Muda Project area:* Part I, MADA KL, 1976.

Yeo, K.W. The grooming of an elite: Malay administrators in the FMS, 1903-41, *Journal of SE Asian Studies*, XI, No.2, 1980.

Yip, Y.H. *The development of the tin mining industry*, KL 1969.

Yoshihara, K. Japanese direct investment in SE Asia, *ISEAS*, No.18 1973.

Young, K., Bussink, W.C.F., Hasan, P. *Malaysia: Growth and Equity in a multiracial society*, WB Report, Geneva, 1980.

Yegar, Moshe, *Islam and Islamic Institutions in British Malaya,* 1979, Jerusalem.

Zaidi, S.J.H. 'MTUC',1975, Kuala Lumpur.

Index

ASIA TITLES FROM ZED PRESS

POLITICAL ECONOMY

BEN KIERNAN AND CHANTHOU BOUA
Peasants and Politics in Kampuchea, 1942–1981
Hb and Pb

DAVID SELBOURNE
Through the Indian Looking Glass
Pb

HASSAN GARDEZI AND JAMIL RASHID (EDITORS)
Pakistan: The Roots of Dictatorship
The Political Economy of a Praetorian State
Hb and Pb

STEFAN DE VYLDER
Agriculture in Chains
Bangladesh — A Case Study in Contradictions and Constraints
Hb

REHMAN SOBHAN AND MUZAFFER AHMAD
Public Enterprise in an Intermediate Regime:
A Study in the Political Economy of Bangladesh
Hb

SATCHI PONNAMBALAM
Dependent Capitalism in Crisis:
The Sri Lankan Economy, 1948–1980
Hb

DAVID ELLIOT
Thailand: Origins of Military Rule
Hb and Pb

A. RUDRA, T. SHANIN AND J. BANAJI ET AL.
Studies in the Development of Capitalism in India
Hb and Pb

BULLETIN OF CONCERNED ASIAN SCHOLARS
China: From Mao to Deng
The Politics and Economics of Socialist Development
Hb and Pb

RUTH AND VICTOR SIDEL
The Health of China:
Current Conflicts in Medical and Human Services for
One Billion People
Hb and Pb

BETSY HARTMANN and JAMES K. BOYCE
A Quiet Violence:
View from a Bangladesh Village
Hb and Pb

REHMAN SOBHAN
The Crisis of External Dependence
Hb and Pb

ELISABETH CROLL
The Family Rice Bowl
Food and the Domestic Economy in China
Hb and Pb

W.F. WERTHEIM AND MATTHIAS STIEFEL
Production, Equality and Participation in Rural China
Pb

CONTEMPORARY HISTORY/REVOLUTIONARY STRUGGLES

SUMANTA BANERJEE
India's Simmering Revolution:
The Naxalite Uprising
Pb

WILFRED BURCHETT
The China, Cambodia, Vietnam Triangle
Pb

SELIG HARRISON
In Afghanistan's Shadow:
Baluch Nationalism and Soviet Temptation
Hb and Pb

MUSIMGRAFIK
Where Monsoons Meet:
History of Malaya
Pb

LAWRENCE LIFSCHULTZ
Bangladesh: The Unfinished Revolution
Pb

HUA WU YIN
Malaysia: The Politics of Imperialist Domination
Hb and Pb

HUMAN RIGHTS

PERMANENT PEOPLE'S TRIBUNAL
Philippines: Repression and Resistance
Pb

JULIE SOUTHWOOD AND PATRICK FLANAGAN
Indonesia: Law, Propaganda and Terror
Hb and Pb

SATCHI PONNAMBALAM
The Tamil Question
Hb and Pb

WOMEN

BOBBY SIU
Women of China:
Imperialism and Women's Resistance, 1900–1949
Hb and Pb

ELSE SKJONSBERG
A Special Caste?
Tamil Women in Sri Lanka
Pb

GAIL OMVEDT
We Will Smash this Prison!
Indian Women in Struggle
Hb and Pb

AGNES SMEDLEY
Portraits of Chinese Women in Revolution
Pb

MARIA MIES
The Lacemakers of Narsapur:
Indian Housewives Produce for the World Market
Pb

PATRICIA JEFFREY
Frogs in a Well:
Indian Women in Purdah
Hb and Pb

ARLENE EISEN
Women in the New Vietnam
Hb and Pb

ELISABETH CROLL
Chinese Women
Hb and Pb

Zed titles cover Africa, Asia, Latin America and the Middle East, as well
as general issues affecting the Third World's relations with the rest of the
world. Our Series embrace: Imperialism, Women, Political Economy, Histor
Labour, Voices of Struggle, Human Rights and other areas pertinent to the
Third World.

**You can order Zed titles direct from Zed, 57 Caledonian
Road, London, N1 9DN, U.K.**

MARRAM BOOKS

Permanent People's Tribunal
**PHILIPPINES: REPRESSION AND
RESISTANCE**

The first formal application of established
international legal norms in assessing the
Marcos regime in the Philippines. Set out in
the form of a trial, the book is based on the
eloquent testimony of Filipino workers and
peasants, backed up by the expert evidence
of specialists in banking, international law
and industrial relations. The result is a
comprehensive picture of economic and
political repression in the Philippines.

312pp Map Glossary Bibliography Index
Pb 0 906968 03 8 £4.95   US$8.95
1982

Musimgrafik
**WHERE MONSOONS MEET: History
of Malaya**

'A cartoon/text history of Malaya, it is at
once very funny, accurate, and thought-
provoking. In fact it is probably the best
introduction to Malayan history there
is . . . .Everyone interested in Malaya must
read *Where Monsoons Meet*, and so should
those claiming any interest in Third World
Struggles.'

176pp Distributed by Zed Press for Grassroots
Pb 0 906968 00 3   £3.50   US$6.50
1979

Kinfe Abraham

**FROM RACE TO CLASS: Links and
Parallels in African and Black
American Protest Expression**

'A critical survey of the major trends in the
development of black literature .... Presents
a revealing panorama of black writing where
literary beauty and the agonies of the black
soul are interwoven.' *Professor Hailu Araya,*
Dean, Institute of Language Studies, Addis
Ababa University, Ethiopia.
'An original and integrated approach to the
study of the black experience and the
development of black consciousness on both
sides of the Atlantic.' *Independent Review*
This portrait of black literature from the 19th
Century to the present day is remarkable on
the one hand for its systematic comparison
of African and Afro-American poetry, drama
and fiction, and on the other hand for its use
of a Marxist interpretation to relate this great
body of literature to the history of black
people.

272pp Index
Pb 0 90698 02 X £6.95 US$12.50
1982

**THE REPORT OF THE INTER-
NATIONAL MISSION OF LAWYERS
TO MALAYSIA**

Increasing international concern by Human
Rights organizations throughout the world
about the numbers of persons executed
and those awaiting execution by the
Malaysian government in Malaysia, resulted
in an international mission of lawyers
visiting Kuala Lumpur in August 1982. The
aim of the mission was primarily to examine
the working of the national security
legislation as it relates to those charged
with offences under the Internal Security
Act 1960, the mandatory nature of the
death sentences for certain of those
offences and the trial procedures in security
cases which lead to the mandatory death
sentence as well as other sentences. The
mission also investigated the position of
those detained without trial under the
Internal Security Act. Their findings are
presented in this book.

72pp
ISBN 0 906968 04 6 £2.95 US$5.95
March 1983